The Execution of Illegal Orders and International Criminal Responsibility

Hiromi Satō

The Execution of Illegal Orders and International Criminal Responsibility

Springer

Assoc. Prof. Hiromi Satō
National Defense Academy
Department of International Relations
Hashirimizu 1-10-20
239-8686 Yokosuka, Kanagawa
Japan
hiromi@nda.ac.jp

ISBN 978-3-642-16752-2 e-ISBN 978-3-642-16753-9
DOI 10.1007/978-3-642-16753-9
Springer Heidelberg Dordrecht London New York

Library of Congress Control Number: 2011921398

Cover design: WMX Design GmbH, Heidelberg, Germany

Printed on acid-free paper

Springer is part of Springer Science+Business Media (www.springer.com)

Foreword

This study is a revised and translated version of my doctoral thesis, which was approved by the University of Tokyo in 2008. The original Japanese version has been published as *Ihō na Meirei no Jikkō to Kokusaikeijisekinin (The Execution of Illegal Orders and International Criminal Responsibility)* (Tokyo: Yūshindō Kōbunsha, 2010). The views expressed in this study are my own and do not necessarily represent those of the Japanese government.

There are many people who I wish to thank for helping me complete this study. Professor Yasuaki Ōnuma, who supervised my work on this study, meticulously read through the early versions of the manuscripts several times and provided invaluable comments. Professor James Crawford, my supervisor at the University of Cambridge, Professor John Dugard, and Professor Hisakazu Fujita, also my supervisor at the University of Tokyo, inspired my study in international criminal law. Professors Yūji Iwasawa, Hitoshi Saiki, Kichimoto Asaka, and Kōji Teraya gave generous amounts of their precious time to discuss the manuscript of the original thesis. I am also indebted to late Professor Yasuhiko Saitō and Professors Toshio Okuhara, Yōzō Yokota, Noriyuki Nishida, Akira Kotera, Junji Nakagawa, Akira Mayama, Kazuhiro Nakatani, and Yoshie Kawade for their helpful comments and support. My colleagues and the staff at the National Defense Academy have always been of great help. Ms. Anke Seyfried and the other staff at Springer-Verlag skillfully helped me publish this study. I would like to express my sincere thanks to all of these people.

September 2010 Hiromi Satō

Contents

Chapter 1
Introduction

Abstract The idea of prosecuting individual state officials directly under international law for their international illegal acts has been a matter of interest in the international society, especially since the Nuremberg Trial was held after World War II. One of the major principles of international criminal law presented by the Trial – the 'Nuremberg Principle' on the superior orders defense – denied immunity on the ground of superior orders in serious international crimes such as war crimes and laid down substantial grounds for the prosecution of state officials. However, detailed discussions on the problem of the superior orders defense have, in fact, long been conflicting. This study aims to describe the whole picture of the conflict of views and examine its implication for international rule-making with regard to international criminal law as well as for the development of international law in general.

1.1 The Subject of the Study

The development of the notion of individual criminal responsibility in international law has reflected the increased intervention of international law into domestic law with respect to the control of human behavior. After World War II, the notion of international common interest was embodied in some international instruments, and international law began to oblige states to criminalize certain acts under the respective national laws. This legal framework was first introduced for the problems of war crimes and genocide.

Before the Trial of the Major War Criminals before the International Military Tribunal (Nuremberg Trial), international law did not generally oblige states to punish war criminals. Some international conventions adopted at the beginning of the twentieth century made it obligatory for state parties to enact the national criminal law to control the violations of the conventions. For example, Article 21 of the *Hague Convention of 1907 (X) for the Adaptation to Maritime Warfare of the Principles of the Geneva Convention* provided as follows:

> The signatory Powers likewise undertake to enact or to propose to their legislatures, if their criminal laws are inadequate, the measures necessary for checking in time of war individual acts of pillage and ill-treatment in respect to the sick and wounded in the fleet, as well as for

H. Satō, *The Execution of Illegal Orders and International Criminal Responsibility*,
DOI 10.1007/978-3-642-16753-9_1, © Springer-Verlag Berlin Heidelberg 2011

> punishing, as an unjustifiable adoption of naval or military marks, the unauthorized use of the distinctive marks mentioned in Article 5 by vessels not protected by the present Convention.

Moreover, Article 29 of the *Convention for the Amelioration of the Condition of the Wounded and Sick in Armies in the Field* of 1929 read as follows:

> The Governments of the High Contracting Parties shall also propose to their legislatures should their penal laws be inadequate, the necessary measures for the repression in time of war of any act contrary to the provisions of the present Convention.[1]

These conventions were confined to regulating the violations of specific international instruments. They did not deal with war crimes in general. Some contemporary academics insisted on an obligation of belligerent parties to punish war criminals of hostile countries,[2] whereas others did not approve of such punishment.[3] In addition, most of the academic arguments that supported the punishment of the war criminals of hostile countries understood this as the 'right' of the belligerent parties.[4] This is why it has often been pointed out that the regulation of war criminals is the same as that of piracy.[5]

However, after the Nuremberg Trial, the principle of universality was introduced through the adoption of the Geneva Conventions of 1949, which oblige state parties to punish war crimes in general under the respective national laws. The trials and punishments for certain war crimes have since been obligated by international law.

On the other hand, immediately after World War II, the Nuremberg Trial realized the international prosecution of war crimes without the mediation of national laws. Further, toward the end of the twentieth century, the United Nations Security Council set up the *International Tribunal for the Prosecution of Persons Responsible for Serious Violations of International Humanitarian Law Committed in the Territory of the Former Yugoslavia since 1991* (ICTY) and the *International Criminal Tribunal for the Prosecution of Persons Responsible for Genocide and*

---

[1]The quoted provision succeeded Article 28 of the *Convention for the Amelioration of the Condition of the Wounded and Sick in Armies in the Field* of 1906.

[2]See, for instance, the Oxford Manual which was adopted by the Institute of International Law in 1880 read '[i]f any of the foregoing rules be violated, the offending parties should be punished, after a judicial hearing, by the belligerent in whose hands they are (J. Scott, *Resolutions of the Institute of International Law* (New York: Oxford University Press, 1916), 41)'.

[3]For instance, E. Colby, 'War Crimes and Their Punishment', *Minnesota Law Review* 8 (1923): 44–5.

[4]For instance, L. Oppenheim, *International Law,* 3rd ed. by R. Roxburgh, vol. 2, *War and Neutrality* (London: Longmans, 1921), 342, note 1; L. Oppenheim, *International Law,* 4th ed. by A. McNair, vol. 2, *Disputes, War and Neutrality* (London: Longman, Green, 1926), 409, note 1 (the following editions expressed the same view) ; H. Lauterpacht, 'The Law of Nations and the Punishment of War Crimes', *British Yearbook of International Law* 21 (1944): 61–2.

[5]The arguments which pointed out the resemblance between war crimes and piracy include W. Cowles, 'Universality of Jurisdiction over War Crimes', *California Law Review* 33 (1945): 188–203; G. Schwarzenberger, *International Law and Totalitarian Lawlessness* (London: Cape, 1943), 59.

Other Serious Violations of International Humanitarian Law Committed in the Territory of Rwanda and Rwandan Citizens Responsible for Genocide and Other Such Violations Committed in the Territory of Neighbouring States, Between 1 January 1994 and 31 December 1994 (ICTR). The activities of these tribunals have introduced a new form of international criminal prosecution under the name of the international society, although various conditions need to be met in order to realize criminal trials before international tribunals.

As international law extended its control to the procedural aspects of national laws, it also gradually laid down clear definitions of international crimes together with the principles of criminal law to be applied at international trials. As stated above, the international conventions adopted before World War II confined themselves to dealing with violations of respective instruments. They neither aimed at formulating a general definition of war crimes[6] nor did they stipulate the general principles of criminal law to be applied. States were required to apply the national criminal laws of their respective countries or to provide for special national laws stipulating specific definitions of war crimes as well as general principles of criminal law to be applied at war crime trials. Some commentators attached great importance to this point and regarded war crimes as 'national crimes'.[7]

In these circumstances, the *Charter of the International Military Tribunal* (Nuremberg Charter) and the judgment of the Nuremberg Trial presented the definitions for relevant crimes and principles of criminal law to be applied at the trial. These rules later gained considerable support and were formulated as the Nürnberg Principles by the United Nations International Law Commission (ILC). The characteristics of the international rule-making process drastically changed after the Nuremberg Trial.

The notion of individual criminal responsibility in international law has special significance when the criminal acts in question relate to state acts as in the case of war crimes. In such a case, the prosecution of individual criminal acts introduces a new form of controlling the acts of sovereign states by international law.

In traditional theories and practice of international law, violations of international law by states basically led to collective responsibility. The responsibility of individual state officials who committed international illegal acts was generally absorbed into collective state responsibility.

However, the Nuremberg Charter and other international instruments adopted since then, such as the *Convention on the Prevention and Suppression of the Crime of Genocide* (Genocide Convention) and the *International Convention on the Suppression and Punishment of the Crime of Apartheid,* provide for some special measures on serious violations of the laws of war as well as crimes against humanity. They clearly stipulate that even if these illegal acts were committed as

---

[6]See the Hague Convention of 1907 (X) and the Geneva Convention of 1929 quoted above.

[7]G. Manner, 'The Legal Nature and Punishment of Criminal Acts of Violence Contrary to the Laws of War', *American Journal of International Law* 37 (1943): 407–410. Garner also emphasized that violations of international law were punished as national crimes (J. Garner, *International Law and the World War*, vol. 2 (London: Longmans, Green and co., 1920), 472–5).

state acts, the very persons who carried out the acts should be held directly responsible under international law. Thus, with respect to international illegal acts of high international concern, individual criminal responsibility can be dealt with at the international level along with the collective state responsibility. It can be said that the regulation of state acts has been much strengthened at least theoretically.

However, the notion of individual criminal responsibility of state officials under international law has faced with serious obstacles. In particular, the process of attributing international obligations directly to individual state officials faced considerable resistance in legal theory. This resistance was based on the theory of the 'impunity of state acts' and the absolute character of military discipline.

In a substantive aspect of international law, such resistance came in the form of the theory of sovereign immunity and an assertion of automatic immunity under the defense of superior orders. The theory of sovereign immunity implied that the official acts of a sovereign state should not result in a problem of individual responsibility under international law. The defense of superior orders was often deemed as unconditionally immunizing persons who committed illegal acts under the orders of a government or other superiors. From the viewpoint of the effective control of war crimes, a negation of these theories or assertion was indispensable.

Bernard Röling highly evaluated the judgment of the Nuremberg Trial in light of these problems of international law, especially that of the defense of superior orders. Röling, who served as a judge at the Tokyo Trial, supported the Nuremberg judgment as having shown the superiority of international law over national legal orders.[8] He emphasized, among other things, that the Nuremberg Tribunal stated that 'the very essence of the Charter is that individuals have international duties which transcend the national obligations of obedience imposed by the individual State'.[9]

Robert Jackson, who participated in the drafting of the Nuremberg Charter in his capacity as the representative of the United States and who later served as a prosecution counsel at the Nuremberg Trial, expressed a similar view. Jackson evaluated the rejection of the superior orders defense by the Charter, as well as the principle of individual responsibility, that of conspiracy, and prohibition of the plea of 'acts of state', as contributing to the legal control of wars. He stated:

> It is quite evident that the law of the charter pierces national sovereignty and presupposes that statesmen of the several states have a responsibility for international peace and order, as well as responsibilities to their own states. It would be idle to deny that this concept carries far-reaching implications.[10]

---

[8]B. Röling, 'Criminal Responsibility for Violations of the Laws of War', *Revue belge de droit international* 12 (1976): 20.

[9]Ibid.

[10]*Report of Robert H. Jackson, United States Representative to the International Conference on Military Trials: London, 1945* (Washington, DC: GPO, 1949) [hereinafter, *Jackson Report*], ix.

The idea that international law directly regulates the state acts of individuals should be deemed significant as showing the development of the international legal system. The idea implies that individual state officials should be obliged by international law bypassing national legal orders and bear sanctions under international law in case of its violations. However, an expression of this notion in international legal instruments could not be realized without obstacles. As already mentioned, the traditional international law absorbed the individual responsibility of state officials into collective state responsibility. A question of individual criminal responsibility had been dealt with by the respective national laws. It was thus natural that states hesitated to regard individuals as independent actors in criminal matters under international law. Concurrent debates on the superior orders defense can be said to have straightforwardly reflected this hesitation.

Article 8 of the Nuremberg Charter provided on the superior orders defense as follows:

> The fact that the Defendant acted pursuant to order of his Government or of a superior shall not free him from responsibility, but may be considered in mitigation of punishment if the Tribunal determines that justice so requires.[11]

This provision refused immunity on the ground of superior orders and bore an effect to broaden the possibility of punishing war crimes. The provision led to lively debates during the trials held under the Charter. After the Nuremberg Trial, the rule of Article 8 came to be widely supported and was consolidated into one of the Nürnberg Principles by the ILC. Nonetheless, the problem of the superior orders defense cannot be said to have been thoroughly concluded in the subsequent international rule-making processes.

Since the Nuremberg Trial, the problem of the superior orders defense has always been a cause of an imbroglio at the drafting of the Genocide Convention, the Geneva Conventions of 1949, and the *Protocol Additional to the Geneva Conventions of August 12, 1949, and Relating to the Protection of Victims of International Armed Conflicts (Protocol I)* (Additional Protocol I). The complications aroused suspicion on the very nature of the 'principle' of the superior orders defense. The notion of international criminal responsibility of state officials has been widely considered at the international level after the Nuremberg Trial. However, the history of international rule-making up to the present even implies that certain counteractions against this idea do exist.

Academic arguments have also been conflicting. First, there have been diverse interpretations of the 'Nuremberg Principle' with regard to the superior orders defense, and second, the understanding of the present legal situation on this topic is also varied.

Some commentators interpret the 'Nuremberg Principle' as having opposed the superior orders defense, while some regard this opposition only for major war

---

[11]Trial of the Major War Criminals before the International Military Tribunal, (Nuremberg, 1947) [hereinafter, IMT], vol. 1, 12.

criminals, that is, for senior state officials. On the contrary, others deem the 'principle' as having conditionally recognized the superior orders defense. Different views have been associated with various understanding of the present situation of the problem, which eventually leads to a wide range of evaluations of the 'Nuremberg Principle'.

What is the 'Nuremberg Principle' with regard to the superior orders defense? Can it be said to have been established as a 'principle'? If there were any problems with the 'Nuremberg Principle' on the said defense, what kind of influence did they have on the subsequent discussions on this topic?

Bearing these questions in mind, this study seeks to reevaluate the whole picture of the problem of the superior orders defense. The first theme of this study is to establish a clear structure for discussion on the superior orders defense and to confirm its present situation. The second theme is to examine what kind of significance the discussions on the superior orders defense since the Nuremberg Trial have had on the development of international law. Such an examination would lead to certain implications with regard to an ideal method of international rule-making in the future.

1.2 Background of the Study

In the 1990s, the United Nations Security Council set up two ad hoc international criminal tribunals through its resolutions. At the beginning of the twenty-first century, the International Criminal Court (ICC), established on the basis of a multilateral convention, commenced operations. At the national level, the application of the notions of international law, such as crimes against humanity and the universality principle, for the prosecution of former heads of states has drawn much attention lately. Major examples are the trials of Nazi war criminals in the 1980s and 1990s[12] and the prosecution of Pinochet.[13] The construction of legal systems on individual criminal responsibility under international law has been accelerated after a period of stagnation for half a century.

However, the introduction of international rules on criminal matters is generally accompanied by many problems in the international society, which is grounded in horizontal structure among sovereign states. Criminal prosecution at international tribunals has been very limited. The Security Council has thus far established only two international tribunals. The application of international criminal law at national

[12]See M. Lippman, 'The Pursuit of Nazi War Criminals in the United States and in Other Anglo-American Legal Systems', *California Western International Law Journal* 29 (1998): 1–100.

[13]With regard to the *Pinochet* case, see, for instance, R. Wedgwood, 'International Criminal Law and Augusto Pinochet', *Virginia Journal of International Law* 40 (2000): 829–47; N. Arriaza, 'The Pinochet Precedent and Universal Jurisdiction', *New England Law Review* 35 (2001): 311–19.

courts has also been limited and has often been arbitrary.[14] Furthermore, negotiations with state leaders accused of international crimes might arguably be key to the peaceful settlement of disputes at least in the short run. In such a case, there is even a possibility that prosecution of such state leaders would obstruct the settlement of disputes.[15]

On the other hand, prosecution under international law does not necessarily exclude other methods of dispute settlement such as negotiations, truth and reconciliation commissions, and civil compensation. Relevant practice has shown that amnesty for individuals responsible for serious human rights violations sometimes facilitates ceasefire or the establishment of truth and reconciliation commissions.[16] Criminal proceedings have been confined to play a complementary role in relation to other dispute settlement methods.[17]

Relevant practice has also revealed that dispute settlement by bypassing criminal proceedings is neither always effective nor appropriate. Examples of this would be the case of Slobodan Milošević of the former Yugoslavia and Foday Sankoh of Sierra Leone. They once evaded prosecutions; however, after committing other criminal acts, they were eventually subjected to criminal proceedings.[18] In Chile and El Salvador, amnesties for individuals responsible for criminal acts further led to serious human rights violations.[19]

The fact that opportunities for prosecution are very limited would be problematic from the viewpoint of strengthening the legitimacy of international criminal

[14]See G. Simpson, 'War Crimes: A Critical Introduction', in T. McCormack & G. Simpson, *The Law of War Crimes, National and International Approaches* (Boston: Kluwer Law International, 1997), 1–30.

[15]D. Forsythe, 'Politics and the International Tribunal for the Former Yugoslavia', in *The Prosecution of International Crimes*, eds R. Clark & M. Sann (New Brunswick: Transaction, 1996), 199; Y. Ōnuma, *Jinken, Kokka, Bunmei – Fuhenshugitekijinkenkan kara Bunsaitekijinkenkan e (Human Rights, State, and Civilization – From Universal Perspective of Human Rights to Transcivilizational Perspective of Human Rights)* (Tokyo: Chikuma Shobō, 1998), 103.

[16]With regard to the problem of amnesties, see J. Dugard, 'Reconciliation and Justice: The South African Experience', *Transnational Law and Contemporary Problems* 8 (1998): 277–311; D. Wippman, 'Atrocities, Deterrence, and the Limits of International Justice', *Fordham International Law Journal* 23 (1999): 473–88; D. Majzub, 'Peace or Justice? Amnesties and the International Criminal Court', *Melbourne Journal of International Law* 3 (2002): 247–79.

[17]See M. Scharf, 'Justice Versus Peace', in *The United States and the International Criminal Court – National Security and International Law*, eds S. Sewall & C. Kaysen (Boston: Rowman & Littlefield Publishers, Inc., 2000), 179–93; S. Ratner & J. Abrams, *Accountability for Human Rights Atrocities in International Law, Beyond the Nuremberg Legacy,* 2nd ed. (Oxford: Oxford University Press, 2001), 228–52; L. Sadat, 'International Criminal Law and Alternative Modes of Redress', in *International Criminal Law and the Current Development of Public International Law*, ed. A. Zimmermann (Berlin: Duncker & Humbolt, 2003), 161–94. Regarding civil remedies, see also R. Wedgwood, 'National Courts and the Prosecution of War Crimes', in *Substantive and Procedural Aspects of International Criminal Law, The Experience of International and National Courts*, vol.1, eds G. McDonald & O. Swaak-Goldman (The Hague: Kluwer Law International, 2000), 410–12.

[18]Sadat, supra n. 17, at 174.

[19]Scharf, supra n. 17, at 182.

law. However, the complete renunciation of prosecutions would be even more harmful. It would not be appropriate to expect too much of the preventive function of international criminal law. Nonetheless, we should not underestimate the risk of the 'culture of impunity' brought about by the total negation of prosecution under international law, which would make would-be criminals bolder and aggravate a chain of violence.[20]

In case international criminal law cannot be effectively executed, it may still be possible to expect certain milder effects as a social norm. That is, international criminal law might offer the grounds on which various actors building international public opinion criticize illegal acts. At this point, international criminal law bears resemblance to international law on armed conflicts, and the notion of *jus cogens* and that of the obligations *erga omnes*. The complete implementation of certain international rules or legal notions is comparatively difficult.[21] In relation to the problem of the superior orders defense, a comment by Yasuaki Ōnuma, who evaluated the Nuremberg and Tokyo Trials from such a point of view, is noteworthy. He argues that the notion of the 'obligation to disobey illegal state orders' would ease mental isolation of individuals who try to implement international obligations, and it could be a measure to impede a general tendency toward war before reaching an extreme situation.[22]

Thus, the implementation of international criminal law appears to bear considerable significance, although it should not be overestimated. Several international tribunals have already implemented judicial proceedings. Moreover, the scope of the application of international criminal law at the national level has gradually been widened. In order to make relevant state practice worthwhile, it is crucial to concretely lay down international rules in criminal matters as well as reexamine basic rule-making methods. Heretofore discussions on the superior orders defense seem to bear an important implication for such a reexamination.

---

[20]See E. Bradley, 'In Search for Justice – A Truth in Reconciliation Commission for Rwanda', *Detroit College of Law Journal of International Law and Practice* 7 (1998): 150–52; Sadat, supra n. 17, at 185–6.

[21]The views which underline the notion of *jus cogens* in international law as 'supplemental arguments' include C. Ford, 'Adjudicating jus cogens', *Wisconsin International Law Journal* 13 (1994): 179–80. Schachter also upholds the notion of the obligations *erga omnes* as strengthening the sense of international obligations (O. Schachter, *International Law in Theory and Practice* (Dordrecht: Martinus Nijhoff Publishers, 1991), 211–3). Ōnuma draws attention to 'the communicative function', 'the function of embodying shared understandings of international society', and 'the justifying and legitimating function' of international law (Onuma Y., 'International Law in and with International Politics: The Functions of International Law in International Society', *European Journal of International Law* 14 (2003): 130–39).

[22]Y. Ōnuma, *Tōkyōsaiban kara Sengosekinin no Sisō e (From the Tokyo Trial to the Idea of Postwar Responsibility)*, 4th ed. (Tokyo: Tōshindō, 1997), 52–4. See also Y. Ōnuma, *Sensōsekininron Josetsu (Introductory Study on the Responsibility for War)* (Tokyo: University of Tokyo Press, 1975), 350.

1.3 Terminology

1.3.1 The Defense of Superior Orders

The 'defense of superior orders' means an assertion of immunity by the accused on the ground that he/she committed criminal acts under the orders of his/her superiors. Occasionally, the word 'plea' is used in stead of 'defense', but in common law, the former usually means a response of 'guilty', 'not guilty', or 'no contest' by the accused in an arraignment. Moreover, in academic arguments and state practice in international law, the term 'superior orders defense' has generally been used when referring to an assertion of the accused to be immunized because of the existence of orders.

A legal consequence of the superior orders defense has been discussed in various ways, as will be seen in the following chapters. However, there has not been any specific conflict of views on the terminology itself.

1.3.2 Defense

The word 'defense' is originally a terminology of common law. 'Defense' refers to a statement by a defendant on why he/she should be acquitted notwithstanding that other elements of a crime have been proved.[23] In the national criminal laws of continental law countries such as Germany, relevant aspects are examined under the notions of the 'definition of the crime (*tatbestand*)', 'wrongfulness or unlawfulness (*rechtswidrigkeit*)', and 'culpability or blameworthiness (*schuld*)'. However, such classification has not been adopted in international criminal law thus far. All relevant factors have been discussed under the term 'defense'.

The use of the term 'defense' as a general ground for immunity naturally reflects the entire framework for analyzing the notion of crime in international law.

In the theory of criminal law in many continental law countries, the analysis of the problem is conducted in terms of the three components stated above. The subjective and objective elements of a crime are examined in light of these components, and the mutual relationship among these elements is investigated. On the other hand, in the theory of criminal law in common law countries, the notions of the 'definition of the crime', 'wrongfulness or unlawfulness', and 'culpability or blameworthiness' are not prominent. In common law, the two factors of *actus reus* (guilty act or deed of the crime) and *mens rea* (guilty mind or mental element) are examined

---

[23]J. Smith & B. Hogan, *Criminal Law*, 6th ed. (London: Butterworths, 1988), 177–8; M. Allen, *Textbook on Criminal Law*, 8th ed. (Oxford; New York: Oxford University Press, 2005), 158–9. J. Dressler, *Understanding Criminal Law*, 3rd ed. (New York: Lexis Publishing, 2001), 201.

first. Then, the notion of 'defense' is contraposed against these elements; this determines whether or not the case is proved.[24]

Some legal theories of continental countries seem to come close to those of common law countries. However, certain differences between the frameworks of analysis of the respective theories make them fundamentally heterogeneous.

For example, the argument that the definition of the crime (*tatbestand*) is identical to wrongfulness (*rechtswidrigkeit*) and can only be prescribed by the objective element[25] may be recognized as unifying objective element and subjective element, respectively. However, this argument analyzes the objective element by making use of the two notions of the definition of crime and wrongfulness. It is different from the common law theory, which deals with the single notion of *actus reus*.

Another argument that understands the objective element as the definition of the crime reflecting wrongfulness, and subjective element as the definition of the crime reflecting culpability,[26] appears to come close to the dual approach of common law theory. However, such an argument as associating the subjective element with the definition of the crime seems peculiar when compared to the other continental law theories. There arises a conflict of views to which common law theory is basically indifferent.[27]

International criminal law has not introduced a method for analyzing the objective and subjective elements of a crime under the three notions used in the theory of continental law countries. Neither the objective element of a crime nor its substantive element is respectively classified into the notions of the definition of the crime, wrongfulness, and culpability. Further, the international legal theory does not classify the consolidated notion of the objective element as well as that of subjective element into one or two of the three notions.

The latest texts of international criminal law tend to discuss international crimes by employing the notions of *actus reus* and *mens rea*, or objective element and subjective element.[28] Recent international judicial practice also uses the terms *actus reus* and *mens rea*.[29] In light of these circumstances, it can be said that

---

[24]With regard to the difference of those theories of criminal law, see G. Fletcher, 'Contemporary Legal Scholarship: Achievements and Prospects: Criminal Law: Criminal Theory in the Twentieth Century', *Theoretical Inquiries in Law* 2 (2001): 265–86.

[25]Y. Takigawa, 'Keihō ni okeru Kōseiyōken no Kinō (The Function of the Definition of the Crime in Criminal Law)', *Keihō Zasshi* 1, no. 2 (1950): 171.

[26]M. Maeda, *Keihō Sōron Kōgi (Lectures on the General Part of Criminal Law),* 2nd ed. (Tokyo: Tokyo University Press, 1994), 100–107; *Ibid.,* 3rd ed. (1998), 51–2.

[27]With regard to the development of the theories of criminal law, see Ryūichi Hirano, *Hanzairon no Shomondai (Jō) Sōron (Problems of the Theories of Crime (First Part) General Part)* (Tokyo: Yūhikaku, 1981), 1–34.

[28]For instance, K. Kittichaisaree, *International Criminal Law* (New York; London: Oxford University Press, 2001); A. Cassese, *International Criminal Law*, 2nd ed. (Oxford; New York: Oxford University Press, 2008).

[29]For instance, the ICTY judgment in *Furundzija* (Judgment (Trial Chamber), *Prosecutor v. Anto Furundzija*, IT-95-17/1 (10 December 1998)).

international criminal law has thus far adopted the terminology and notions of common law countries with respect to the basic structure of the theory of crime.

In the criminal law terminology of common law countries, the expression 'recognize defense' means acquittal of a defendant.[30] On the other hand, the expression 'refuse defense' means conviction of a defendant but does not necessarily deny the possibility of mitigation of punishment.[31] These terminologies have been introduced as they are in international criminal law. For instance, Article 8 of the Nuremberg Charter has generally been understood as having refused the defense of superior orders.[32] The article indeed refused immunity on the ground of superior orders, although it still recognized the possibility of mitigation of punishment. Article 14 of the Draft Code of Crimes against the Peace and Security of Mankind may be cited as a recent example. The article provides for 'defences' separately from Article 15, which stipulates 'extenuating circumstances'.[33]

The refusal of the superior orders defense implies the conviction that a defendant is a 'criminal', even if the punishment is considerably mitigated by taking into account the individual circumstances of a crime. The consequence is fundamentally different if the defense is recognized and the defendant is acquitted. Therefore, whether the superior orders defense exemplifies a defendant or only mitigates his/her punishment is taken into serious consideration.

1.3.3 Views on the Superior Orders Defense

In examining the problem of the superior orders defense, it is necessary to pay attention to the fact that the 'Nuremberg Principle' on the said defense has not been uniformly understood. Article 8 of the Nuremberg Charter provided for the refusal of the superior orders defense in a simple expression, a concrete meaning of which was ambiguous. This ambiguity is one of the causes that led to confusion in the relevant discussions since the Nuremberg Trial. Before analyzing the relevant discussions, it is advisable to clarify what the 'Nuremberg Principle' on the superior orders defense means or to indicate the limitations of such a clarification.

In order to classify the various views expressed on the issue of the superior orders defense, this study makes use of the terminology discussed below.

First, this study classifies the view that denies the automatic acquittal of the accused by the mere fact that he/she committed criminal acts on the orders of his/

[30]The objection to such terminology has been made by D. Husak, 'Partial Defenses', *Canadian Journal of Law & Jurisprudence* 11 (1998): 167–92.

[31]In common law, the notion of 'partial defenses' has been used which leads to the conviction of a lesser offense (Dressler, supra n. 23, at 201, note 2). There has been no such terminology in international law.

[32]See Judgment, IMT, vol. 1, 224; Y. Dinstein, *The Defence of 'Obedience to Superior Orders' in International Law* (Leyden: A.W. Sijthoff, 1965), 152.

[33]Yearbook of International Law Commission [hereinafter, YILC], vol. 2, no. 2 (1996), 39–42.

her superiors as the 'denial of automatic immunity'. This view reserves judgment on the legal consequences of factors such as a lack of the knowledge of illegality and/or a lack of manifest illegality of criminal conduct, and coercion, which are incidental to superior orders. Therefore, the 'denial of automatic immunity' has the potential to develop into either the 'principle of absolute responsibility' or the 'principle of conditional immunity' explained below, depending on the evaluation of the incidental factors.

The 'principle of absolute responsibility' takes into account any incidental factors such as a lack of the knowledge of illegality and/or a lack of manifest illegality of criminal conduct, and coercion, and yet rejects immunity under the superior orders defense. The 'principle of conditional immunity' recognizes the possible immunity by the superior orders defense on the condition that factors such as a lack of the knowledge of illegality and/or a lack of manifest illegality, and coercion accompanied the superior orders.

The 'denial of the principle of automatic immunity', the 'principle of absolute responsibility', and the 'principle of conditional immunity' are opposed to the 'principle of automatic immunity'. The relationship between these notions can be illustrateded as follows:

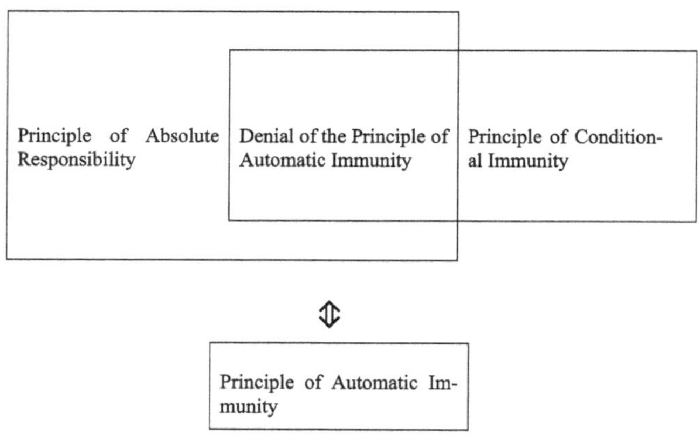

It is necessary to consider the fact that the commentators who discuss the 'principle of absolute responsibility' or the 'principle of conditional immunity' do not refer to the term 'superior orders defense' in the same way as other commentators do. Those who specifically refer to these principles take into consideration a lack of the knowledge of illegality and/or a lack of manifest illegality, and coercion, in addition to the mere fact that the accused was following orders. In consequence, they use the term 'superior orders defense' as a wide notion encompassing these factors. On the other side, reference to the simple 'denial of automatic immunity' does not necessarily clarify whether the issue of the superior orders defense relates to the mere fact that orders were given or also to other incidental factors stated above. Further, the 'principle of automatic immunity' only relates to the fact of the existence of superior orders. Thus, an expression such as the 'refusal of the superior orders defense' would have various implications depending on the range of discussions of the respective commentators.

1.3.4 International Criminal Law

There is a common understanding among international lawyers that the term 'international criminal law' has several implications. This complexity is brought about by the fact that its two characteristics – as national norms protecting national legal interests and as international norms protecting international legal interests – are intermingled in the notion of international criminal law.

The views of commentators in defining international criminal law have nuanced differences. For instance, Georg Schwarzenberger and Kanae Taijudō recognized 'international criminal law' in a substantive sense only in the case that international law is prohibitive or directly defines international crimes, and provides for the proceedings of punitive sanctions.[34]

On the other hand, Sōji Yamamoto recognizes it as an 'international legal norm' or '*droit international penal/Völkerstrafrecht*' where international law obliges states to punish certain acts by providing for the definition of crimes and concrete punishment.[35] The level of intervention, that is, the degree of the obligation of states in both aspects of substantial and procedural criminal rules, is not given so much importance.

However, most of these commentators do not necessarily deny that the term 'international criminal law' is to be used in various ways. Moreover, it has been rather exceptional in practice that international law defines international crimes specifically and conducts prosecutions at any international fora. In light of such circumstances, it does not seem advisable to limit the notion of international criminal law so strictly. It would be more suitable to the realities to give due consideration to the fact that national laws have functioned to a large extent for the implementation of international rules.

Thus, this study does not restrict the meaning of 'international criminal law'. As M. Cherif Bassiouni pointed out, the criminal aspects of international law and the international aspects of national criminal law are inseparably interrelated especially with regard to enforcement.[36] The object of this study is the substantive rules of international criminal law as an international legal norm. However, this does not imply that 'international criminal law' should be understood restrictively.[37]

---

[34] K. Taijudō, 'Kokusaihanzai no Gainen to Kokusaihō no Tachiba 'The Notion of International Crimes and the Perspective of International Law', *Jurisuto (Jurist)* 720 (1980): 71–2; G. Schwarzenberger, 'The Problem of an International Criminal Law', *Current Legal Problems* 3 (1950): 272–4.

[35] S. Yamamoto, *Kokusaikeijihō (International Criminal Law)* (Tokyo: Sanseidō, 1991), 128–37.

[36] M. Bassiouni, 'An Appraisal of the Growth and Developing Trends of International Criminal Law', *Revue internationale de droit penal* 45 (1974): 428.

[37] Regarding the notion of 'international criminal law', see, for instance, M. Bassiouni, 'The Sources and Content of International Criminal Law: A Theoretical Framework', in *International Criminal Law*, 2nd ed., vol. 1, *Crimes*, ed. M. Bassiouni, (New York: Transnational Publishers, Inc., 1999), 4–17; J. Paust et al. (eds), *International Criminal Law, Cases and Materials,* 2nd ed. (Durham, N.C.: Carolina Academic Press, 2000), 3–18.

1.4 Structure of the Study

Chapter 2 surveys the relevant national rules until the end of World War II, of the countries that drafted the Nuremberg Charter; it also reviews the concurrent situation of international rule-making. This would be a necessary step for the examination of the preparatory work of the Charter. The survey will not lead to any finding of an international rule on the superior orders defense at the time. Nonetheless, in order to specify the characteristics of the Charter's provisions, it would be meaningful to identify what sort of legal situations surrounded the drafters of the Charter.

Chapter 3 consults the preparatory work of the Nuremberg Charter and the Nuremberg Trial conducted under the Charter. The so-called Subsequent Proceedings conducted by the United States and France in their respective occupation zones in Germany as well as the Tokyo Trial are to be investigated. It is aimed to examine the essence of the 'Nuremberg Principle' with regard to the superior orders defense by obtaining the overview of these proceedings. Further, by contrasting them with relevant academic discussions, the theoretical meanings of the 'Nuremberg Principle' on the superior orders defense as well as its limitations will be considered.

Chapter 4 seeks to find out what kind of influence the above mentioned judicial proceedings had on the subsequent international rule-making, judicial practice, and academic arguments. The examination will be carried out from the point of view of two questions: how has the idea that was clearly worked out by the 'Nuremberg Principle' been evaluated, and has a contradiction of the 'Nuremberg Principle' on the superior orders defense been solved?

These examinations will not eventually lead to a meaningful conclusion from the viewpoint of clarifying the present international rules on the superior orders defense. Nonetheless, they will at least imply the basic position of the international society with regard to this issue.

Since the Nuremberg Trial, the international society considered the punishment of state officials for serious international crimes as an important proposition of modern international law. Nonetheless, such a proposition has consistently been accompanied by conscious or unconscious 'hesitation'. As will be seen below, this hesitation manifested in the most conspicuous way immediately before and after the Nuremberg Trial and has not been eradicated in the subsequent international rule-making processes. The subsequent chapters try to clarify such characteristics of the discussions on the superior orders defense, which has not been given enough attention thus far. The final purpose of this study is to identify the genuine meaning of the 'Nuremberg Principle' on the superior orders defense and an implication of the whole picture of the relevant discussion.

Chapter 2
Before the Adoption of the Nuremberg Charter

Abstract This chapter first surveys the national legal situations of the countries that drafted the Nuremberg Charter before the end of World War II, in preparation for the examination of the Charter's preparatory work. It is observed that the national judicial precedents or military legal materials of these countries commonly recognized the possibility of immunization under the superior orders defense on certain conditions. On the other hand, the concurrent international rule-making on the issue of the superior orders defense was in its infancy. Although there were some international legal instruments adopted at the time, they did not fully contribute to the formulation of relevant international rules.

2.1 National Laws of the Drafting Countries of the Nuremberg Charter

As a preliminary step for the examination of the Nuremberg Trial, this section seeks to grasp the legal situations of the countries that drafted the Nuremberg Charter – the United States, the United Kingdom, France, and the Soviet Union. The outcome of the examination described below is probably what influenced the debates of the drafters of the Nuremberg Charter or, what the drafters intentionally overlooked.

2.1.1 The Defense of Superior Orders in the United Kingdom

Studies that have analyzed domestic laws on the superior orders defense in the United Kingdom have often highlighted that the relevant provision of the British Manual of Military Law was drastically revised during World War II.[1] They

[1]For instance, G. Williams, *Criminal Law, The General Part*, 2nd ed. (London: Stevens & Sons, 1961), 299–300; L. Green, 'Superior Orders and the Reasonable Man', *Canadian Yearbook of International Law* (1970): 81–3; B. Röling, 'Criminal Responsibility for Violations of the Laws of War'. *Revue belge de droit international* 12 (1976): 18 L. Green, 'Superior Orders and Command Responsibility', *Canadian Yearbook of International Law* (1989): 176–80.

H. Satō, *The Execution of Illegal Orders and International Criminal Responsibility*,
DOI 10.1007/978-3-642-16753-9_2, © Springer-Verlag Berlin Heidelberg 2011

underline the fact that the Manual abolished the notion of automatic immunity on the ground of superior orders in its 1944 edition and vested it with only an effect of conditional immunity along with mitigation of punishment. However, this revision cannot be said to have reflected the overall development of legal situations in the United Kingdom. The precedents laid down by the civil courts of this country, irrespective to the revision of the Manual, had already shown a certain trend by the time. The revision of the Manual in 1944, as will be seen below, was rather a recurrence to the general trend of judicial practice in the United Kingdom.

Before the end of World War II, there had been few judicial precedents dealing with the issue of the superior orders defense in British civil courts, especially in military affairs. N. Dunbar commented on this fact:

> The few relevant cases leave one with the impression that English Courts, especially in the early part of last century [nineteenth century], did not welcome litigation involving an examination of military affairs or which might set an unhealthy precedent by encouraging members of the armed forces to air their grievances in public and to bring actions tending to impair respect for military discipline.[2]

In these circumstances, commentators often refer to the judgment of the Supreme Court of the Cape of Good Hope (South Africa) on the case of *Queen v. Smith* as an authority on the issue of the superior orders defense.[3] Academic arguments that criticize the Manual's provision before its revision in 1944 generally stand on the ground of the *Smith* judgment.[4]

In the following section, we will survey the relevant judicial precedents of British civil courts, and contrapose them to the revision of the Manual of Military Law.

2.1.1.1 Judicial Precedents in the United Kingdom

As stated above, up to the mid-twentieth century, the judicial precedents of British civil courts dealing with the issue of the superior orders defense in military affairs

---

[2] N. Dunbar, 'Some Aspects of the Problem of Superior Orders in the Law of War', *Judicial Review* 63 (1951): 238. Other arguments that pointed out a paucity of relevant judicial precedents of the United Kingdom include C. Kenny, *Outlines of Criminal Law*, 15th ed. (Cambridge: Cambridge University Press, 1936), 81; Williams, supra n. 1, at 297. Battle further drew attention to the inconsistency among those limited number of judicial precedents. (G. Battle, 'The Trial before the Leipsic Supreme Court of Germans Accused of War Crimes', *Virginia Law Review* 8 (1921): 21–2).

[3] For instance, H. Stephen, 'Superior Orders as Excuse for Homicide', *Law Quarterly Review* 17 (1901): 87–9; Dunbar, supra n. 2, at 239–40; K. Kittichaisaree, *International Criminal Law* (New York; London: Oxford University Press, 2001), 266.

[4] H. Bellot, 'War Crimes: Their Prevention and Punishment', *Transactions of Grotius Society* 2 (1917): 45–8; Address by Lord Cave, Minutes of the Proceedings of the Seventh Annual General Meeting, *Transactions of the Grotius Society* 8 (1923): xxiii; S. Glueck, *War Criminals, Their Prosecution & Punishment* (New York: Alfred A. Knopf, 1944) 149–50; Green, supra n. 1, 'Reasonable Man', at 78–83.

were considerably limited. Further, the views expressed in the relevant precedents had not been standardized.

For instance, there was a judgment that recognized immunity by the fact of superior orders in some cases. The judgment in *Keighly v. Bell*, which was a civil case in the late nineteenth century treating false imprisonment by a military person, showed such an idea:

> Were I compelled to determine that question, I should probably hold that the orders are an absolute justification in time of actual war – at all events, as regards enemies, or foreigners – and, I should think, even with regard to English-born subjects of the Crown, unless the orders were such as could not legally be given. I believe that the better opinion is, that an officer or soldier, acting under the orders of his superior – not being necessarily or manifestly illegal – would be justified by his orders.[5]

This judgment expressed the view that superior orders were to be recognized as immunizing factors where the conduct in question had not been manifestly illegal.[6]

On the other hand, other judgments denied immunity on the ground of superior orders, for example, the judgment in *Rex v. Thomas*. In this case of murder by an English marine, the court convicted the accused by rejecting the jury's view that the accused was carrying out his duty.[7]

In these circumstances, many commentators evaluate the 1900 judgment in *Smith* as an authoritative view.[8] The judgment was made by the Supreme Court of the Cape of Good Hope, a special court of the colony of the British Empire at the time. The accused, a private soldier, was charged with the murder of a local who had not immediately obeyed his order. The accused asserted that he had acted in obedience of his superior's orders. The Supreme Court admitted this assertion, reasoning that the superior orders defense could be recognized under the conditions of a lack of the knowledge of the illegality of his/her conduct and a lack of manifest illegality of the conduct in question[9]:

> I think it is a safe rule to lay down that if a soldier honestly believes he is doing his duty in obeying the commands of his superior, and if the orders are not so manifestly illegal that he

---

[5]*Keighly v. Bell* (1866), 4 F&F 763, 790, 176 ER 781, 793.

[6]Lauterpacht quoted *Keighly v. Bell* as representing concurrent judicial precedents in the United Kingdom. See H. Lauterpacht, 'The Law of Nations and the Punishment of War Crimes', *British Yearbook of International Law* 21 (1994): 72.

[7]Dunbar, supra n. 2, at 239; J. Turner, *Russell on Crime*, 12th ed., vol. 1 (London: Stevens, 1964), 87–8. Regarding to this case, see *Rex. v. Thomas* (1816), 4 M&S 441, 105 ER [KB] 897.

[8]See the academic arguments referred to in Footnotes 3 and 4 of this chapter.

[9]Although the judgment of *Keighly v. Bell* used the word 'justification' whereas the *Smith* judgment made use of the expression 'excuse', it is not required to strictly differentiate the notion of a justification from that of an excuse in British criminal law (J. Smith, *Justification and Excuse in the Criminal Law* (London: Stevens, 1989), 7–8). As both the notions of a justification and of an excuse are included in the notion of 'defense' (*ibid.*, 1; M. Allen, *Textbook on Criminal Law*, 8th ed. (Oxford; New York: Oxford University Press, 2005), 158–9), it does not seem to be necessary to pay attention so much to the difference of the terminology of the judgments in question.

> must or ought to have known that they were unlawful, the private soldier would be protected by the orders of his superior officer.[10]

This view resembles the judgment given in *Keighly v. Bell*. The *Smith* judgment underlined the importance of military discipline as the ground for recognizing the superior orders defense. The court explained that it would be a subversion of military discipline if a soldier hesitated in obeying orders, although 'it is monstrous to suppose that a soldier would be protected where the order is grossly illegal'.[11] The court concluded that immunizing a soldier who had obeyed 'not necessarily or manifestly illegal' orders was 'a well-established principle of law'.[12] The judgment in *Smith* mentioned that the *Keighly v. Bell* judgment had shown this 'principle of law'. This is the principle of conditional immunity. A difference between these two judgments was that the *Smith* judgment, in contrast to the other judgment, limited the possibility of immunity by also considering subjective factors such as the 'knowledge' of the accused. This rule denoted in the *Smith* judgment would be an exception in common law, which generally does not recognize a mistake of law as an immunizing factor.[13]

The judgment given in *Smith,* which represented a 'well-established principle of law', has been upheld by many commentators. Nonetheless, this precedent cannot be deemed binding in the United Kingdom under the doctrine of precedent (*stare decisis*).[14] Moreover, commentators have not clarified why *Smith* should be recognized as a leading case.[15] In fact, the judgments of the Dominions and other units of the British Empire had sometimes been attached importance as 'persuasive precedents'[16] or 'authorities'.[17] However, high esteem for the *Smith* judgment seems, after all, as Hugh Bellot pointed out,[18] owing to the fact that it had been the only

---

[10] 17 Cape Rep. (1900) 561, 568.

[11] Ibid., 566–7.

[12] Ibid., 568.

[13] J. Appleman, *Military Tribunals and International Crimes* (Indianapolis: Bobbs-Merrill Company, Inc., 1954), 59; Allen, supra n. 9, at 91–2. Regarding this point, German *Criminal Code* recognizes a mistake of law as an exempting factor if the mistake in question was unavoidable (§17, *Strafgesetzbuch*). It is also the case with criminal laws of other countries that have been influenced by German criminal law. (M. Osiel, 'Obeying Orders: Atrocity, Military Discipline, and the Law of War', *California Law Review* 86 (1998): 960). On the variety of academic arguments and judicial precedents in Japan, see N. Nishida, *Keihō Sōron (Criminal Law, General Part)* (Tokyo: Kōbundō, 2006), 222–30.

[14] With regard to the judicial precedents of the Dominions and colonies of the British Empire, *stare decisis* in relation to judicial organs of the United Kingdom only matters with the precedents of the Privy Council (K. Takayanagi, *Eibeihōgen Riron (Theory of the Source of Anglo-American Law)* (Tokyo: Yūhikau, 1938), 97–8; C. Allen, *Law in the Making,* 6th ed. (Oxford: Clarendon Press, 1958), 243–5; H. Tanaka, *Eibeihō Sōron (Introduction to Anglo-American Law)*, vol.2 (Tokyo: University of Tokyo Press, 1980), 477.

[15] See, for instance, Glueck, supra n. 4, at 149–50.

[16] Takayanagi, supra n. 14, at 98.

[17] Allen, supra n. 14, at, 260–61.

[18] Bellot, supra n. 4, at 47–8. See also Dunbar, supra n. 2, at 239.

judicial precedent dealing with the issue of the superior orders defense at the time. A more important case from the viewpoint of the doctrine of precedent would be, as Hersch Lauterpacht denoted, the *Keighly v. Bell* case.[19] However, this was a judgment on a civil case and it would not be appropriate to consider its judgment as directly applicable to criminal cases.

Thus, the judgment given in *Smith* cannot be deemed indisputably established as a leading case in the United Kingdom. On the other hand, there were no relevant precedents during the time in question, whereas *Smith* had been positively evaluated by many commentators. All in all, one can possibly regard the judgments in *Smith* and *Keighly v. Bell* as indicating a concurrent trend in the opinions of the civil courts of the United Kingdom to some extent – that is, a trend to recognize the superior orders defense under the criteria of 'knowledge of illegality' and/or 'manifest illegality'. It can be said that, although the judicial precedents of the United Kingdom had not been fully established on the issue of the superior orders defense, it had given certain direction until World War II.

2.1.1.2 Oppenheim's *International Law* and the British Manual of Military Law

Oppenheim and the Manual of 1914

The British Manual of Military Law of 1914 recognized automatic immunity under the superior orders defense. The British Manual was drawn up in 1884 by the Parliamentary Counsel Office under the request of the Secretary of State for War. It surveyed the Army Act, 1881, the Rules of Procedure, and the history of military law and organizations.[20] The Manual first provided for the superior orders defense in its 1914 edition.[21] Its previous fifth edition of 1907 shelved relevant provisions in light of the fact that important issues of international law had just been considered at the Hague Conference.[22] Its fourth edition of 1899 contained no provisions on the superior orders defense.[23]

Section 443 of the Manual of 1914 in principle approved the punishment of enemy soldiers who carried out state acts. However, the provision did not recognize acts committed under superior orders as war crimes:

---

[19] Lauterpacht, supra n. 6, at 72.

[20] 'Preface to the First Edition', in War Office, Manual of Military Law (London: Printed for His Majesty's Stationery Office by Harrison and Sons, 1899), iii.

[21] Bellot, supra n. 4, at 47; Glueck, supra n. 4, at 150; Lauterpacht, supra n. 6, at 69.

[22] 'Note', in War Office, Manual of Military Law (London: Printed for His Majesty's Stationery Office by Harrison and Sons, 1907), 222.

[23] War Office, Manual of Military Law (London: Printed for His Majesty's Stationery Office by Harrison and Sons, 1899).

members of the armed forces who commit such violations of the recognized rules of warfare as are ordered by their Government or by their commander are not war criminals and cannot therefore be punished by the enemy. He may punish the officials or commanders responsible for such orders if they fall into his hands, but otherwise he may only resort to the other means of obtaining redress [complaints, good offices, reprisals, and so forth] which are dealt with in this chapter.[24]

This provision was elaborated on by Brigadier-General Sir James Edmonds. Edmonds, as per the decision of the Secretary of State for War, sought Lassa Oppenheim's opinions on the Manual before its publication.[25]

Oppenheim, in the first edition of his *International Law, Vol. 2, War and Neutrality*, stated the following on the orders of the government or superiors:

Violations of rules regarding warfare are war crimes only when committed without an order of the belligerent Government concerned. If members of the armed forces commit violations *by order* of their Government, they are not war criminals and cannot be punished by the enemy; the latter can, however, resort to reprisals. In case members of forces commit violations ordered by their commanders, the members cannot be punished, for the commanders are alone responsible, and the latter may, therefore, be punished as war criminals on their capture by the enemy.[26]

The third edition of Oppenheim's *International Law* in 1921 emphasized that the reason for recognizing the superior orders defense was the existence of compulsion by law: 'The law cannot require an individual to be punished for an act which he was compelled by law to commit'.[27] Violations of the laws of war committed under the orders of governments or superiors shall not be deemed as war crimes; only the person who committed such illegal acts without any orders may be punished by adversaries.[28] The rule of the British Manual of Military Law which recognized automatic immunity under the superior orders defense can be said to have reflected this view of Oppenheim at the time.[29]

---

[24]War Office, Manual of Military Law (London: Printed for His Majesty's Stationery Office by Harrison and Sons, 1914), Art. 443.

[25]Lord Hankey's Speech, Parliamentary Debates, House of Lords 168 (19 July 1950): 467.

[26]L. Oppenheim, *International Law,* vol.2, *War and Neutrality* (London: Longmans, Green and Co., 1906), 264–5.

[27]L. Oppenheim, *International Law*, 3rd ed. by R. Roxburgh, vol.2, *War and Neutrality* (London: Longmans, 1921), 343. Its fourth and fifth editions expressed the same argument (L. Oppenheim, *International Law*, 4th ed. by A. McNair, vol.2, *Disputes, War and Neutrality* (London: Longman, Green, 1926) 410; L. Oppenheim, *International Law*, 5th ed. by H. Lauterpacht, vol.2, *Disputes, War and Neutrality* (London: Longmans, Green, 1935) 454).

[28]Oppenheim, supra n. 26, at 264.

[29]It is the common understanding among commentators that the provision on the superior orders defense in the Manual reflected the view of Oppenheim. *See* Bellot, supra n.4, at 46; Lauterpacht, supra n. 6, at 69; Dunbar, supra n. 2, at 242; Green, supra n. 1, 'Reasonable Man', at 81.

Revision of the Manual in 1944

A considerable number of concurrent commentators were critical of the Manual provision that recognized automatic immunity under the superior orders defense. The criticism reflected the view of British civil courts, which had developed but not yet established certain trend by that time.[30] Some commentators who pointed out the disparity between the Manual provision and British judicial precedents also asserted that the Manual did not hold any legal effect or official authority.[31]

Meanwhile, Coleman Phillipson criticized the Manual from the viewpoint of the necessity of punishing war crimes:

> It has been contended in some quarters that a combatant's acts, no matter how heinous, outrageous, and abominable, do not possess a criminal character if they are committed under orders from superior officers. But this argument carried to its logical conclusion would lead to ineptitude and absurdity; the successive shifting of responsibility would exculpate every one until we reached the ultimate cause – in the case of Germany let us say, for example, the Kaiser.[32]

Phillipson implied that the superior orders defense should not be recognized in principle so that it does not impede punishments for war crimes. However, he termed the conduct as 'heinous, outrageous, and abominable' and did not necessarily deny the superior orders defense for acts whose illegality was not manifest. His view was surely critical of the relevant provision of the Manual. But it did not apparently conflict with the trend of the British judicial precedents,[33] which conditionally allowed the superior orders defense on the test of manifest illegality.

A fatal blow to the 1914 edition of the Manual provision on the superior orders defense was the report of the British Government Committee of Enquiry into 'War Crimes' of 1918–1919 (Birkenhead Committee). The Committee reported that the relevant provision of the Manual did not have the authority and the Committee could not back the view expressed by the Manual.[34]

It is noteworthy that the Birkenhead Committee report, along with Phillipson's view, possibly coincided with concurrent judicial precedents of British civil courts. That is, the report denied the superior orders defense only if the illegal conduct in question led to manifest violation of laws and customs of war.[35]

---

[30] See the academic arguments referred to in Footnote 4 of this chapter.

[31] Bellot, supra n. 4, at 46; Cave, supra n. 4, at xxiii.

[32] C. Phillipson, *International Law and the Great War* (London: T. Fisher Unwin, 1915), 260–61.

[33] See the judgment of *Keighly v. Bell* of 1866.

[34] J. Morgan, 'Nuremberg and After', *Quarterly Review* 285 (1947): 330. The report of the Committee supported the 'Opinion' of Morgan which had been requested by Lord Birkenhead (*ibid.*, 329–30).

[35] *Ibid.*

The notion of automatic immunity under the superior orders defense did not gain support, except in the military circle.[36] Under such circumstances, the editor of the sixth edition of Oppenheim's *International Law* of 1940, Lauterpacht, revised the description of the superior orders defense. He took a 180° turn on the relevant lines that had been maintained until the treatise's fifth edition of 1935. The sixth edition rejected the view adopted by the British Manual of Military Law, stating that 'it is difficult to regard it as expressing a sound legal principle':[37]

> The fact that a rule of warfare has been violated in pursuance of an order of the belligerent Government or of an individual belligerent commander does not deprive the act in question of its character as a war crime; neither does it, in principle, confer upon the perpetrator immunity from punishment by the injured belligerent.[38]

It is to be noted that the above quote uses the expression 'neither does it, *in principle*, confer upon the perpetrator immunity [italics by the author]'. It implies that the clause does not categorically reject the superior orders defense, which is parallel to the positions of Phillipson and the report of the Birkenhead Committee that criticized the 1914 edition of the British Manual. The sixth edition of *International Law* stated that when considering the issue of superior orders, it was necessary to take into account:

> the fact that obedience to military orders, not obviously unlawful, is the duty of every member of the armed forces and that the latter cannot, in conditions of war discipline, be expected to weigh scrupulously the legal merits of the order received; that rules of warfare are often controversial; and that an act otherwise amounting to a war crime may have been executed in obedience to orders conceived as a measure of reprisals. Such circumstances are probably in themselves sufficient to divest the act of the stigma of a war crime.[39]

Lauterpacht thus indicated the possibility of allowing the superior orders defense in exceptional cases. This view was also apparently in line with the trend that had been developed by the judicial precedents in the United Kingdom.

Oppenheim's *International Law* revised its description on the superior orders defense in 1940. In 1944, and in concert with this revision, the British Manual of Military Law was also revised. Both revisions were made after the outbreak of World War II. This change of course has been explained as a measure for preventing enemy soldiers from appealing for defense, which had conventionally been allowed for British soldiers.[40] Such a comment seems to stand to reason. However,

---

[36]Bellot, supra n. 4, at 47; G. Finch, 'Superior Orders and War Crimes', *American Journal of International Law* 15 (1921): 441. For instance, see the argument of Commander Graham Bower in G. Bower, 'The Laws of War: Prisoners of War and Reprisals', *Transaction of Grotius Society* 1 (1916): 24.

[37]L. Oppenheim, *International Law*, 6th ed. by H. Lauterpacht, vol.2, *Disputes, War and Neutrality* (London: Longman, Green & Co., 1940), 453–4.

[38]*Ibid.*, 453.

[39]*Ibid.*, 454.

[40]A. Knieriem, *The Nuremberg Trials* (Chicago: Henry Regnery Company, 1959), 246–9; H. Jescheck, *Die Verantwortlichkeit der Staatsorgane nach Völkerstrafrecht – Eine Studie zu den*

even if there were political motives behind the revision of the Manual, a consequence of the revision eventually conformed to the rule laid down by British courts.[41] We should be careful about this point.

The opening of Section 443 of the Manual was revised to reflect verbatim the description of the sixth edition of Oppenheim/Lauterpacht's *International Law*.[42] With respect to the exceptional cases where the superior orders defense would be recognized, Section 443 basically used the sixth edition of *International Law* verbatim.

Thus, it can be said that the notion of automatic immunity under the superior orders defense much reflected Oppenheim's view from the 1900s to the 1910s. However, such a notion did not conform to the judicial precedents of British civil courts. What the civil courts had been developing was the principle of conditional immunity on the tests of the knowledge of illegality and/or manifest illegality. In consequence, and against the background of a change in circumstances caused by the outbreak of war, the Oppenheim's view and the British Manual of 1914, which reflected his view, were much criticized. Eventually, Oppenheim's treatise and the Manual were amended in 1944. It can be said that in the United Kingdom, the prevalent view on the superior orders defense toward the end of World War II was the principle of conditional immunity on the tests of the knowledge of illegality and/or manifest illegality.

Such a change in the legal situations in the United Kingdom led to a similar change in the United States to some extent. However, the development of judicial precedents on the superior orders defense in the latter bore independent characteristics. It was rather substantial in contrast to the case of the United Kingdom.

2.1.2 Superior Orders Defense in the United States

As discussed above, the British Manual of Military Law was revised just before the end of World War II in reflecting the trend of British civil courts. Almost the same can be said about the United States' Rules of Land Warfare. Moreover, as in the British case, critics of the US Rules before their revision based their arguments on the judicial precedents of US civil courts.[43]

As the British judicial precedents up to the end of the war had been limited, it was difficult to even identify the standpoint of courts on the superior orders defense.

Nürnberger Prozessen – (Bonn: Ludwig Röhrscheid Verlag, 1952), 260. See also Parliamentary Debates, House of Lords 168 (19 July 1950): 442.

[41]Glaser drew attention to this point. See S. Glaser, 'L'ordre hiérarchique en droit pénal international', *Revue de droit pénal et de criminologie* 33 (1952–3): 294–8.

[42]The United Nations War Crimes Commission, *History of the United Nations War Crimes Commission and the Development of the Laws of War* (London: HMSO, 1948), 282.

[43]Glueck, supra n. 4, at 140–49; J. Berger, 'The Legal Nature of War Crimes and the Problem of Superior Command', *American Political Science Review* 38 (1944): 1203; Dunbar, supra n. 2, at 240–43.

The situation was somehow different in the United States. The view of US civil courts on the superior orders defense was conspicuously in contrast to the relevant provision of the Rules.

We will now survey the development of the Rules of Land Warfare and the judicial precedents of US courts on the issue of the superior orders defense before the end of World War II.

2.1.2.1 Change in the Rules of Land Warfare

The Rules of Land Warfare is a manual first adopted in 1914 for use by officers of the US land forces. The provisions were based on the *Instructions for the Government of Armies of the United States in the Field* (Lieber Code).[44] The Lieber Code, promulgated by President Lincoln during the Civil War, was the first US code regulating military actions in the field.[45] The Code was effective only for the US Army. Nonetheless, it much influenced the adoption of military manuals of countries such as Prussia, France, and Russia.[46] The Lieber Code confined itself to recognizing the superior orders defense for specific criminal acts in Articles 44 and 69.[47] It did not provide for the said defense in a general manner.

In contrast to the Lieber Code, the Rules of Land Warfare stipulated general rules on the superior orders defense. Section 366 of the Rules allowed automatic immunity under the superior orders defense regardless of individual circumstances in the respective cases:

> Individuals of the armed forces will not be punished for these offenses in case they are committed under the orders or sanction of their government or commanders. The commanders ordering the commission of such acts, or under whose authority they are committed by their troops, may be punished by the belligerent into whose hands they may fall.[48]

This provision is similar to Section 443 of the 1949 edition of the British Manual of Military Law. Commentators such as George Finch expressed that Section 443 of the British Manual 'was substantially copied into the Rules of Land Warfare'.[49]

---

[44]'Preface', in War Department: Office of the Chief of Staff, Rules of Land Warfare (Washington, DC: GPO, 1914), 7.

[45]L. Green, *The Contemporary Law of Armed Conflict,* 2nd ed. (New York: Juris Publishing, 2000), 29.

[46]*Ibid.*, 29–30.

[47]Instructions for the Government of Armies of the United States in the Field, Prepared by Francis Lieber, Promulgated as General Orders No.100 by President Lincoln, 24 April 1863, in *The Laws of Armed Conflicts, A Collection of Conventions, Resolutions and Other Documents*, eds D. Schindler & J. Toman (Dordrecht : Nijhoff, 1988), 10, 12.

[48]War Department: Office of the Chief of Staff, Rules of Land Warfare (Washington, DC: GPO, 1914), Sec. 366.

[49]Finch, supra n. 36, 'Superior Orders', at 441; A. Sack, 'Punishment of War Criminals and the Defence of Superior Order', *Law Quarterly Review* 60 (1944) 66; Berger, supra n. 43, at 1203; Glueck, supra n. 4, at 150.

However, toward the end of World War II, the treatment of war criminals of the Axis Powers had been focused as of vital importance, and the provision on the superior orders defense of the Rules was deemed to be an obstacle to the punishment of war criminals of those adversaries. The view that the recognition of the superior orders defense would hedge war crimes trials was specifically expressed by Colonel Archibald King, Chief of War Plans Division of the Judge Advocate General's Department of the United States Army, which proposed the revision of the Rules of Land Warfare. King, in his memorandum for the Judge Advocate General in October 1944, emphasized the necessity of revising Section 366 of the Rules, which, in his argument, (1) did not reflect the judicial precedents of the United States, (2) did not conform with the concurrent views of international law, and (3) was likely to be used for the prevention of proper punishment of Axis war criminals.[50] With regard to the concurrent 'views of international law', King referred to the revision of the British Manual of Military Law in April 1944.

The eventual proposal for the revision by the Judge Advocate General to the Assistant Chief of Staff of the War Department – which reflected the memorandum of King – had a provision that denied the superior orders defense for 'acts which violate accepted rules of warfare or are otherwise clearly illegal'.[51] The memorandum of King for the Commanding General of the Army Service Forces denoted that the proposed change would deny the superior orders defense 'where the superior's order is clearly illegal or would obviously violate accepted rules of warfare'.[52]

Consequently, after the discussion in the War Department, Section 366 of the Rules of Land Warfare was revised as follows:

> Individuals and organisations who violate the accepted laws and customs of war may be punished therefore. However, the fact that the acts complained of were done pursuant to order of a superior or government sanction may be taken into consideration in determining culpability, either by way of defence or in mitigation of punishment. The person giving such orders may also be punished.[53]

Similar to the British Manual, this revision realized a change from automatic immunity to conditional immunity. A person who committed criminal acts may possibly be immunized on the ground that he/she was following the orders of the government or superiors. However, he/she cannot expect automatic immunity any longer, which was recognized by the Rules of 1914.

The Rules of 1944 did not clarify the circumstances under which the accused may be immunized on the ground of superior orders or government sanction. King's proposal relied on the test of manifest illegality. Nonetheless, the final provision did

---

[50]Memorandum for the Judge Advocate General, 4 Oct. 1944, in RG 153, *JAG*, Box 1606, Case File 103-24 (United States National Archives and Records Administration).

[51]Memorandum for the Assistant Chief of Staff, G-1, WDGS, 4 Oct. 1944, in ibid.

[52]Memorandum for the Commanding General, Army Service Forces, 4 Oct. 1944, in ibid.

[53]Memorandum for General Henry, 2 November 1944, in RG 165, *WDGS/WDSS*, *Personnel*, Box 313 (United States National Archives and Records Administration); The United Nations War Crimes Commission, supra n. 42, at 282.

not refer to this point. As will be seen below, the US courts argued on the lack of the knowledge of illegality and/or lack of manifest illegality, and coercion from superiors as the grounds of immunity by that time. However, it would not be appropriate to conclude on the content of Section 366 by analogy with those arguments. It seems difficult to specify the grounds of immunity from the wording of the Rules.

As King pointed out, automatic immunity, which was adopted by the Rules of Land Warfare of 1914, did not conform with the concurrent judicial precedents of US civil courts. This point will be clarified in the next section. The most significant difference was that the courts, in contrast to the Rules, deemed the function of the superior orders defense to be restrictive.

2.1.2.2 Judicial Precedents of US Courts

'Denial of Superior Orders Defense' and Judicial Precedents

The judgment given in *Wirz* in 1865 has often been referred to as the first precedent of US courts dealing with the issue of the superior orders defense.[54] In this case, Major Henry Wirz was charged on the count of persecuting Union prisoners of war during the Civil War. The judgment was delivered by a military commission and the grounds for conviction as well as the reasoning behind the judgment were not clearly presented. Therefore, it is difficult to find out the details of the discussion. However, Leslie Green and M. Cherif Bassiouni interpret the Wirz's conviction as the denial of the superior orders defense for enemy soldiers.[55]

Some people argue that the US courts had not recognized the superior orders defense by soldiers on violations of the laws of war up to the end of World War II,[56] whereas others contend the opposite.[57] However, the judicial precedents, which were raised by the former, seem to have been shelved in a disorderly fashion in

[54]Green, supra n. 1, 'Reasonable Man', 77–8; M. Bassiouni, *Crimes against Humanity in International Criminal Law* (Dordrecht; Boston: Martinus Nijhoff Publishers, 1992), 418–9. See also Finch, supra n. 36, 'Superior Orders', at 444–5; S. Gregory, 'Criminal Responsibility of Sovereigns for Willful Violations of the Laws of War', *Virginia Law Review* 6 (1919): 403–5.

[55]Green, supra n. 1, 'Reasonable Man', at 78; Bassiouni, supra n. 54, at, 419.

[56]Berger, supra n. 43, at 1203. See also A. Dinstag, '*Fedorenko v. United States*: War Crimes, the Defense of Duress, and American Nationality Law', *Columbia Law Review* 82 (1982), 145. As to this point, Bassiouni restricted himself to listing the cases in which the superior orders defense had been denied. See Bassiouni, supra n. 54, at, 416–9.

[57]The arguments which deem that conditional immunity was recognized include Battle, supra n. 2, at 22–4; Green, supra n. 1, 'Reasonable Man', at 73–7. Colby restricted himself to listing the cases in which the superior orders defense was allowed. See E. Colby, 'War Crimes', *Michigan Law Review* 23 (1924–5): 606–7.

defiance of the respective character of the cases. The examples are the judgments in *Little et al. v. Barreme et al.*,[58] *Mitchell v. Harmony*,[59] and *US v. Bevans*.[60]

Little et al. v. Barreme et al. dealt with the illegal capture of a Danish brigantine by the US frigates. The Supreme Court judged that the defendant who had captured the Danish brigantine under superior orders should be answerable for damages. The court rejected the superior orders defense by the defendant, delivering that 'the instructions cannot change the nature of the transaction, or legalize an act which without those instructions would have been a plain trespass'.[61] The judgment deemed that the order of the capture, which eventually had directed a manifest trespass, was illegal.

In *Mitchell v. Harmony*, the judgment recognized that the US officer who had seized the plaintiff's property in Mexico during the war between the United States and Mexico was responsible for compensation. In *US v. Bevans*, a sentry was convicted for murdering a person who had abused him using reproachful words on board a US naval vessel. In both cases, the judgment rejected the superior orders defense of soldiers as in *Little et al. v. Barreme et al.*.

However, it would be problematic to reject the superior orders defense in a general way by consulting the judgments in *Little et al. v. Barreme et al.* and *US v. Bevans*. To be sure, the judgment in *US v. Bevans*, for example, denied the superior orders defense. It delivered that an order that directs the killing of a person in response to abuse through reproachful words would be 'illegal and void, and not binding upon any person; and the party who should give the order, equally with the party who should execute it, would be involved in the guilt of murder'.[62] However, the judgment restricted the argument of the quote to the orders that are 'against the express provisions of law, and against natural justice'.[63] This was also the case with *Little et al. v. Barreme et al.* As already noted, the judgment in *Little et al. v. Barreme et al.* dealt with the acts 'which without those instructions would have been a plain trespass'. As will be seen below, a question of weather or not the illegality of the criminal conduct was manifest has been treated as crucial in discussing the superior orders defense. It would be inappropriate to regard these two judgments as having completely denied the superior orders defense.

In contrast to these cases, the judgment in *Mitchell v. Harmony* generally rejected the superior orders defense irrespective of whether or not the conduct in question had been manifestly illegal.[64] However, it should be noted that the

---

[58] 6 US (2 Cranch) 170 (1804).

[59] 54 US (13 How) 115 (1851).

[60] 24 F. Cas. 1138 (No. 14,589)(C.C.D.Mass., 1816).

[61] 6 US (2 Cranch) 170, 179 (1804). The cases which specifically supported *Little et al. v. Barreme et al.* include *US v. Bright*, 24 F.Cas. 1232, 1238 (No. 14,647)(C.C.D.Pa. 1809).

[62] 24 F. Cas. 1138, 1140 (No. 14,589)(C.C.D.Mass. 1816).

[63] Ibid.

[64] 54 US 115, 137 (1851).

judgment was made for civil proceedings, a conclusion of which does not necessarily conform to the precedents of criminal cases.[65]

Criminal Cases and Superior Orders Defense

Oft-cited criminal cases of US courts that dealt with the issue of the superior orders defense by soldiers are *US v. Jones,*[66] *McCall v. McDowell et al.,*[67] and *In re Fair et al.*[68]

In *US v. Jones,* a US officer was indicted for piracy upon a Portuguese vessel. The court reasoned in its judgment that 'the participation of the inferior officer, in an act which he knows, or ought to know, to be illegal, will not be excused by the order of his superior'.[69]

McCall v. McDowell et al. treated a false imprisonment by a US officer. The court resolved in its judgment that the accused had 'acted not as a volunteer':

> Except in a plain case of excess of authority, where at first blush it is apparent and palpable to the commonest understanding that the order is illegal, I cannot but think that the law should excuse the military subordinate when acting in obedience to the orders of his commander. Otherwise he is placed in the dangerous dilemma of being liable in damages to third persons for obedience to an order, or to the loss of his commission and disgrace for disobedience thereto.[70]

The judgment made use of the notion of 'commonest understanding' in deciding whether or not the illegality of the conduct was manifest.[71]

Further, the court gave a reason as to why the superior orders defense should be approved in cases where the illegality of the criminal conduct had not been manifest. The court underlined the importance of the obligation of obeying orders in the army and drew attention to the fact that such an obligation made subordinates vulnerable to 'coercion':

> The first duty of a soldier is obedience, and without this there can be neither discipline nor efficiency in an army. If every subordinate officer and soldier were at liberty to question the

[65] Glueck, supra n. 4, at 144; Dunbar, supra n. 2, at 235–6. On the other hand, Bartlett understood the defense of superior orders as that of coercion. He explained on *Mitchell v. Harmony* that the accused had not faced urgent or immediate danger by superior orders so that the defense could not be recognized. See H. Bartlett, 'Liability for Official War Crimes', *Law Quarterly Review* 35 (1919): 191).

[66] 26 F.Cas. 653 (No. 15,494)(C.C.D.Pa. 1813).

[67] 15 F.Cas. 1235 (No. 8,673)(C.C.D.Cal. 1867).

[68] 100 Fed. 149 (C.C.D.Neb. 1900).

[69] 26 F.Cas. 653, 657-8 (No. 15,494)(C.C.D.Pa. 1813).

[70] 15 F.Cas. 1235, 1240 (No. 8,673)(C.C.D.Cal. 1867). The same view was shown in the judgment in *In re Fair et al.* (100 Fed. 149, 154-5 (C.C.D.Neb. 1900)).

[71] See the *In re Fair et al.* judgment that held the same test (100 Fed. 149, 155 (C.C.D.Neb. 1900)).

> legality of the orders of the commander, and obey them or not as they may consider them valid or invalid, the camp would be turned into a debating school, where the precious moment for action would be wasted in wordy conflicts between the advocates of conflicting opinions.[72]

The judgment attached importance to the fact that soldiers were possibly required to act in contravention of his/her own intention because of the coercion under which they were placed. Eventually, the court recognized the superior orders defense on the test of manifest illegality. The factor of coercion was referred to only as the ground for adopting the test of manifest illegality, that is, the reason why the superior orders defense should be allowed in cases where the illegality of the conduct was not manifest. However, the issue of coercion was revealed as an independent topic on the superior orders defense later in the drafting of the Nuremberg Charter.

Thus, it can be said that some major precedents of US civil courts that dealt with the issue of the superior orders defense by US soldiers had been developing a view as follows: If a soldier who committed a criminal act was not aware of the illegality of the act, and/or if the act was not manifestly illegal, the soldier may appeal under the defense of superior orders. Whether or not the illegality of the act was manifest should be judged by the test of 'commonest understanding'.[73]

The Rules of Land Warfare of 1914 introduced a provision that allowed automatic immunity under the superior orders defense. This provision can be said to have been contrary to the general trend of the judicial precedents of US civil courts since the nineteenth century. The revision of the Rules in 1944 and the eventual denial of the superior orders defense in principle could not avoid criticism as was the case with the revision of the British Manual of Military Law. Critics regarded the revisions as political expediencies foreseeing the prosecution of enemy war criminals after World War II.[74] Nonetheless, as seen above, the view that the British Manual of 1944 adopted was in conformity with the developing trend of the judicial precedents of British civil courts. The same may be said with the legal situations in the United States. A change from automatic immunity to conditional immunity could be described as a highly political measure, but it was in fact a recurrence to the major view of the US judicial precedents.

---

[72] 15 F.Cas. 1235, 1240-41 (No. 8,673)(C.C.D.Cal. 1867).

[73] The arguments which conclude that conditional immunity had come to be recognized especially in criminal cases include Glueck, supra n. 4, at 144–9; Dunbar, supra n. 2, at 235–7. See also J. Insco, 'Defense of Superior Orders before Military Commissions', *Duke Journal of Comparative & International Law* 13 (2003): 399–406.

[74] See, for instance, the statement of the Earl of Cork and Orrery that '[r]evenge is sweet, and the rules laid down in the British and American Manuals were an obstacle to its attainment' (Parliamentary Debates, House of Lords 168 (19 July 1950): 442). The American 'Manual' is identical with the US Field Manual 27-10, that is, the US Rules of Land Warfare.

2.1.3 Superior Orders Defense in France

In France, the issue of the punishment of enemy soldiers for war crimes had been focused on since World War I. First, it was discussed whether or not French judicial organs had jurisdiction for war crimes that had been committed by enemy soldiers. If the answer was positive, the next question was whether or not such jurisdiction covered criminal acts that had been committed outside French territory. Further, in relation to the issue of the superior orders defense, it was questioned if the provision on an excuse in the French *Penal Code (Code pénal (anciene))* could be applied to the trials of enemy soldiers. These problems were much discussed especially towards the end of World War I.

Principal debaters on the topic of war crimes prosecution at the time in France were Alexandre Mérignhac and Louis Renault.[75] This section surveys the academic debates mainly between these two commentators and the eventual legislation promulgated by the French government just before the establishment of the Nuremberg Charter.

2.1.3.1 Academic Debates

Until World War II, there were various arguments in France about superior orders with respect to the French *Penal Code*. For instance, commentators such as Henri Donnedieu de Vabres[76] recognized immunity or mitigation of punishment on the test of manifest illegality. On the other hand, Émile Garçon[77] and others recognized immunity on the ground of coercion incidental to orders.[78] There were also discussants such as Léon Duguit who completely denied the illegality of the acts committed under superior orders.[79]

However, since World War I, the issue of punishment of enemy war criminals came to be intensively discussed and the question of the superior orders defense by

---

[75]See A. Mérignhac, 'De la sanction des infractions au droit des gens commises, au cours de la guerre européenne, par les empires du centre', *Revue générale de droit international public* 24 (1917): 5–56 ; L. Renault, 'De l'application du droit pénal aux faits de guerre', *Revue générale de droit international public* 25 (1918): 5–29.

[76]H. Donnedieu de Vabres, *Traité élémentaire de droit criminel et de législation pénale comparée* (Paris: Librairie du recueil sirey, 1937), 246–7. He recognized mitigation of punishment in the case the illegality was not manifest and immunity in the case the factor of coercion mattered.

[77]E. Garçon, *Code pénal*, tome premier (Paris: Librairie de la société du recueil général des lois et arrêts, 1901–6), 184–5.

[78]The arguments which recognized immunity on the tests of manifest illegality and/or coercion include J. Barthélémy, 'L'influence de l'ordre hiérarchique sur la responsabilité des agents', *Revue du droit public et de la science politique en France et a l'étranger* 31 (1914): 506–7; I. Poljokan, *La responsabilité pour les crimes et délits de guerre* (Paris: Jouve et c[ie], Éditeurs, 1923), 155–6, 165.

[79]L. Duguit, *Etudes de droit public,* vol.2, *L'État, les gouvernants et les agents* (Paris: A. Fontemoing, 1903), 633–4.

enemy soldiers were treated independent of the relevant national law. First, automatic immunity, as Duguit maintained, had hardly been supported in this context. Second, the issue of the superior orders defense in international law had been treated mainly as the question of whether or not Article 64 of the French *Penal Code* which recognized immunity on the ground of coercion should be applied.

With respect to war crimes committed during World War II, the problem of coercion drew attention much more than the issues of the knowledge of illegality and/or manifest illegality. Article 327 of the French *Penal Code* recognized a justification for 'the homicide, the wounding and striking that was ordered by the law and commanded by the legitimate authority (l'homicide, les blessures et les coups étaient ordonnés par la loi et commandés par l'autorité légitime) (translated by the author)'. However, as Paul Coste-Floret argued that the order of the law (l'ordre de la loi) was apparently lacking with regard to war crimes,[80] there were hardly any commentators who referred to that provision concerning war crimes trials. Under such circumstances, it was unlikely that the view that recognized immunity on the tests of the knowledge of illegality and/or manifest illegality could be widely supported. Cost-Floret's argument that the illegality of superior orders on war crimes was manifest in most cases[81] seemed to reflect the views prevalent at the time.

Eventually, the debates on the superior orders defense developed around the question of whether or not an excuse on the ground of coercion in national law could be allowed for enemy soldiers. As was noted before, Anglo–American judicial precedents had concurrently been shaping a rule to immunize soldiers on the tests of the knowledge of illegality and/or manifest illegality. It was an exceptional rule for soldiers. In contrast, discussions in France did not presuppose that some special rules should be applied for military orders. Here, the point was whether the accused who appealed under the superior orders defense was a French national or an enemy soldier. The issue of coercion was treated as the question of whether the rule in the French *Penal Code* would likewise be applicable for its adversaries.

Article 64 of the French *Penal Code* recognized an excuse on the ground of coercion under which the accused had been placed:

> There is no felony nor misdemeanor when the defendant was in a state of insanity at the time of the action, or when he was coerced by a force which he could not resist (Il n'y a ni crime ni délit, lorsque le prévenu était en état de démence au temps de l'action, ou lorsqu'il a été contraint par une force à laquelle il n'a pu resister). (translated by the author)

The question was whether enemy soldiers could be immunized on the ground of this provision if they appealed under the superior orders defense for their war crimes.

---

[80]P. Coste-Floret, 'La répression de crimes de guerre et le fait justificatif tiré de l'ordre supérieur', *Recueil dalloz de doctrine de jurisprudence et de legislation – Chronique* (1945): 21. See also Barthélémy, supra n. 78, at 33; Donnedieu de Vabres, supra n. 76, at 246.

[81]Coste-Floret, supra n. 80, at 21.

Commentators, including Renault, who recognized the superior orders defense, emphasized the absolute character of military discipline.[82] Soldiers were not usually allowed to question the orders of their superiors. Moreover, the knowledge on the laws of war was not fully popularized in the army. Even if soldiers were aware of the illegality of the orders, the violation of a duty to obey them would lead to severe penalties. Considering these points, we should bear in mind that soldiers were under immediate coercion (contrainte immédiate). Having said so, Renault contended to apply Article 64 of the *Penal Code*.[83] There may be a view, he argued, that the usual penal provision should not be applied to war crimes committed by enemy soldiers. Surely, international law allows reprisals for violations of the laws of war by belligerent parties. Nonetheless, it is deceptive to resort to reprisals behind a mask of judicial measures. In such a case, 'the violence and the arbitrariness bear a particularly odious character ([l]a violence et l'arbitraire prennent un caractère particulièrement odieux)'.[84]

On the other hand, Mérignhac represented another view that did not recognize the defense of coercion. He assumed that it was abusive to apply ordinary rules of French criminal law for war crimes committed by its enemy country, particularly, Germany. He argued that German state organs under Kaiser's rule would evade prosecution under Article 64 of the French *Penal Code*. In turn, Kaiser himself would evade prosecution because he only accomplished 'a collective act (un acte collectif)' or 'an act of government (un acte de gouvernement)'.[85]

The fact that the conduction of war is grounded in the intention of a head of state would not necessarily lead to the assumption that war crimes committed by state organs should be immunized by Article 64 of the French *Penal Code*. War crimes would not always be committed by the orders of a head of state. Moreover, the argument that deems the defense of coercion to be always applicable regardless of the degree of coercion at the time of the criminal conduct cannot be said to be in keeping with Article 64. The article used the expression, 'when he was coerced by a force which he could not resist'.

However, where state acts, especially military acts, matter, the treatment of the coercion defense would substantially influence the eventual number of conviction. In the army, military discipline has decisive importance. This point has been equally agreed upon by both the commentators who supported the application of the coercion defense and those who did not. Wide-ranging recognition of the coercion defense on war crimes implies drastic restriction of the cases for punishment. It would mean, depending on the situation, a denial of punishment for almost all violations of the laws of war.

---

[82]Renault, supra n. 75, at 27.

[83]*Ibid.*

[84]*Ibid.*, 28. The same view was expressed in Comment by F. du Saint, *Réforme sociale* 69 (1915): 212. See also M. Nast, 'Le sanctions penales de l'enlèvement par les allemands du matériel industriel en territoires français et belges occupés par leurs troupes', *Revue générale de droit international public* 26 (1919): 123.

[85]Mérignhac, supra n. 75, at 52.

The coercion in question is not physical or mental coercion among private persons. Superior orders in military organizations are accompanied by legal coercion backed by the power of state and national laws, which are grounded on this power. In recognizing automatic immunity under the superior orders defense in the third edition of his *International Law*, Oppenheim emphasized that soldiers were 'compelled by law to commit' the conduct in question under superior orders.[86] It is thus undeniable that coercion generally accompanies acts committed under superior orders. Mérignhac's rejection of the coercion defense for enemy soldiers could be considered as his concern for this specific aspect of the coercion in question. If one aims at prosecuting individuals for their state acts, the coercion defense emerges as a serious obstacle for trials.

The problem of how to deal with the coercion defense and the superior orders defense, which is closely related to the former, leads to the question with regard to the significance of prosecuting state acts. What should the prosecution of state organs who committed war crimes aim at, and where should the limit of such prosecution be set?

2.1.3.2 The *Ordonnance* of 1944

Should national rules on the coercion defense consistently be applied for war crimes by enemy soldiers or should some peculiar rules that give the highest priority to punishing enemy soldiers be applied? French military commissions during World War I took the latter position with regard to war crimes by German soldiers and rejected the application of Article 64 of the French *Penal Code*.[87] *Ordonnance du 28 août 1944 relative à la répression des crimes de guerre* which was stipulated for trials of enemy war criminals during World War II allowed immunity on the ground of superior orders. However, the relevant provisions did not clarify the relationship between the superior orders defense and coercion defense.

The French judicial organs that had jurisdiction over war crimes during World War II were the Military Government Tribunals set up in the French-occupied zone of Germany and the Permanent Military Tribunals.[88] The *ordonnance* of 1944 provided for jurisdiction and other legal competence of the latter. Article 3 of the *ordonnance* states the following on the superior orders defense:

> The laws, decrees or regulations issued by the enemy authority, the orders or authorizations issued by that authority or the authorities, which are or which had been subordinated to it, cannot be invoked as justifying factors within the meaning of Article 327 of the *Penal Code*, but can only, in suitable cases, be invoked as extenuating circumstances or as absolute excuses (Les lois, décrets ou règlements émanant de l'autorité ennemie, les ordres ou autorisations donnés par cette autorité ou par les autorités qui en dépendent ou qui en ont

---

[86] Oppenheim, supra n. 27 (1921), at 343.

[87] Mérignhac, supra n. 75, at 53.

[88] The United Nations War Crimes Commission, *Law Reports of Trials of War Criminals*, vol. 3 (London: HMSO, 1948), 93.

dépendu ne peuvent être invoqués comme faits justificatifs au sense de l'art. 327 c. pén., mais seulement, s'il y a lieu, comme circonstances atténuantes ou comme excuses absolutoires). (translated by the author)

As previously noted, Article 327 of the French *Penal Code* recognized unconditional justification under the superior orders defense. In contrast, the *ordonnance* of 1944 did not recognize a justification by the said defense with regard to war crimes by enemy soldiers. Article 3 of the *ordonnance* denoted that superior orders should only be considered for an excuse or mitigation of punishment depending on the situations of the respective cases. However, the provision did not provide any criteria for judgment on the allowance of the said defense. Some commentators understand the provision as relevant to the issue of coercion.[89] However, in light of the fact that the French military commissions did not allow enemy soldiers the coercion defense during World War I, it would not be appropriate to instantly judge on this point.

Thus, in France, before the adoption of the Nuremberg Charter, the problem of the superior orders defense manifested mainly as that of the coercion defense. The situation was different from that of the Anglo–American judicial precedents which treated the problem under the topics of the knowledge of illegality and/or manifest illegality, but while bearing in mind the importance of military discipline and the existence of coercion. However, the *ordonnance* of 1944 eventually did not clarify the relationship between the superior orders defense and coercion defense. The question was whether or not to take into consideration the fact of coercion in recognizing superior orders as an excuse. The situation is reminiscent of the fact that the British Manual of Military Law and the US Rules of Land Warfare revised in the same year also did not clarify the conditions under which the superior orders defense could be recognized.

In the United Kingdom, the United States, and France, the topics of the knowledge of illegality and/or manifest illegality, and coercion, were put forth in regard to the superior orders defense. These topics gained prominence again in the drafting of the Nuremberg Charter as unresolved problems at the international level.

2.1.4 Superior Orders Defense in the Soviet Union

The Russian Empire, in its *Military Criminal Code* of 1910 – which was based on its 1869 edition – stipulated that subordinates who were not conscious of the illegality of the orders that they had received should not be punished.[90] After the

[89]Coste-Floret, supra n. 80, at 21.

[90]See Article 69 of the Russian *Military Criminal Code* (R. Klibanski, *Das Russische Militär-Strafrecht, Übersetzt und Bearbeitet* (Berlin: J.Guttentag, 1913), 29). See also P. Fuhrmann, *Der Höhere Befehl als Rechtfertigung im Völkerrecht* (Berlin: C. H. Beck'sche Verlagsbuchhandlung, 1963), 61.

formation of the Union of Soviet Socialist Republics, however, the *Regulations on the Military Crime* of 1927 did not provide for the superior orders defense, whereas a few judicial precedents relevant to the issue had not yet formed the case law.[91]

In such circumstances, the *Kharkov* trial conducted in Ukraine during World War II deserves special mention; this trial drew international attention as a trial of German war criminals in Soviet territory.

In the Moscow Declaration, the United States, the United Kingdom, and the Soviet Union declared to punish war crimes committed during World War II. The Declaration clearly put forth the Allied Powers' intention to punish persons responsible for atrocities during the war after peace was made with Germany.[92] However, Soviet military tribunals tried and convicted German war criminals in 1943 before the conclusion of peace with Germany.[93] In particular, *Kharkov* drew much attention as a war crimes trial 'directed' by the Soviet regime.[94] Three German and Soviet corroborators were sentenced to death on the counts of atrocities against Soviet citizens and Soviet prisoners of war. After the *Kharkov* trial, the Soviet government changed its policy – it suspended war crimes trials until the end of World War II and did not mention the *Kharkov* trial any more.[95] With regard to this change in policy, it has been pointed out that the aim to demonstrate a strict attitude by the Soviet Union toward war crimes trials had been accomplished to some extent and that German retaliation for the *Kharkov* trial had proved to be a new menace for the Allied Powers.[96]

In *Kharkov*, the prosecution tried to assign the criminal conduct with an organizational character and emphasized the responsibility of the German government. In having done so, the prosecution often guided the accused to admit that they committed criminal acts under superior orders.[97] However, this did not mean that they attached importance to superior orders as a ground for immunity. On the contrary, the prosecution relied on the judgment of the Reipzig Trials and rejected the superior orders defense under which the accused sought refuge.[98] The judgment of the Reipzig Trials, as will be seen later, denoted a test of the knowledge of illegality in deciding on the question of immunity under the superior orders defense.

[91] R. Maurach, Die Kriegsverbrecherprozesse gegen deutsche Gefangene in der Sowjetunion (Hamburg, 1950), 32–5, 37–41.

[92] 'Great Britain – Soviet Union – United States, Tripartite Conference in Moscow, Anglo-Soviet-American Communiqué, November 1, 1943', *Supplement to the American Journal of International Law* 38 (1944): 3, 7–8.

[93] G. Ginsburg, *Moscow's Road to Nuremberg, The Soviet Background to the Trial* (The Hague: Martinus Nijhoff Publishers, 1996), 52.

[94] On the Kharkov trial, an audience was made rotate to maximize the attendance, and foreign correspondents were also admitted to attend (*ibid.*, 52–5).

[95] *Ibid.*, 55–6.

[96] *Ibid.*, 56.

[97] *Ibid.*, 53–4.

[98] *Ibid.*, 54; Glueck, supra n. 4, at 150–51.

The judgment in *Kharkov* convicted all four accused. The significance of *Kharkov* lies in the fact that it clarified that the superior orders defense should not immunize war criminals.[99] Academic arguments in the Soviet Union at the time generally denied the superior orders defense for manifestly illegal acts.[100] Commentators attached importance to *Kharkov* as a precedent that backed this academic view.[101]

2.1.5 Conclusion

As seen in this section, at least the three countries that drafted the Nuremberg Charter – the United Kingdom, the United States, and France – had been forming basic views on the superior orders defense by 1944, although with some contradictions and confusion.

In the United Kingdom, as the judicial precedents were inconclusive, the British Manual of 1944 recognized the principle of conditional immunity just like the US judicial precedents, the US Rules of Land Warfare, and the French *ordonnance* on war crimes. This principle denied automatic immunity under the superior orders defense but allowed immunity or mitigation of punishment on the ground of orders depending on the situations of the respective cases.

However, the national legislation or precedents of these three countries did not fully present the grounds on which immunity or mitigation of punishment was to be recognized. The British and US judicial precedents had developed criteria such as the knowledge of illegality and/or manifest illegality. The French academic society focused on the factor of coercion by superiors. Nonetheless, these arguments were not reflected on the relevant military documents in a specific way.

The civil courts of the United Kingdom and the United States generally judged on the superior orders defense on the basis of the tests of the knowledge of illegality and/or manifest illegality. This appears to be fundamentally different from the arguments of the French academic society which had mainly dealt with the problem of coercion. However, it is noteworthy that some US judicial cases such as *McCall v. McDowell et al.* associated the issue of manifest illegality with coercion. The judgment in *McCall v. McDowell et al.* was, in referring to the test of manifest

---

[99]Ginsburg, supra n.93, at 64.

[100]*Ibid.*, 63–4. For instance, Trainin recognized the strictness of military discipline but still denied immunity on the ground of superior orders, arguing that manifestly illegal act was not that of the army but instigation of a crime (A. Trainin, *Hitlerite Responsibility under Criminal Law* (First published in Russian for the Institute of Law, Academy of Sciences of the U.S.S.R., Translated by A. Rothstein) (London: Hutchinson & Co. Ltd., 1945), 90). In so arguing, he referred to the Reipzig Trials and Section 47 of the German *Military Criminal Code* as the prosecution in the *Kharkov* trial did.

[101]Ginsburg, supra n. 93, at 63–4.

illegality of the criminal conduct, grounded on the fact that soldiers had been placed under coercion by military discipline.[102] The court emphasized the importance of the obligation of obedience as well as military discipline, and pointed out that soldiers acted under actual coercion especially during armed conflicts. It then delivered that the superior orders defense should be allowed if the illegality of the conduct in question had not been manifest.

The factor of coercion bears a peculiar character in the case of superior orders. As seen before, Oppenheim in his third edition of *International Law* which significantly influenced the provisions of the British Manual underlined the 'compulsion by law' as a ground for recognizing the superior orders defense.[103] Indeed, as far as military conduct is concerned, it should be noted that soldiers are placed in a specific environment – the army – where military discipline is vital. In addition, military discipline is backed by the fact that superior orders in the army reflect state acts. Military orders are given on the basis of national laws. These facts give a peculiar character to the 'coercion' which is to be considered with regard to the superior orders defense. Such coercion bears legal character along with physical and mental character. The US courts did not pay attention to whether or not there had been actual coercion – physical or mental – in recognizing the superior orders defense on the test of manifest illegality. The courts simply emphasized that soldiers had acted under coercion, which is a part of military discipline. Such an argument could be said to relate to the peculiar character of the coercion discussed here. It may be understood that the court meant that legal coercion, together with a lack of the knowledge of illegality and/or a lack of manifest illegality, brought about a multiplier effect of immunity.

Meanwhile, it is also noteworthy that the judgment in *McCall v. McDowell et al.* recognized immunity on the test of manifest illegality, underlining the importance of military discipline besides coercion. The concurrent writing of William Winthrop, which has been dubbed as the 'Blackstone of Military Law'[104] recognized the superior orders defense on the test of manifest illegality because of the importance of military discipline.[105] It would be reasonable to consider that from the viewpoint of state interest, immunity should be allowed exceptionally in the case of superior orders because of a lack of the knowledge of illegality and/or a lack of manifest illegality.

---

[102]It is noteworthy that the *Smith* judgment of the Supreme Court of the Cape of Good Hope also recognized conditional immunity by emphasizing the importance of military discipline. However, the *Smith* judgment did not specifically connect the issue of military discipline with that of coercion.

[103]Oppenheim, supra n. 27 (1921), at 343. Green also argues on legal compulsion that 'both duress and orders involve some measure of compulsion upon the actor, the former by way of a direct threat against his personal security, and the latter by way of legal compulsion accompanied by an implied sanction for non-compliance (L. Green, *Superior Orders in National and International Law* (Leyden: A. W. Sijthoff, 1976), 15)'.

[104]*Reid v. Covert*, 354 U.S. 1, 19, n.38 (1957); *Hamdan v. Rumsfeld*, 126 S.Ct. 2749, 2777 (2006).

[105]W. Winthrop, *Military Law and Precedents, Second ed.* (Washington, DC: GPO, 1920), 296–7.

Various arguments surveyed in this section put forth a significant question dealing with the issue of the superior orders defense at the international level: how to deal with conflict between international obligations and the coercion by or obligations under national law? Conceptual priority on international obligations does not instantly lead to the dissolution of conflicts between international and national obligations. Should the ideal of international law precede and should international legal order attain its goal, or should one make a compromise in realizing the ideal of international law, facing a complex construction of international legal order, which has been considerably influenced by national legal orders? These questions were to be answered by the international rule-making on the issue of the superior orders defense.

In the national laws of the United Kingdom, the United States, and France, automatic immunity under the superior orders defense had been rejected and conditional immunity had been introduced by the end of World War II. The national legislation or other legal materials of these countries did not clarify the conditions on which immunity could be allowed. However, they were basically accorded in recognizing superior orders as a defense in certain situations.

One should bear in mind that the relevant legal instruments of the three countries were revised in 1944. In the United Kingdom and the United States, the Manual and the Rules, respectively, were revised mostly in conformity with the judicial precedents of civil courts. In contrast, the new *ordonnance* of France was specially promulgated for the cases of enemy soldiers. Nonetheless, the countries had common grounds for adopting the principle of conditional immunity in anticipating the postwar trials of enemy war criminals. Thus, it can be said that the positions of these three countries on the superior orders defense, which had been formed by 1944, possibly had considerable influence on the drafting of the Nuremberg Charter and the proceedings of the Nuremberg Trial.

2.2 Situation of International Law

Toward the end of World War II, legislations on the superior orders defense were far from established at the international level. The situation was even more confused than that of the drafting countries of the Nuremberg Charter. The United Kingdom, the United States, and France – the three of those drafting countries –, together with Japan and Italy, proposed an agreement on the laws of armed conflict, which recognized automatic immunity under the superior orders defense on the one hand, while on the other, they proposed another agreement that categorically denied immunization. The Treaty of Versailles, which was concluded in consequence of World War I, did not provide for the superior orders defense. As a result, war crimes trials were conducted in Germany by German judicial organs that applied their national law.

The two instruments mentioned above did not take effect. Moreover, German war crimes trials after World War I were not conducted by directly applying international law. Such precedent does not offer decisive materials in examining international rules on the superior orders defense.

Nonetheless, it would be possible to determine what the governments of the relevant countries expressed on the issue of the superior orders defense in the rule-making process of those documents. Further, the German trials drew much attention in the international society as alternative proceedings to those of the Allies.[106] This section will examine the above-mentioned precedent for considering the international legal situation before the establishment of the Nuremberg Charter. We will consult the *Washington Treaty in Relation to the Use of Submarines and Noxious Gases in Warfare* and the *Rules for the Control of Radio in Time of War,* which were adopted in the 1920s, together with the war crimes trials conducted in Germany – the so-called Leipzig Trials – following the conclusion of the Versailles Treaty.

2.2.1 Proposals of Treaties and Superior Orders Defense

2.2.1.1 Washington Treaty in Relation to the Use of Submarines and Noxious Gases in Warfare

In 1922, the United Kingdom, the United States, and France – which later participated in the drafting of the Nuremberg Charter – along with Japan and Italy, signed the Washington Treaty. The Treaty was concluded at the Washington Naval Conference. The Conference considered 'the rules adopted by civilized nations for the protection of the lives of neutrals and noncombatants at sea in time of war, and to prevent the use in war of noxious gases and chemicals' as a part of its agenda[107] and specifically dealt with the problems of submarines and gases.

The Washington Treaty prohibited attacks against merchant vessels without warning by submarines. Article 3 of the Treaty thoroughly denied the superior orders defense for violations of relevant provisions. Article 3 read as follows:

> The Signatory Powers, desiring to insure the enforcement of the humane rules of existing law declared by them with respect to attacks upon and the seizure and destruction of merchant ships, further declare that any person in the service of any Power who shall

---

[106]Regarding German war crimes trials conducted in Germany, *see* Battle, supra n. 2, at 1–26; Finch, supra n. 36, 'Superior Orders', at 440–45; Y. Dinstein, *The Defence of 'Obedience to Superior Orders' in International Law* (Leyden: A.W. Sijthoff, 1965), 10–20. On the drafting process of international agreements between World War I and World War II, *see* J. Shinobu, *Senjikokusaihō Kōgi (Lectures on International Laws of War),* vol. 3 (Tokyo: Maruzen, 1941), 405–411; Dinstein, supra n. 106, at 97–103; E. Fukatsu & Y. Kita, '"Jōkanmeirei no Kōben" ni Kansuru Kokusaihōtenka wo Meguru Shomondai – Dainijisekaitaisen Izen no Sagyo – (Problems on International Codification on "Superior Orders Defense" – The Process before World War II –)', *Hōgaku Kiyō (Nihon Daigaku Hōgakubu Hōgaku Kenkyujo)* 34 (1993): 187–99.

[107]H. Malkin, 'The Washington Conference (November 12, 1921—February 6, 1922)', *British Yearbook of International Law* 3 (1922–3): 179.

> violate any of those rules, whether or not such person is under orders of a governmental superior, shall be deemed to have violated the laws of war and shall be liable to trial and punishment as if for an act of piracy and may be brought to trial before the civil or military authorities of any Power within the jurisdiction of which he may be found.

As the clause 'whether or not such person is under orders of a governmental superior, shall be deemed to have violated the laws of war and shall be liable to trial and punishment as if for an act of piracy' indicated, the Treaty meant to oblige punishment of violations without any consideration for the circumstances prevailing at the time of the criminal conduct. As seen in the previous section, the British Manual of Military Law and the US Rules of Land Warfare specifically allowed automatic immunity under the superior orders defense in the 1920s. As both countries had signed the Washington Treaty, this instrument would be deemed to be rather stringent on the responsibility of the subordinates who had acted under superior orders. During World War I, the United States and the United Kingdom suffered serious damages from a submarine sink-on-sight policy of the German Navy.[108] The Washington Treaty was proposed by these two countries for regulating submarines. Stringency in terms of equating attacks against merchant vessels with 'piracy'[109] and rejecting the superior orders defense could be considered as the strong repulsion of these countries against unrestricted submarine warfare.

The Washington Treaty was signed by the said five countries. Nonetheless, France did not ratify the instrument and it was not put into effect eventually. A reason for the French refusal was that the Treaty generally prohibited the commerce destruction by submarines.[110] France was unwillingly restricted on its warship tonnage through the Washington Conference. The French delegate thus occasionally tried to avoid excessive regulations on submarines.[111] The provisions of the Washington Treaty, which declared that the commerce destruction by

[108]In particular, these two countries received a severe blow with the sinking of the British cargo and passenger ship *Lusitania* because of German submarine attacks. Out of over 1,200 casualties, approximately 150 were US citizens. In response to this incident, the United States broke off relations with Germany and entered World War I. For more information on the relationship between the *Lusitania* incident and the Washington Treaty, see Shinobu, supra n. 106, at 382–95; A. Mérignhac, 'Le désarmement, les traités de paix de 1919–1920, la conférence de Washington de 1921–1922', *Revue général de droit international public* 29 (1922): 136–7. France also suffered serious damages from a submarine sink-on-sight policy of Germany (Shinobu, supra n. 106, at 389–90). However, as will be seen later, the French government placed importance on the commerce destruction by submarines and stood on a different position from the United States and the United Kingdom.

[109]It was criticized on this point that state acts should not be identified with private piracy which was irrelevant with state power. See K. Yokota, 'Rondonkaigi to Sensuikanshiyōhōki (The London Conference and the Rules on the Use of Submarines)', *Kokusaihō Gaikō Zasshi* 29, no. 6 (1930): 13; R. Genet, 'The Charge of Piracy in the Spanish Civil War', *American Journal of International Law* 32 (1938): 257; Shinobu, supra n. 106, at 406.

[110]Yokota, supra n. 109, at 8; Mérignhac, supra n. 75, at 142–5.

[111]Mérignhac, supra n. 75, at 136–9; J. François, 'L'Avenir du sous-marin', *Revue general de droit international public* 30 (1923): 39–40.

submarines was practically impossible under the rules of the Treaty, were far from acceptable for France, which took submarine warfare very seriously.[112]

2.2.1.2 Rules for the Control of Radio in Time of War

The Washington Treaty ultimately did not come into effect. However, the adopted provisions at least clarified its denial of the superior orders defense for the material jurisdiction of the Treaty. What sharply contrasted with this Treaty was the draft of the *Rules for the Control of Radio in Time of War* of 1923. This proposal was adopted by the Commission of Jurists, which comprised of the delegates of the United Kingdom, the United States, France, Japan, and Italy.[113] The tasks of the Commission were to report on (1) whether or not concurrent international law kept up with the advent of new measures for warfare and (2) if not, then what kind of provisions for rules should be made.[114]

The Commission finally prepared the drafts of the *Rules for the Control of Radio in Time of War* and the *Rules of Aerial Warfare*. With respect to the superior orders defense, Article 12 of the former read that '[r]adio operators incur no personal responsibility from the mere fact of carrying out the orders which they receive in the performance of their duties as operators'.[115]

Did the quoted expression mean that the fact of the execution of orders indicated immunity of the subordinates, or that some additional factors such as voluntariness on the part of the subordinates were necessary for the establishment of their responsibility? A commentary attached to the provision made it clear that it was only the superiors that should be held accountable. Article 12 thus can be construed as recognizing automatic immunity under the superior orders defense.[116] The commentary included the following explanation and underlined the peculiar character of the duties of radio operators who executed orders in cabins:

> The operator works in his cabin where he executes the orders of those above him. Consequently it is right that he should incur no personal responsibility merely because he

[112]According to Genet, the French delegate contended that commanders on board submarines should not bear individual responsibility for orders from their superiors (Genet, supra n. 109, at 256). In light of the relevant provisions of the British Manual and the US Rules of Land Warfare at the time, and of the fact that the British government once recognized the superior orders defense for German commanders of submarines (*ibid.*), such contention of the French delegate would not be deemed as peculiar. It could be said that the United Kingdom and the United States that had faced the incident of *Lusitania* changed their conventional attitude.

[113]Commission of Jurists to Consider and Report upon the Revision of the Rules of Warfare, 'General Report', *American Journal of International Law, Supplement* 32 (1938): 1.

[114]*Ibid.*

[115]*Ibid.*, 11.

[116]The arguments which deemed the article as recognizing automatic immunity on the ground of superior orders include F. Shick, 'War Criminals and the Law of the United Nations', *University of Toronto Law Journal* 7 (1947–8): 48–9; Dinstein, supra n. 106, at 101–2.

> has executed orders which he has received in the discharge of his duties as radio operator. Liability to punishment for acts which contravene rules such as Articles 9 or 10 falls on those who have given the orders for such acts.[117]

However, this proposal did not clarify the relationship between these rules and the general international law. Did the draft Rules presuppose that the superior orders defense was generally recognized for violations of the laws of war, or did it specially allow the said defense for radio operators? These questions have been left unanswered.

The draft Rules of 1923 were not made into effect as a treaty. The final report of the Commission of Jurists, which comprised of the drafts of the *Rules for the Control of Radio in Time of War* and the *Rules of Aerial Warfare,* was much criticized on the whole. It was said that the regulation of the warfare based on airplanes and radio technology was unrealistic since such technology developed rapidly.[118] Moreover, the content of the instruments was considered to be ambiguous.[119]

Eventually, none of the five countries accepted the final report of the Commission. Even if Article 12 of the draft Rules was put into effect, the provision could not be deemed to contribute to the general understanding of the concurrent international rules.

2.2.2 *The Versailles Treaty and the Reipzig Trials*

2.2.2.1 The Versailles Treaty

The Washington Treaty and the draft Rules were attended to with the common problems on the issue of the superior orders defense. These instruments did not clarify whether they denied/supported this defense as a general rule or restricted themselves to partially conclude on this defense just in the scope of their material jurisdiction. In addition, the two instruments ultimately did not come into force as a treaty or a rule.

Another attempt to establish a multinational rule on the superior orders defense was the drafting of the Versailles Treaty at the end of World War I. It was a significant multilateral conference that examined the issue of the superior orders defense in the violation of the laws of war in general. However, it has already been noted that the conclusion of the Washington Treaty and the draft Rules that

117 Commission of Jurists to Consider and Report upon the Revision of the Rules of Warfare, supra n. 113, at 11.

118 R. Wyman, 'The First Rules of Air Warfare', *Air University Review* (1984, March – April): 99–100.

119 *Ibid.*, 100. See also W. Rodgers, 'The Laws of War Concerning Aviation and Radio', *American Journal of International Law* 17 (1923): 629–40.

followed the Versailles Treaty was extremely difficult. Even among the victorious countries, it was not easy to express specific ideas on the issue of the superior orders defense.

The Preliminary Peace Conference of 1919 established the Commission on the Responsibility of the Authors of the War and on Enforcement of Penalties, comprising the delegates of the United States, the United Kingdom, France, Italy, and Japan, in order to inquire into the issue of individual responsibility with regard to the breach of the laws and customs of war during World War I.[120]

The Commission expressed its basic idea on the superior orders defense in dealing with the issue of individual responsibility:

> the trial of the offenders might be seriously prejudiced if they attempted and were able to plead the superior orders of a sovereign against whom no steps had been or were being taken. ... We desire to say that civil and military authorities cannot be relieved from responsibility by the mere fact that a higher authority might have been convicted of the same offence. It will be for the court to decide whether a plea of superior orders is sufficient to acquit the person charged from responsibility.[121]

The first part of the paragraph appears to have generally denied the superior orders defense. However, it primarily indicated the necessity of prosecuting the head of state and simply underlined that a combination of the immunity of the head of state and the superior orders defense would be harmful. In fact, the latter part of the paragraph showed that the report recognized the superior orders defense in some cases. Although a person who violated the laws of war could not be immunized solely on the ground of superior orders, he/she could be immunized if some other factors had accompanied the superior orders. The report did not clarify the 'other factors' and entrusted courts to use their discretion. Nonetheless, it is worth bearing in mind that the courts were allowed to decide 'whether a plea of superior orders is sufficient to acquit the person charged from responsibility'.[122]

As per the author's knowledge, there are no other records on the Commission's discussion relevant to this issue. However, it has already been seen above that the Allied Powers expressed various views on the superior orders defense at that time. In such circumstances, it was fully foreseeable that the conclusion of a unified idea on this issue was not easily expected.

Eventually, the Versailles Treaty stipulated on trials and punishment of war criminals in Articles 227–30 of Section 7. It contained no provision on the superior orders defense. Some commentators argued that it should not be construed that the superior orders defense was denied, since there was no provision in the Treaty that

[120] Commission on the Responsibility of the Authors of the War and on Enforcement of Penalties, 'Report Presented to the Preliminary Peace Conference', *American Journal of International Law* 14 (1920): 95.

[121] *Ibid.*, 117.

[122] The arguments which deem the line in question as recognizing conditional immunity under the superior orders defense include S. Glaser, *Introduction a l'étude du droit international pénal* (Paris: Sirey, 1954), 128; Fukatsu & Kita, supra n. 106, at 182–3.

conflicted with the Commission's report.[123] However, considering that a unified international rule on the said defense had not been formed by that time, a final judgment of the Allied Powers on this problem could not be instantly estimated.

An international rule on the superior orders defense was not clearly formulated on the occasion of World War I. As we will see below, German national courts eventually tried German war crimes during the war. These national courts applied the nation's criminal law in dealing with the problem of the superior orders defense.

2.2.2.2 The Reipzig Trials

Articles 228 and 229 of the Versailles Treaty provided that the Allied Powers would try German war criminals and Germany should extradite German nationals for trials to the Allied Powers:

> Article 228
> The German Government recognizes the right of the Allied and Associated Powers to bring before military tribunals persons accused of having committed acts in violation of the laws and customs of war. Such persons shall, if found guilty, be sentenced to punishments laid down by law. This provision will apply notwithstanding any proceedings or prosecution before a tribunal in Germany or in the territory of her allies.
> The German Government shall hand over to the Allied and Associated Powers, or to such one of them as shall so request, all persons accused of having committed an act in violation of the laws and customs of war, who are specified either by name or by the rank, office or employment which they held under the German authorities.
> Article 229
> Persons guilty of criminal acts against the nationals of one of the Allied and Associated Powers will be brought before the military tribunals of that Power.
> Persons guilty of criminal acts against the nationals of more than one of the Allied and Associated Powers will be brought before military tribunals composed of members of the military tribunals of the Powers concerned.
> In every case the accused will be entitled to name his own counsel.

However, as the Allied Powers sent Germany a list of suspects, the German government disapproved the extradition on the ground of its domestic political conditions. The German government contended that the extradition of major figures of the German Army and Navy in the list would stir up public opinion and the new regime in Germany would become unstable.[124] In addition, it had often been argued in Germany that the extradition of German war criminals, including those who were not in the list, was in conflict with international law and the general principle of law.[125]

---

[123] G. Manner, 'The Legal Nature and Punishment of Criminal Acts of Violence Contrary to the Laws of War', *American Journal of International Law* 37 (1943): 417.

[124] A. Mérignhac, 'De la responsabilité pénale des actes criminels commis au cours de la guerre de 1914–1918', *Revue de droit international et de législation comparée, Troisième serie* 1 (1920): 61–8; Cave, supra n. 4, at xxviii; E. Colby, supra n. 57, at 615; Jescheck, supra n. 40, at 64.

[125] J. Bell (ed.), *Völkerrecht im Weltkrieg 1914-1918,* vol.3 (Deutsche Verlagsgesellschaft für Politik und Geschichte M.B.H., 1927), 57; Lauterpacht, supra n. 6, at 61.

The German government itself contended at the Peace Conference that such an extradition would contradict Section 9 of the German *Criminal Code*.[126] Consequently, the Allied Powers accepted the German government's contention and decided to let the German Supreme Court at Leipzig try German war criminals. However, the Allies reserved to begin with their independent proceedings, depending on the progress of German trials.

Thus, the trials, which had been decided under the Versailles Treaty, were finally conducted by German national courts, which applied the German national laws. On the issue of the superior orders defense, the German Supreme Court naturally applied the relevant provisions of the German criminal law. Therefore, the judgments of the Reipzig Trials should not be deemed to directly reflect the concurrent international law. Nonetheless, the trials were conducted under the Versailles Treaty and drew much attention of the relevant countries. This section will examine the Reipzig Trials as a significant precedent that influenced subsequent discussions on the superior orders defense.

The Reipzig Trials ended up with the conviction of only six of the accused.[127] The Supreme Court expressed its view on the superior orders defense in the *Dover Castle*[128] and *Llandovery Castle* cases.[129]

In the *Dover Castle* case, Karl Neumann, the First Lieutenant of the German Navy, was indicted for having torpedoed and sunk the English hospital ship *Dover Castle* from the submarine he commanded. Neumann contended that he had only carried out the order of the German Admiralty. The court first emphasized the importance of military discipline in the army and expressed its basic idea that only superiors would bear responsibility if an execution of orders violated criminal law.[130] This idea conformed to Paragraph 1, Section 47 of the German *Military Criminal Code*. The court also expressed the view that the idea was in accordance with 'the legal principles of all other civilized states', including Section 443 of the concurrent British Manual of Military Law.[131]

---

[126]Document 57, German Counterproposals of May 29, 1919, in A. Luckau, *The German Delegation at the Paris Peace Conference* (New York: H. Fertig, 1971), 370.

[127]The Allied Powers listed 896 of the accused, whereas the list prepared by the German government showed 45 accused (J. Descheemaeker, 'Le Tribunal Militaire International des grands criminels de guerre', *Revue générale de droit international public* 50 (1946), 213). Only 12 out of the listed accused were eventually tried at Reipzig (*ibid*).

[128]Judgment in the Case of Commander Karl Nemann, Hospital Ship 'Dover Castle', *in* 'Judicial Decisions Involving Questions of International Law', *American Journal of International Law* 16 (1922): 704–8.

[129]Judgment in the Case of Lieutenants Dithmar and Boldt, Hospital Ship 'Llandovery Castle', *id.*, 708–24.

[130]*Ibid.*, 707.

[131]*Ibid.* However, as was seen in Sect. 2.1, the United Kingdom, the United States, France, and the Soviet Union among those 'civilized states' had not fully clarified the 'the legal principles' on the superior orders defense. With regard to Section 47 of the German *Military Criminal Code*, see M. Mayer, 'Der rechtswidrige Befehl des Vorgesetzten', in *Festschrift Paul Laband* (Tübingen: Verlag von J. C. B. Mohr, 1908), 148–62; O. Thielke, *Gehorsam und Schuld des Staatsbeamten*

Having said so, the court pointed out that there were two exceptional cases on Section 47 of the German *Military Criminal Code*: one was where the accused had deviated from the orders that he/she had received, and the other was where the accused was conscious of the illegal character of the conduct in question. Then, the court judged that the *Dover Castle* case did not fall in these exceptions. Neumann thought that the measure taken by the German Navy against the hospital ship was a legal reprisal in light of the circumstances prevailing at the time. The court decided that he was not responsible for having executed orders without the knowledge of their illegality.[132]

The judgment in the *Llandovery Castle* case convicted the accused. However, it was basically the same with the judgment in the *Dover Castle* case on the problem of the superior orders defense. It is noteworthy that the *Llandovery Castle* judgment decided on the knowledge of illegality of the accused by referring to an additional test – the test of whether or not the illegality of the conduct in question is universally known:

> It is true that according to para. 47 of the Military Penal Code, if the execution of an order in the ordinary course of duty involves such a violation of the law as is punishable, the superior officer issuing such an order is alone responsible. According to No. 2, however, the subordinate obeying such an order is liable to punishment, if it was known to him that the order of the superior involved the infringement of civil or military law. This applies in the case of the accused. It is certainly to be urged in favor of the military subordinates, that they are under no obligation to question the order of their superior officer, and they can count upon its legality. But no such confidence can be held to exist, if such an order is universally known to everybody, including also the accused, to be without any doubt whatever against the law. This happens only in rare and exceptional cases. But this case was precisely one of them, for in the present instance, it was perfectly clear to the accused that killing defenceless people in the life-boats could be nothing else but a breach of the law.[133]

Further, Neumann insisted that he had been forced by his superiors to execute the illegal act. However, the court did not recognize the existence of such coercion.[134]

Eventually, only six were convicted in the Reipzig Trials, and they were meted out with comparatively light punishments. The Allied Powers called off the proceedings at the German Supreme Court and expressed their intention to execute Articles 228–30 of the Versailles Treaty on their own.[135] However, eventually, they

---

und des Soldaten bei gesetzwidrigen Befehlen des Vorgesetzten (Königsberg: Druck von Karg und Manneck, 1911), 62–72.

[132]Judgment in the Case of Commander Karl Nemann, Hospital Ship 'Dover Castle', 'Judicial Decisions Involving Questions of International Law', *American Journal of International Law* 16 (1922): 707–8.

[133]Judgment in the Case of Lieutenants Dithmar and Boldt, Hospital Ship 'Llandovery Castle', *id.*, 721–2.

[134]*Ibid.*, 722–3.

[135]*Journal du droit international* (1921): 1077–8; 'Vermischtes, Deutsche Juristen!', *Deutsche Juristen - Zeitung* (1922): 106–7; Jescheck, supra n. 40, at 67. Regarding the criticism of the

did not request Germany to extradite the suspects.[136] Public opinion in Germany resisted strongly. It was difficult to collect evidence from abroad and the Reipzig Trials were considerably behind schedule.[137] By the time the Allied Powers changed its policy to realize the provisions of the Versailles Treaty to the letter, international arguments on war crimes punishment had fairly toned down.[138]

2.2.3 Conclusion

International rule-making on the superior orders defense had been in its infancy until World War I. The countries that suffered serious damages because of a submarine sink-on-sight policy of Germany during the war expressed their categorical denial of the superior orders defense in the Washington Treaty. However, the same countries unconditionally allowed the said defense in the draft Rules. The countries that participated in the drafting of the Washington Treaty bore in mind the attacks carried out by German submarines without any warning given to merchant vessels. It is understandable to some extent that the treatment of the superior orders defense in this legal instrument was rather stringent. In any event, the relationship between the provisions of this Treaty as well as the draft Rules on one hand and general international law on the other was not fully clarified.

In such circumstances, it seemed difficult from the beginning to set up general rules on international law with respect to the superior orders defense. The Versailles Treaty did not even introduce a provisional rule that widely allowed the discretion of courts. The Treaty was concluded without any relevant stipulation on the issue. Finally, the German national court conducted partial proceedings on war crimes during the war. The court expressed that the superior orders defense should be allowed mainly on the test of the knowledge of illegality.

It is worth noting that such a position of the German national court was similar to that of the civil courts of the United Kingdom and the United States, the countries that were directly involved in the drafting of the Nuremberg Charter. As seen in Section 1 of this chapter, the British and US civil courts had conditionally been recognizing the superior orders defense on the tests of the knowledge of illegality and/or manifest illegality toward the end of World War II. It can be said that these

Reipzig Trials by the Allied Powers (for instance, E. Clunet, 'Les criminels de guerre devant le Reichsgericht, à Leipzig', *Journal du droit international* (1921): 440–2; Descheemaeker, supra n. 127, at 213), the German Minister of Justice made a refutation that the Allies were not positive on mutual assistance on criminal matters with Germany ('Vermischtes, Das Reichsgericht und die Prozesse gegen die sog. Kriegsverbrecher', *Deutsche Juristen – Zeitung* (1922): 611–2; Bell, supra n. 125, at 61–2. See also C. Mullins, *The Leipzig Trials* (London: H. F. & G. Witherby, 1921), 43.

[136]Jescheck, supra n. 40, at 67. In France and Belgium, there were some trials *in absentia* (*Journal du droit international* (1921): 781–2, 1076–7).

[137]Battle, supra n. 2, at 5-6; Cave, supra n. 4, at xxviii.

[138]Mullins, supra n. 135, at 23. Jescheck, supra n. 40, at 67.

three countries held common positions in restrictively allowing the superior orders defense.

The German trials were a part of the postwar management of the Allied Powers and drew much international attention. The precedent of the Reipzig Trials should have had an even greater impact on the subsequent international rule-making as compared to the national judicial precedents of the other relevant countries. The drafters of the Nuremberg Charter might not have paid much attention to such national precedents in general. However, they should not have easily overlooked the fact that the Reipzig Trials supported conditional immunity in the superior orders defense.

Chapter 3
Formation of the 'Nuremberg Principle'

Abstract The judgment of the Nuremberg Trial of the Major War Criminals clearly denied immunity on the mere fact of orders and presented the possibility of 'moral choice' as the 'true test'. However, the judgment did not explain what the notion of 'moral choice' concretely meant and whether immunity should be approved on this test. The Subsequent Proceedings held in the occupied zones of Germany further brought about serious conflict on the problem, and the Tokyo Trial did not resolve the confusion of the 'principle' on the superior orders defense. What can at least be said is that the 'Nuremberg Principle' on the superior orders defense denied automatic immunity on the ground of superior orders, which would objectively be deemed to be a rejection of the immunity of state acts and the absolute character of military discipline.

3.1 Preparatory Work of the Nuremberg Charter

As seen in Section 2.2 of the previous chapter, international rule-making on the superior orders defense was characterized by chaos until the establishment of the Nuremberg Charter. The views of the relevant countries differed widely – some recognized automatic immunity on the defense, while others categorically denied it. Such disparity in views was not dispelled at the Nuremberg Trial that tried 'major war criminals of the European Axis' after World War II. Although the disparity in views narrowed, it still influenced the formulation of the 'Nuremberg Principle' on the superior orders defense.

The view that construes the Nuremberg Charter as 'having denied superior orders defense' has almost been common among studies that refer to this topic. On the other hand, various interpretations have been made on the relevant part of the judgment of the Nuremberg Trial which was conducted under the Charter. As will be seen below, a problem lies in understanding the judgment that presented the test of 'moral choice'. Depending on the interpretation of this part of the judgment, the essence of the 'Nuremberg Principle' comes to be different. Furthermore, the interpretation of the notion of 'moral choice' will possibly influence the evaluation of the 'Nuremberg Principle' as the 'principle'.

H. Satō, *The Execution of Illegal Orders and International Criminal Responsibility*,
DOI 10.1007/978-3-642-16753-9_3,

In order to analyze these points, it is necessary to correctly grasp the essence of the provision of the Nuremberg Charter on the superior orders defense.[1] Section 3.1 will survey the drafting process of Article 8 of the Charter. Then, the subsequent sections will examine the judgment of the Nuremberg Trial of the Major War Criminals, the Subsequent Proceedings, and the Tokyo Trial, which will be juxtaposed with the conclusion of Section 3.1. Through an examination of these trials, it will be clarified that the 'principle' that the four Allied Powers – the United States, the United Kingdom, France, and the Soviet Union – had shown remained ambiguous on some important points. Even among the four countries, it was difficult to establish a general rule on the superior orders defense.

3.1.1 The United Nations War Crimes Commission

Close to the end of World War II, the Allied Powers established the United Nations War Crimes Commission to address the problems of the prosecution and punishment of war criminals.[2] The Commission started its study in 1944 on the issues of investigation, detection, apprehension, trial, and punishment of persons responsible for war crimes. It dealt with the problem of the superior orders defense in its first meeting and entrusted the examination to the Legal Committee, a subordinate organization of the Commission. Meanwhile, another subordinate organization, the Committee on Enforcement, dealt with the problem of the superior orders defense at the same time.

At the beginning, the idea presented by Article 30 of the draft submitted by the United States government to the Committee on Enforcement was supported by the War Crimes Commission in general. The article approved conditional immunity on the test of manifest illegality. In addition, it recognized possible immunity or mitigation of punishment if the accused had been under coercion at the time of the criminal conduct:

> 1. The plea of superior orders shall not constitute a defence ... if the order was so manifestly contrary to the laws of war that a person of ordinary sense and understanding would know or should know, given his rank or position and the circumstances of the case, that such an order was illegal.

---

[1]Earlier studies of the Nuremberg Charter in relation to the superior orders defense which pay attention to the preparatory work of the Charter are restricted. See, for instance, Y. Dinstein, *The Defence of 'Obedience to Superior Orders' in International Law* (Leyden: A.W. Sijthoff, 1965), 104–119; E. Fukatsu & Y. Kita, '"Jōkanmeirei no Kōben" ni Kansuru Kokusaihōtenka wo Meguru Shomondai – Dainijisekaitaisen Izen no Sagyō – Problems on International Codification on "Superior Orders Defense" – The Work before World War II –', *Hōgaku Kiyō (Nihondaigaku Hōgakubu Hōgakukenkyūjo)* 34 (1993): 204–227.

[2]Australia, the United Kingdom, the United States, Belgium, China, Czechoslovakia, France, Greece, India, Luxembourg, the Netherlands, Norway, Poland, Yugoslavia participated the Commission in1944 (The United Nations War Crimes Commission, *History of the United Nations War Crimes Commission and the Development of the Laws of War* (London: HMSO, 1948), 118).

2. It shall be for the Tribunal and its Divisions to consider to what extent irresistible compulsion shall be a ground for mitigation of the penalty or for acquittal.[3]

On this proposal, the Chinese delegate expressed that some guideline, not a unified rule, should be formulated considering the complexity of the issue and the variety of national rules. The Legal Committee approved this view and reported that it supported Article 30(1) of the US draft as a guideline that conformed to general state practice.[4]

However, this recommendation of the Committee was not adopted unanimously. For example, the Czech delegate was against the Committee's idea on the ground that some national laws of the Allies were severer than that of the recommendation. The Czech draft recommendation recognized the coercion defense but did not approve immunity on the test of manifest illegality as the US proposal did.[5]

These proposals were further discussed at the Committee on Enforcement. Eventually, the Committee inclined to denote as a basic guideline that superior orders should not automatically exempt the accused.[6] The War Crimes Commission supported this conclusion of the Committee on Enforcement and officially reported as follows to the relevant countries:

> Having regard to the fact that many, if not most, of the member States have legal rules on the subject, some of which have been adopted very recently, and that in most cases these rules differ from one another, and to the further consideration that the question how far obedience to the orders of a superior exonerates an offender or mitigates the punishment must depend on the circumstances of the particular case, the Commission does not consider that it can usefully propound any principle or rule.[7]

That is, the function of automatic immunity should not be admitted for the fact of superior orders, whereas immunity or mitigation of punishment should possibly be admitted if the orders had been accompanied by some incidental factors. The War Crimes Commission did not clarify what those incidental factors and their individual influence on criminal responsibility were.

The position of the War Crimes Commission as a whole was similar to what the national laws or other legal precedents of the United Kingdom, the United States, and France – three of the countries that participated in the drafting of the Nuremberg Charter – supported at the time. Moreover, it resembled the judgment of the Reipzig Trials that were conducted by the German Supreme Court. The Supreme Court recognized immunity under the superior orders defense on the condition that some additional factors – a lack of the knowledge of illegality and a lack of manifest illegality – had accompanied the orders.[8]

---

[3] *Ibid.*, 278.

[4] *Ibid.*, 278–9.

[5] *Ibid.*, 279.

[6] *Ibid.*

[7] *Ibid.*, 280.

[8] The International Commission for Penal Reconstruction and Development as well as the London International Assembly upheld the same position. The former emphasized the issue of manifest

3.1.2 Preparatory Work of the Nuremberg Charter

3.1.2.1 Proposals of the United States and the Soviet Union

The United States, the United Kingdom, France, and the Soviet Union held an international conference at London from 26 June to 8 August 1945, with the aim of establishing an international military tribunal for the punishment of 'the major war criminals of the European Axis'. The agenda of the conference was an examination of the substantive rules on prosecution and trials. The London Conference also dealt with the issue of defenses under which the accused appeal, together with the topics of criminal act, punishment, organization of the tribunal, trial proceeding, and so forth. However, at the conference, which was urgently held just before the end of the war, the four countries did not substantially consult the problem of defenses.

As was in the case with the War Crimes Commission, the United States positively proposed draft provisions of an agreement at the London Conference. The proposal, which the US delegate showed to the other three countries in April 1945,[9] provided for the superior orders defense in Section 11:

> The fact that a defendant acted pursuant to order of a superior or government sanction shall not constitute an absolute defense but may be considered either in defense or in mitigation of punishment if the tribunal before which the charges are being tried determines that justice so requires.[10]

This proposal basically followed what the War Crimes Commission finally agreed upon, with some changes made to the wordings. The Commission recognized the possibility of conditional immunity, but did not clarify the condition on which to recognize immunity. The US proposal at the London Conference also supported conditional immunity. It used an abstract and the general expression of 'requirement of justice', and entrusted the decision on this point with the respective courts.

The US delegate, Jackson, reported to the president of the United States on the government plan of prosecuting war criminals. Considering that Jackson participated in the drafting of the above-quoted US proposal,[11] it might not be wrong to

---

illegality and the latter focused on the issue of coercion (The Work of the International Commission for Penal Reconstruction and Development, in *ibid.*, 98; The Work of the London International Assembly, in *ibid.*, 101). The London International Assembly did not allow immunization on the ground of coercion if the criminal act in question was 'so obviously heinous' (*ibid*).

[9]American Draft of Definitive Proposal, Presented to Foreign Ministers at San Francisco, April 1945, in *Report of Robert H. Jackson, United States Representative to the International Conference on Military Trials: London, 1945* (Washington, DC: GPO, 1949) [hereinafter, *Jackson Report*], 22.

[10]*Ibid.*, 24.

[11]*Ibid.*, 22.

deem Jackson's report to have explained an intention of the US proposal to some extent. The report criticized the superior orders defense and immunity of a head of state as intolerably expanding the scope of immunity of state officials. However, the report pointed out that there could be a case where the superior orders defense should be allowed:

> There is doubtless a sphere in which the defense of obedience to superior orders should prevail. If a conscripted or enlisted soldier is put on a firing squad, he should not be held responsible for the validity of the sentence he carries out. But the case may be greatly altered where one has discretion because of rank or the latitude of his orders. . . . An accused should be allowed to show the facts about superior orders. The Tribunal can then determine whether they constitute a defense or merely extenuating circumstances, or perhaps carry no weight at all.[12]

Jackson argued that the superior orders defense should not be allowed if the accused had certain discretion in executing the orders. Contrasting this argument to Section 11 of the US proposal, the expression 'if the tribunal ... determines that justice so requires' may be construed as relevant to the cases in which it was judged that the accused did not have any discretion.[13]

At the London Conference, the Soviet Union basically backed this US proposal. However, the Soviet delegate requested some emendations and proposed a substitute draft which read, '[t]he fact that the accused acted under orders of his superior or his government will not be considered as justifying[14] the guilt circumstance'.[15] At this stage, the meaning of the Soviet proposal was not clear enough. Did the proposal only deny automatic immunity under the superior orders defense, or did it propose absolute responsibility, which denies immunity notwithstanding the factors that accompanied the orders? Later, the final draft of the Soviet Union specifically provided that immunity should not be recognized even if the subordinate 'acted blindly'.[16]

Responding to this Soviet proposal, the United States changed its position in its revised draft of 30 June. Its revised position did not allow immunity on the fact of superior orders:

---

[12] *Ibid.*, 47.

[13] The lack of discretion would be related to the issue of coercion, although the relationship between the lack of discretion and the issues of the knowledge of illegality and/or manifest illegality is ambiguous. Shick construed the quoted statement of Jackson as relevant to the knowledge of illegality (F. Shick, 'War Criminals and the Law of the United Nations', *University of Toronto Law Journal* 7 (1947–8): 46, note 67).

[14] The Soviet delegate used the word 'justify' but did not make any objection to the terminology of 'defense' which was later used by the US delegate. It seems that the Soviet delegate did not necessarily persist in the use of the word 'justify'. With respect to the terminologies of 'justification', 'excuse', and 'defense', see note 9 of Chapter 2.

[15] Aide-mémoire from the Soviet Government, June 14, 1945, in *Jackson Report*, 62.

[16] Executive Agreement, Last Soviet Draft, in *ibid.*, 181. The meaning of the words 'acted blindly' is ambiguous. However, it would be understood as indicating, at least, the situation in which subordinates acted without their own judgments, that is, under coercion.

> The fact that a defendant acted pursuant to order of a superior or to government sanction shall not constitute a defense per se, but may be considered in mitigation of punishment if the Tribunal determines that justice so requires.[17]

Different from the US proposal in April, this revised draft rejected immunity even if 'justice so requires'. An effect of the notion of 'justice' was restricted to mitigation of punishment.

The United States changed its position from conditional immunity to absolute responsibility, apparently responding to the Soviet proposal. In light of the details of the discussion, it would be appropriate to deem that the change in the position of the United States was the consequence of the Soviet proposal.[18] However, the US revised draft did not denote any theoretical reasons for the change.

3.1.2.2 Requirement of Justice

The principle of absolute responsibility, which denies immunity under the superior orders defense even if 'justice' so requires, was approved in the drafts proposed by the Drafting Subcommittee as well as the United Kingdom.[19] However, the meaning of the word 'justice' was not fully explained. Jackson referred to the discretion of the accused at an early stage of the conference. The Soviet draft employed the expression 'blind action', which was at least more concrete than 'requirement of justice'. However, these comments and proposals were far from adequate to explain the substance of 'justice'.

At the final stage of the London Conference on 24 July 1945, the delegates of the four Allied Powers again discussed the conditions under which the mitigation of punishment under the superior orders defense should be allowed. However, they did not spare enough time for the issue of the defense. Finally, they supported the idea of not specifically providing the grounds for mitigation of punishment.[20]

Only the British delegate, David Maxwell Fyfe, referred to concrete grounds for mitigation of punishment at the final stage of the discussion. He raised an objection to the Soviet delegate's view that even mitigation of punishment should not be allowed for major war criminals. Fyfe argued that a general rule indicated by the texts of international law was that those who had been threatened to be shot if they had not executed Hitler's orders should be spared their lives and allowed mitigation of punishment.[21] According to Fyfe's view, 'justice' in the draft

---

[17]Revised Draft of Agreement and Memorandum Submitted by American Delegation, June 30, 1945, in *Jackson Report*, 124.

[18]See Dinstein, supra n. 1, at 116–7; Fukatsu & Kita, supra n. 1, at 219.

[19]Draft of Agreement and Charter, Reported by Drafting Subcommittee, July 11, 1945, in *Jackson Report*, 197; Draft Agreement and Charter, Proposed by British Delegation, July 11, 1945, in *ibid.*, 205; Redraft of Charter, Submitted by British Delegation, July 23, 1945, in *ibid.*, 352.

[20]Minutes of Conference Session of July 24, 1945, in *ibid.*, 368.

[21]*Ibid.*, 367–8. However, the sixth and seventh editions of Oppenheim's *International Law* which Fyfe relied on did not deny the possibility of conditional immunity (L. Oppenheim, *International*

Charter would require the mitigation of punishment if the accused had been threatened by superiors.

An overview of the discussion of the delegates indicates that they had slightly varying views on the evaluation of the rules provided in the Nuremberg Charter. As the debate on 24 July showed, the Soviet delegate who had consistently asserted the severe responsibility of war criminals held that even mitigation of punishment should not be allowed for the major war criminals. It seems that he only bore in mind that the Nuremberg Charter aimed solely at the prosecution of major war criminals. In contrast, the British delegate on the same day expressed his idea on the Charter as reflecting 'the general rule on superior orders in international law books'. It was also the case with the US delegate. As will be seen later, when Jackson was involved in the trial proceeding as the US chief prosecutor, he implied that the Charter's provision in question was related to the responsibility of a squad soldier.

On this point, Röling and some other commentators argued that the provision of the Charter on the superior orders defense was intended to be applied for major war criminals and the same rule should not be applied for lower state organs.[22] As the basis for his arguments, Röling referred to the facts that the Nuremberg Charter targeted the major war criminals and that the Special Court of Cassation of the Netherlands underlined this point in its judgment. However, these points did not necessarily mean that some rules apart from those stipulated in the Charter should be applied for trials of lower state organs. As Röling mentioned, circumstances would fairly be different if superior orders that were received by lower state organs, not major war criminals, mattered. Such a difference would possibly influence the degree of responsibility of the respective state organs. In reality, the Subsequent Proceedings after the Nuremberg Trial could be said to have consciously dealt with the difference. Nonetheless, as far as the discussion at the London Conference is concerned, it is doubtful whether the four delegates had such a common understanding. It would be more appropriate to construe that the final provision was concluded with some ambiguity; this is because the understanding or premise of each delegate was not completely unified on the question of whether or not the

Law, 6th ed. by H. Lauterpacht, vol. 2, *Disputes, War and Neutrality* (London: Longman, Green & Co., 1940), 453–4; L. Oppenheim, *International Law,* 7th ed. by H. Lauterpacht, vol.2, *Disputes, War and Neutrality* (London: Longmans, 1952), 568–9).

[22]B. Röling, 'The Law of War and the National Jurisdiction since 1945', *Recueil des cours de l'académie de droit international de la Haye, 1960, II*, 100 (1961): 372–3. McCoubrey construes the personal jurisdiction of Article 8 of the Nuremberg Charter as restrictive, emphasizing that major war criminals did issue orders and they apparently knew the illegality of the conduct. See H. McCoubrey, 'From Nuremberg to Rome: Restoring the Defence of Superior Orders', *International and Comparative Law Quarterly* 50 (2001): 386–94. Garraway underlines, on this point, the statement of the Soviet delegate at the London Conference. See C. Garraway, 'Superior Orders and the International Criminal Court: Justice Delivered or Justice Denied', *International Review of the Red Cross* 836 (1999): 785–94. Weber also argues that the rule of Article 8 of the Nuremberg Charter only applies to serious crimes (H. Weber, 'Die Strafrechtliche Verantwortlichkeit für Handeln auf Befehl', *Monatsschrift für Deutsches Recht* 2 (1948): 39). However, the grounds for these arguments have not been shown.

Charter provisions reflected the general rules that were applicable to other state officials as well and not just major war criminals.

Eventually, the four Allies provided for the superior orders defense in Article 8 of the Nuremberg Charter, but without specifying concrete grounds for mitigation of punishment:

> The fact that the Defendant acted pursuant to order of his Government or of a superior shall not free him from responsibility, but may be considered in mitigation of punishment if the Tribunal determines that justice so requires.[23]

As already noted, it is not clear what kind of situations the phrase 'justice so requires' indicated. Indeed, during the London Conference, the US, the Soviet, and the British delegates referred to the possible 'discretion' of subordinates, 'blind action', and 'threatening to be shot', respectively. If these aspects were connected to the factors of the knowledge of illegality and/or manifest illegality, and coercion – at least it would not be disputable that the restriction of 'discretion' and 'threatening' is related to coercion – Article 8 of the Charter could be deemed to have followed the state practice that was observed in the previous chapter in considering these factors. However, the Nuremberg Charter, which was stipulated for the punishment of Nazi war criminals, was different from this state practice in one significant respect: the Charter did not recognize conditional immunity under the superior orders defense. 'Justice' could only be taken into account as a ground for the mitigation of punishment.[24]

During the London Conference, the US view on the superior orders defense changed from conditional immunity to absolute responsibility. The Soviet Union proposed absolute responsibility, and the United States as well as the other countries immediately followed it. However, no theoretical grounds for rejecting any possibility of immunity were presented.

As noted before, the provision on the superior orders defense in the Nuremberg Charter was prepared under the apprehension that the said defense would make the prosecution of war crimes impossible. During the London Conference, Jackson addressed the United States president as follows:

> With the doctrine of immunity of a head of state usually is coupled another, that orders from an official superior protect one who obeys them. It will be noticed that the combination of these two doctrines means that nobody is responsible. Society as modernly organized cannot tolerate so broad an area of official irresponsibility.[25]

Such a motive, which partially directed the Charter provision, was shared by many academic arguments that had been expressed until the establishment of the

---

[23]Agreement and Charter, August 8, 1945, in *Jackson Report,* 424.

[24]The arguments which criticize that Article 8 of the Charter did not clearly provide for the immunization on the tests of the knowledge of illegality and/or manifest illegality include V. Maugham, *U.N.O. and War Crimes* (London: John Murray, 1951), 45, 48; G. Williams, *Criminal Law, The General Part*, 2nd ed. (London: Stevens & Sons, 1961), 300.

[25]Report to the President by Mr.Justice Jackson, June 6, 1945, in *Jackson Report*, 47.

Charter. As will be seen later, commentators who rejected the superior orders defense either emphasized that the said defense would make enforcement of the laws of war impossible or restricted themselves to contend that the defense went against the 'great principle of natural justice', 'spirit of justice', 'sound legal principle', and so on.[26] It is difficult to find any theoretical observation on criminal responsibility, which was seen in the discussion on the national legal situations of the United Kingdom, the United States, and France.

From the very beginning, the US government had examined the summary trial of German major war criminals until a plan for a formal international military trial was put forth. At the conference of foreign ministries of the United States, the United Kingdom, and the Soviet Union held at Moscow, the US Secretary of State, Cordell Hull, had already expressed his view that the leaders of Germany, Japan, and Italy should be brought 'before a drumhead court-martial. And at sunrise on the following day there would occur an historic incident'. He repeated the same statement at cabinet meetings.[27] At the Teheran Conference, which was held among the leaders of the three countries in the same year, Joseph Stalin said, '[a]t least 50,000 and perhaps 100,000 of the German Commanding Staff must be physically liquidated'. Franklin Roosevelt jokingly replied that he 'would put the figure of the German Commanding Staff which should be executed at 49,000 or more'.[28] The US Secretary of Treasury, Henry Morgenthau, Jr., recorded in his memorandum in September 1944 that the US president definitely supported his idea when he asserted that German war criminals should immediately be shot upon capture and identification.[29]

Morgenthau's stringent plan for postwar Germany was leaked and utilized by Nazi Germany for propaganda against the Allied Powers. In the United States, Morgenthau's plan was criticized for its character of collective revenge. Public opinion threatened to get more critical if Germany stiffened its resistance and casualties of US soldiers increased.[30] Since then, the US Secretary of Army, Henry Stimson, who proposed a trial and not a summary execution, led the issue of German war crimes in the government.[31] While the US government thus changed its policy, public opinion in the country still supported the execution of war criminals rather than a trial.[32] Jackson was fully aware of the outcry in the

---

[26]See Sect. 3.5.

[27]*The Memoirs of Cordell Hull*, vol. 2 (New York: The MacMillan Company, 1948), 1289–90.

[28]*Foreign Relations of the United States, Diplomatic Paper, The Conferences at Cairo and Teheran, 1943* (Washington, DC: GPO, 1961), 553–4.

[29]H. Stimson & M. Bundy, *On Active Service in Peace and War* (New York: Happer & Brothers, 1947, 1948), 584–5. See also *The Henry Lewis Stimson Diaries in the Yale University Library* (Yale University Library, 1973), roll 9, vol. 48, 20 Sep. 1944 (Microfilm: Modern Japanese Political History Materials Room, National Diet Library, Japan, DHS-1), 92.

[30]See B. Smith, *The Road to Nuremberg* (New York: Basic Books, Inc., Publishers, 1981), 54.

[31]*Ibid.*, 54–5.

[32]See W. Bosch, *Judgment on Nuremberg, American Attitudes toward the Major German War-Crime Trials* (Chapel Hill: The University of North Carolina Press, 1970), 91–4.

government and public opinion as well as the peril of lynching 'justice'. He addressed the US president in his memorandum of April 1945 as follows:

> Time is of the essence. Someone must make an effective and unambiguous move to deal with war criminals, promptly after surrender. It must be on a basis acceptable to people whom we would discourage from taking the law into their own hands with resultant anarchy and civil bloodshed.[33]

Jackson's criticism of the superior orders defense and immunity of a head of state can be said to have reflected similar discussions in the government, a trend of public opinion, and the contemporary academic arguments. At the London Conference, the US position changed from conditional immunity to absolute responsibility without any specific reasons. In light of the circumstances that surrounded Jackson at the time, any such reasons could be considered to have been unnecessary.[34] A combination of the superior orders defense and immunity of a head of state meant a fatal impasse for war crimes trials. The four Allied Powers should have done the utmost to avoid such an impasse.

3.2 The Nuremberg Trial

The Nuremberg Charter stipulated that mitigation of punishment would be admitted on the fact of superior orders only 'if the Tribunal determines that justice so requires'. Immunity, however, could not be allowed. At the stage of the Trial of the Major War Criminals, which was conducted under the Charter, the defense counsels repeatedly contended for immunity under the superior orders defense. Eventually, the judgment of the Nuremberg Trial did not provide a definite conclusion. If one tried to grasp the 'Nuremberg Principle' by taking into account the Charter's provisions and the whole judicial proceedings that applied the Charter, its character as a 'principle' would take on a questionable aspect.

The judgment of the Nuremberg Trial did not meddle with the issue of the superior orders defense. It did not offer enough information to confirm the essence of Article 8 of the Charter. Meanwhile, the defense counsels positively developed arguments on the superior orders defense, seeking for the immunity of the defendants or mitigation of their punishment. The arguments of the defense counsels could not directly be consulted for the interpretation of the judgment. Nonetheless, the Nuremberg Trial was a significant judicial proceeding in light of the development of international law, and both the arguments of the prosecution and the defendant, as well as the judgment itself, drew wide attention. Considering their

[33] E. Gerhart, *America's Advocate: Robert H. Jackson* (Indianapolis; New York: The Bobbs-Merrill Company, Inc., 1958), 309.

[34] Nill-Theobald deems the rigidity of Article 8 to be expressing the intention of the Allied Powers to avoid the impossibility of punishment of war criminals. See C.Nill-Theobald, *'Defences' bei Kriegsverbrechen am Beispiel Deutschlands und der USA, Zugleich ein Beitrag zu einem Allgemeinen Teil des Völkerstrafrechts* (Freiburg im Breisgau: Edition Iuscrim, 1998), 107.

influence on the subsequent international rule-making processes, it would be worth tracing the arguments on both sides.

Moreover, a survey of the debates between the prosecution and the defendant would help in investigating the complications that the tribunal faced in delivering a rather ambiguous judgment on the superior orders defense. In order to clarify the contentious points that raised conflict between the prosecution and defendant, we will first look at their arguments in the trial.[35]

3.2.1 The Argument of the Prosecution

3.2.1.1 Manifest Illegality of the Conduct

It is worth noting that the chief prosecutors of the United Kingdom, France, and the Soviet Union emphasized the manifest illegality of the criminal conduct of the accused.

Hartley Shawcross, the British chief prosecutor, used restrictive expression in denying the superior orders defense. He stated that the orders that 'are manifestly contrary to the very law of nature' should not be a ground for immunity.[36] The French chief prosecutor François de Menthon also underlined that the national laws severely limited the immunizing function of the superior orders defense and rejected the said defense if the orders in question had been manifestly illegal.[37] However, these statements were not necessarily relevant to the understanding that the Nuremberg Charter only focused on the cases of manifest illegality.

With regard to this point, the Soviet chief prosecutor, Roman Rudenko, clearly expressed his view to deem the character of the Charter to be restrictive. He stated that the drafters of the Charter put forth 'a special proviso to the effect that the execution of an obviously criminal order does not exonerate one from criminal responsibility' in order to prevent the accused from seeking refuge under the cover of Hitler's orders.[38] He indicated that the provision in question denied immunity on the superior orders defense in presupposing that the Nuremberg Trial only dealt with the cases of manifest illegality. He appeared to have reserved his opinion for the cases in which the illegality of the conduct had not been manifest.

---

[35]The studies which closely examine the proceedings of the Nuremberg Trial in relation to the superior orders defense include Dinstein, supra n. 1, at 125–56; H. Jescheck, *Die Verantwortlichkeit der Staatsorgane nach Völkerstrafrecht – Eine Studie zu den Nürnberger Prozessen –* (Bonn: Ludwig Röhrscheid Verlag, 1952), 385–6. See also Weber, supra n. 22, at 34–42; R. Woetzel, *The Nuremberg Trials in International Law with a Postlude on the Eichmann Case* (London: Stevens & Sons Limited, 1962), 118–9.

[36]Final Speech of H. Shawcross, Trial of the Major War Criminals before the International Military Tribunal, (Nuremberg, 1947) [hereinafter, IMT], vol. 19, 465–6.

[37]Opening Speech of F. de Menthon, IMT, vol. 2, 418.

[38]Final Speech of R. Rudenko, IMT, vol. 19, 577.

It is not certain whether or not the British and French chief prosecutors shared Rudenko's views. However, the arguments of these three prosecutors were common at least in denying immunity under the superior orders defense while emphasizing the manifest illegality of the conduct.

The US chief prosecutor Jackson expressed an apparently different view on the interpretation of the Charter. He implied that Article 8 of the Nuremberg Charter would also be applicable to the person who had not had discretionary power at the time of the criminal conduct:

> A conscripted private on a firing squad cannot expect to hold an inquest on the validity of the execution. The Charter implies common sense limits to liability just as it places common sense limits upon immunity. But none of these men before you acted in minor parts. Each of them was entrusted with broad discretion and exercised great power.[39]

Regarding the person with 'broad discretion', the Charter did not limit his/her responsibility. It was only for the person who did not have broad discretionary power at the time of criminal conduct that responsibility should be limited. Meanwhile, Article 8 of the Charter only allowed mitigation of punishment. Thus, according to Jackson, the Charter did not allow immunity even for those who were not expected to ponder on the legality of their conduct. Jackson seemed to understand that the Charter only recognized mitigation of punishment even if the accused had not been conscious of the illegality of his/her conduct or the illegality of the conduct had not been manifest.

Thus, the prosecutors' positions were not necessarily unified on the realm of the Charter's provision on the superior orders defense. The views of the British and French prosecutors were not fully clarified, whereas the US and Soviet prosecutors were seemingly different in their understanding of the Charter.

3.2.1.2 Coercion

Meanwhile, the prosecutors, in principle, unanimously denied immunity on the ground of coercion incidental to superior orders.

First, at the trial proceedings, Jackson repeated the statement that he had made at the drafting of the Nuremberg Charter. As noted before, he implied that mitigation of punishment under Article 8 of the Charter was applicable for soldiers of a firing squad who were not allowed to judge the legality of their conduct. Another characteristic of those soldiers that he cited was that they were neither 'entrusted with broad discretion' nor 'exercised great power'. According to Jackson, the Charter only recognized mitigation of punishment under the superior orders defense for soldiers with limited discretion.

The views of the British and French prosecutors were even more severe. The British chief prosecutor Shawcross strongly criticized the defense presented by the accused, stating that it would be better than participating in the execution of orders

[39] Justice Jackson's Opening Speech, IMT, vol. 2, 150–1.

even if he would have been put in jail for disobedience.[40] Further, the French chief prosecutor, Auguste Champetier de Ribes, while admitting that the accused had been threatened or coerced, still argued that these factors did not exempt him nor mitigate punishment. He stated, 'Hitler might have governed their bodies but not their souls. By disobeying him they might perhaps have lost their liberty or even their lives but they would at least have saved their honor. Cowardice has never been an excuse, nor even an extenuating circumstance'.[41]

Such a view, where he did not recognize the possibility of mitigation of punishment, was different from that of Jackson. Moreover, it can be said that the view of the French chief prosecutor deviated from Article 8 of the Nuremberg Charter in light of its drafting process. As was seen in the previous section, the expression 'if the Tribunal determines that justice so requires' in Article 8 can be thought to be relevant to the situation of coercion at least. It would be more natural to deem that the drafters of the Charter intended to allow mitigation of punishment by the fact of coercion.

Nonetheless, it is necessary to prudently interpret the contention of the British and French prosecutors in the background of their relevant statements. It is worth noting that they underlined that the conduct in question had been manifestly illegal as they denied exemption or mitigation of punishment. For instance, Shawcross stated that immunity could not be allowed in the case that the orders were 'manifestly contrary to the very law of nature from which international law has grown'.[42] With respect to the French prosecutors, a denial of the coercion defense and mitigation of punishment was expressed by de Ribes. However, prior to the statement by de Ribes, another French prosecutor, de Menthons, asserted that the conduct of the accused had been manifestly illegal.[43]

The real intention behind each statement of these prosecutors cannot be definitely determined. It would not be possible to declare that they upheld the test of manifest illegality and consciously denied immunity or mitigation of punishment only for the cases wherein the illegality of the act was obvious.

As seen above, the prosecutors unanimously denied the superior orders defense if the criminal conduct had been manifestly illegal, while reserving their positions for the cases in which the illegality had not been manifest. However, the prosecutors' views were ambiguous on the scope of the Charter's provision. With respect to the problem of coercion, the prosecutors generally denied immunity by the coercion defense at least for the cases of manifest illegality. The details of the discussion of the respective prosecutors might have been varied. However, it is at least certain that they supported the principle of absolute responsibility in the case of coercion regarding the criminal conduct in question. On this point, the prosecutors' view correctly reflected the intention of the drafters of the Charter.

---

[40] Final Speech of H. Shawcross, IMT, vol. 19, 466.

[41] Final Speech of C. de Ribes, *ibid.*, 534.

[42] IMT, vol. 19, 466. See also IMT, vol. 3, 144.

[43] IMT, vol. 2, 418.

3.2.2 The Argument of the Defendants

3.2.2.1 The Knowledge of Illegality and/or Manifest Illegality

The defense counsels contended the immunity of the accused, pointing out that the accused were not conscious of the illegality of their conduct and/or that the conduct in question had not been manifestly illegal. As already seen, the chief prosecutors of the United Kingdom, France, and the Soviet Union underlined the manifest illegality of the criminal conduct in arguing on the responsibility of the accused. They did not specifically mention the cases in which the illegality of the criminal conduct had been obscure. It can be said that the arguments of the defendants did not necessarily contradict those of the prosecutors in theory. A critical difference between them could be found in their judgment on legal facts, particularly whether or not the criminal conduct had been manifestly illegal. The prosecutors unanimously determined that the conduct in question had been manifestly illegal, while the defense counsels expressed different views.

One of the causes of such conflicting views was associated with the problem of reprisals. The prosecutors did not refer to the issue of reprisals in this context. In contrast, some defense counsels argued that it had been difficult for the accused to determine whether or not the conduct in question would have been deemed to be reprisals. Then, they contended that the illegality of the conduct had not been manifest.

For instance, Otto Kranzbühler, the defense counsel for defendant Karl Dönitz, presented his argument as follows. He stated that a soldier who received orders at the front could not decide whether or not the orders were in conflict with the Geneva Convention:

> If no one but the leadership of the State is competent to order reprisals, then hundreds or thousands of German officers cannot be required today to have considered themselves also competent, and to have been presumptuous enough to verify orders whose actual and legal basis was entirely unknown to them. In this case the principle prevails, at least for the frontline commanders, that the subordinate may, when in doubt, rely on the order as given.[44]

Moreover, Franz Exner, the defense counsel for defendant Alfred Jodl, referred to this problem in terms of crimes against peace. He argued that a general would seldom be in a position to judge whether or not the state to be attacked had violated neutrality or threatened to attack.[45]

Some argued on the knowledge of illegality separately from the issue of reprisals. They asserted that it had been difficult for the accused to be aware of the illegality of the conduct because it had borne a character of state acts. Such an

---

[44]Kranzbühler's Final Speech on Behalf of Dönitz, IMT, vol. 18, 362.

[45]Exner's Final Speech on Behalf of Jodl, IMT, vol. 19, 21.

assertion was made by Hans Laternser, the defense counsel for the General Staff and High Command of the German Armed Forces. He argued that the Führer's orders had a legislative effect and the military leaders should have obeyed such a 'law'.[46] Laternser thus associated the notion of state acts with the problem of the knowledge of illegality.

The defense counsels thus asserted that the defendants' conduct possibly bore the character of reprisals or that it had been difficult for the defendants to be aware of the illegality of their conduct as a state act. The arguments differed from those of the prosecution in considering the circumstances under which the criminal act had been committed. The prosecutors did not reply to the contention of the defendants. However, as already noted, the British delegate relied on Oppenheim's *International Law*, which drew attention to the problem of reprisals, in discussing the superior orders defense during the drafting of the Nuremberg Charter.[47] The arguments of defense counsels that referred to the possibility of reprisals can be said to have been considerably persuasive in theory.

3.2.2.2 Coercion

Meanwhile, most of the defendants contended immunity on the ground of coercion. For instance, the defense counsel Exner compared defendant Jodl to a soldier who retreated by throwing away his rifle and argued that they would both have been executed for disobeying orders during battle.[48]

The defense counsel, Rudolf Merkel, associated the problem of obedience to orders with that of 'duress induced by official duties'.[49] He questioned whether the defendants could be expected 'to take upon themselves loss of livelihood, family suffering, concentration camp, and perhaps even a shameful death'.[50] He argued, '[i]t is true that cowardice is not a virtue; but it is equally true that heroism and martyrdom in the world of human beings are the exception', and emphasized that the extra-legal state of emergency had been recognized as an exempting factor.[51]

---

[46] Laternser's Final Plea on Behalf of General Staff and OKW, IMT, vol. 22, 83.

[47] Oppenheim, supra n. 21 (1940), at 454.

[48] Exner's Final Speech on Behalf of Jodl, IMT, vol. 19, 24–5.

[49] In common law, the 'coercion' defense is deemed restrictive that may be allowed for wives who committed specific crimes under the coercion of their husbands. See G. Williams, *Criminal Law, The General Part*, 2nd ed. (London: Stevens & Sons, 1961), 751–69; J. Smith & B. Hogan, *Criminal Law*, 7th ed. (London: Butterworths, 1992), 232–45. There has not been such differentiation in international law and the terms of 'duress' and 'coercion' have been used interchangeably. However, during the drafting of the ICC Statute, it was proposed to give comprehensive meaning to the term 'duress' and use it separately from other terminologies. See note 107 of Chapter 4.

[50] Merkel's Final Plea on Behalf of Gestapo, IMT, vol. 21, 536–7.

[51] Ibid., 537.

Such an argument of Merkel identified 'duress induced by official duties' with 'physical compulsion'.

The characteristic of Merkel's view was that he understood exempting coercion as a derivation of official duties backed by state power; that is, such coercion was based on national laws. It was not only Merkel who underlined the legal character of coercion. The defense counsel Hermann Jahrreiss, who defended Jodl, also emphasized the absolute character of the despot's orders. He argued that subordinates could not judge the legality of such orders except when the orders deviated from 'every human order' and 'a genuine question of right or wrong did not arise, so that no genuine examination was called for'.[52] He then questioned whether or not the Nuremberg Charter, which denied immunity under the superior orders defense, should be applied to the Führer's orders.[53] Jahrreiss repeatedly emphasized that the Führer's orders had been 'legally binding'.[54] He seriously considered the point that even if the orders had been in contravention of international law or other conventional values, they still had absolute power over subordinates at the national level: 'His orders were law'.[55]

Thus, these defense counsels emphasized the binding force, which concurrent German laws had for state organs of the country. In relevant discussions, they bore in mind the fact that the persons who resisted coercion by state power or national laws could not be protected at the international level. According to Exner, soldiers who found themselves caught between obligations to their own country and those under international law were driven into a 'really tragic position'. He argued that those soldiers should not be prosecuted.[56]

The coercion incidental to the orders of the government or those in military organizations bears legal character. As a consequence, subordinates are likely to be judged as being under coercion. However, the notion of 'coercion by law' should not be abstractedly overemphasized. Such an argument might lead to the conclusion that superior orders automatically exempt the accused regardless of whether or not they were under actual coercion. This conclusion is similar to the view expressed in Oppenheim's *International Law* of 1921. Oppenheim noted that '[t]he law cannot require an individual to be punished for an act which he was compelled by law to commit'[57] and recognized automatic immunity by the superior orders defense. It goes without saying that this position contradicts Article 8 of the Nuremberg Charter in principle.

[52]Jahrreiss' Speech on Juridical Question of Breach of Peace, IMT, vol. 17, 489.

[53]Ibid.

[54]Ibid., 491.

[55]Ibid., 494.

[56]Exner's Final Speech on Behalf of Jodl, IMT, vol. 19, 22.

[57]L. Oppenheim, *International Law*, 3rd ed. by R. Roxburgh, vol.2, *War and Neutrality* (London: Longmans, 1921), 343.

3.2.2.3 The Realm of Discussion on Coercion

It should be noted that the defense counsels' views on the realm of immunity on the ground of coercion varied. As already seen, the British chief prosecutor emphasized that the criminal conduct in question had been manifestly illegal in arguing that coercion did not have an exempting effect. His argument may possibly be understood as having denied immunity only for the cases of manifest illegality. Among the defense counsels, Jahrreiss shared a similar view.

Jahrreiss underlined the fact that the Führer's order had absolute influence on his subordinates and doubted whether the persons who had acted under such orders could be held individually accountable. However, Jahrreiss made an exception of the cases 'in which the monocrat placed himself, according to the indisputable axioms of our times, outside every human order and in which a genuine question of right or wrong did not arise, so that no genuine examination was called for, either'.[58] In other words, he doubted the responsibility of the accused only for the cases in which the illegality of the criminal conduct had not been manifest. His position would have possibly been the same as that of the British chief prosecutor.

Kurt Kauffman, the defense counsel for Ernst Kaltenbrunner, showed such a view even more specifically:

> there yet remains an absolute obligation to resist an order the purport of which, clearly recognizable to a subordinate, amounts to the materialization of evil and obviously violates the healthy sentiments which aim at humanity and peace among people and individuals. The phrase 'in a life-and-death struggle of a nation there can be no legality' is an untrue thesis not thought out to the end, no matter who expresses it. Even immediate danger to the life of the person receiving the order could not induce me to change my conviction.[59]

On the other hand, defense counsels such as Exner and Merkel expressed a clearly conflicting view on coercion against that of the prosecutors. For instance, Exner denied Jodl's responsibility[60] in stating that the accused would have been executed for disobeying orders even if he had been sure about the illegality of the war.[61] Merkel contended that 'duress induced by official duties' could be an exempting factor of the 'extra-legal state of emergency'. Further, he contended that the accused had lost the free will to judge on a legal and moral value of criminal orders:

> Added to this deep-rooted attitude [the strictest obedience to orders] was the devilish atmosphere which by hypnotic power turned particularly the small officials into tools without a will of their own. All of these motives were added to the threat emanating from the very nature of the occupation and they all combined to create a duress so oppressive that the Gestapo official no longer retained the freedom of will to examine a criminal order as to its legal and moral value and to refuse obedience.[62]

---

[58]Jahrreiss' Speech on Juridical Question of Breach of Peace, IMT, vol. 17, 489.

[59]Kauffmann's Final Speech on Behalf of Kaltenbrunner, IMT, vol. 18, 68.

[60]Exner's Final Speech on Behalf of Jodl, IMT, vol. 19, 22.

[61]Ibid., 24.

[62]Merkel's Final Plea on Behalf of Gestapo, IMT, vol. 21, 537.

According to Merkel, no matter how manifest the illegality and immorality of the conduct had been, the accused should not be deemed responsible since he could not have been able to judge on these values. Exner and Merkel thus recognized immunity on the ground of coercion even in the cases where the accused was aware of the illegality of the conduct or that illegality had been manifest. On this point, their position was squarely opposed to that of the prosecutors.

Thus, during the trial proceedings, the prosecutors and defense counsels much debated on the issues of the knowledge of illegality and/or manifest illegality, and coercion. With regard to the first two issues, the defense counsels opined that the accused should be responsible only in the cases where they were conscious of the illegality of the conduct or that the illegality had been manifest. The prosecution did not clarify its position on this point as a whole. However, at least the British and French chief prosecutors emphasized the manifest illegality of the conduct in discussing the responsibility of the accused. Consequently, one can construe that the prosecutors, probably except the US chief prosecutor, decided on the problem of immunity in light of the manifest illegality of the conduct as the defense counsels did.

The prosecutors' views were also not clear on the issue of coercion. Their basic idea was that coercion could not be deemed as an immunizing factor. However, it was unclear whether or not they denied the mitigation of punishment alike. Moreover, they did not clarify whether immunity or mitigation of punishment should not be recognized even if the illegality of the criminal conduct had not been manifest. Meanwhile, the defense counsels also had varying views on these questions, especially on the latter one. Some defense counsels contended the immunity of the accused on the ground of coercion regardless of the knowledge of illegality and/or manifest illegality of the conduct. Others restrained themselves from asserting immunity with regard to the cases in which illegality had been manifest.

The provision of Article 8 of the Nuremberg Charter did not specifically answer these questions. Then, what about the judgment of the Nuremberg Trial? Did the Nuremberg Tribunal provide for clear answers to the questions that had been put forth by the prosecutors and defense counsels? As we will see below, the ambiguity of the 'Nuremberg Principle' on the superior orders defense was mainly caused by the noncommittal arguments of the Tribunal on this issue.

3.2.3 The Judgment

The judgment of the Nuremberg Trial is largely composed of two parts. The former is the general part which comprises the analysis of the Nazi Regime, its policy as well as its violation of treaties, and the interpretation of the Nuremberg Charter. The latter part judged on criminal organizations and the individual responsibility of each defendant. The issue of the superior orders defense was first treated in the former part in explaining Article 8 of the Nuremberg Charter.[63]

[63]Judgment, IMT, vol. 1, 171, 223–4.

As was seen above, in light of the Charter's preparatory work, it would be undisputable that Article 8 meant to adopt the principle of absolute responsibility in the case of coercion. Nonetheless, the International Military Tribunal (IMT) interpreted the article more restrictively. The Tribunal noted that Article 8 only rejected immunity on the ground of the existence of superior orders. Thus, factors incidental to superior orders should be considered to be outside the scope of the article. The Tribunal delivered on this point as follows in the section titled 'The Law of the Charter':

> The Charter specifically provides in Article 8:
> 'The fact that the Defendant acted pursuant to order of his Government or of a superior shall not free him from responsibility, but may be considered in mitigation of punishment.'
>
> The provisions of this article are in conformity with the law of all nations. That a soldier was ordered to kill or torture in violation of the international law of war has never been recognized as a defense to such acts of brutality, though, as the Charter here provides, the order may be urged in mitigation of the punishment. The true test, which is found in varying degrees in the criminal law of most nations, is not the existence of the order, but whether moral choice was in fact possible.[64]

Then, what was the meaning of the expression 'whether moral choice was in fact possible'? The notion of 'moral choice' had not generally been used in international law until then. It had neither been widely used in national criminal laws. Did the possibility of 'moral choice' relate to the question of whether or not the accused was conscious of the illegality of his/her conduct or if the illegality of the conduct had been manifest? Did it relate to the question of whether or not the accused had been under coercion caused by superior orders? Otherwise, did it relate to the cases in which the illegality of the conduct had not been manifest and, at the same time, the accused had been under coercion?

On the other hand, does a lack of 'moral choice' imply the immunity of the accused, or is it only the mitigation of punishment that was to be approved?

There may be some variations in the interpretation of the expression in question.

First, in light of the expression 'a defense to such acts of brutality' in the judgment, it can be construed that the Tribunal understood the Charter as only dealing with the cases of manifest illegality.[65] In such a case, a major issue relevant to 'moral choice' would be coercion. There have been a considerable number of commentators who understand the judgment as such.[66] For example, as Christiane

---

[64]Ibid.

[65]The arguments which emphasize that the Nuremberg Trial dealt with manifestly illegal acts committed by high-ranking officials were referred to in note 22 above However, as Jescheck pointed out, the material jurisdiction of the Nuremberg Trial was not restricted to manifestly illegal orders. (Jescheck, supra n. 35, at 386). Article 6 of the Nuremberg Charter actually provided for the punishment of conventional war crimes, the illegality of which was sometimes obscure.

[66]C. Eustathiades, 'Quelques aspects de la jurisprudence concernants les criminels de guerre: L'exception des ordres reçus et autres moyens de défense similaires', in D. Constantopoulos, & H. Wehberg, *Gegenwartsprobleme des internationalen rechtes und der rechtsphilosophie: Festschrift für Rudolf Laun zu Seinem Siebzigsten Geburtstag* (Hamburg: Girardet & Co., 1953), 414–5;

Nill-Theobald notes that 'moral choice' could only matter in the cases of coercion,[67] they acknowledge that it is only natural that 'moral choice' relates to the problem of coercion. Meanwhile, a concrete explanation has been given by Yoram Dinstein. He explains that a person who was coerced to conduct a criminal act with a sword on his/her head would have had to choose between saving his/her life by committing the act and his/her own death by not committing the act. Nonetheless, it is impossible in many cases to expect a person to choose one's own death. The person does not have a choice from a moral viewpoint. We should not but admit the person to save his/her own life.[68]

What if the 'moral choice' in the judgment was a test to decide on immunity and not of mitigation of punishment? This interpretation is what the ILC later showed in its Nürnberg Principle of 1950 and in the drafting of the Draft Code of Crimes (Offences) against the Peace and Security of Mankind.[69]

An examination of the wording of Article 8 of the Charter reveals that immunity is denied on the ground of *the existence of orders*. It is fully possible to construe that the recognition of the coercion defense would not conflict with the Charter provision. This is an understanding that if 'moral choice' was not possible, the accused may rely on the defense of coercion and not on the superior orders defense.[70]

However, the conclusion would be substantially different if one interprets Article 8 by taking into account the Charter's preparatory work. If one deems that the Tribunal recognized immunity on the ground of coercion, the Tribunal's view would turn out to be contrary to the intention of the four countries that drafted the Nuremberg Charter. In other words, it would result in a conflict with the principle of

---

Röling, supra n. 22, at, 376; P. Fuhrmann, *Der Höhere Befehl als Rechtfertigung im Völkerrecht* (München; Berlin: C. H. Beck'sche Verlagsbuchhandlung, 1963), 83; Dinstein, supra n. 1, at 152–3; M. McDougal and F. Feliciano, *The International Law of War, Transnational Coercion and World Public Order* (Dordrecht: Martinus Nijhoff Publishers, 1994), 693; Nill-Theobald, supra n. 34, at 166; A. Zimmermann, 'Superior Orders', in *The Rome Statute of the International Criminal Court: A Commentary*, eds A. Cassese, P. Gaeta & J. Jones (Oxford: Oxford University Press, 2002), 962. Jescheck construed the line in question as relevant to the principle of necessity (Jescheck, supra n. 35, at 386).

[67] Nill-Theobald, supra n. 34, at 166.

[68] Dinstein, supra n. 1, at 152.

[69] See also H. Donnedieu de Vabres, 'Le proces de Nuremberg devant les principes modernes du droit pénal international', *Recueil des cours* 70 (1947): 568–9; S. Glaser, 'L'ordre hiérarchique en droit pénal international', *Revue de droit pénal et de criminologie* 33 (1952–3): 327–8; Q. Wright, 'The Outlawry of War and the Law of War', *American Journal of International Law* 47 (1953): 373–4; M. Greenspan, *The Modern Law of Land Warfare* (Los Angeles: University of California Press, 1959), 493–5; Röling, supra n. 22, at, 376; M. Bassiouni, *Crimes against Humanity in International Criminal Law*, 2nd revised ed. (The Hague: Kluwer Law International, 1999), o 472; L. Sadat, *The International Criminal Court and the Transformation of International Law: Justice for the New Millennium* (New York: Transnational Publishers, Inc., 2002), 220. However, the grounds for their arguments have not been indicated.

[70] K. Kittichaisaree, *International Criminal Law* (New York; London: Oxford University Press, 2001), 268.

absolute responsibility in the case of coercion that had been put forth during the drafting of the Charter.

Meanwhile, one can also assume that the Tribunal examined the issues of the knowledge of illegality and/or manifest illegality as *obiter dictum* in addressing the notion of 'moral choice', while excluding from the realm of Article 8 the cases in which the illegality of the conduct had not been manifest.[71] If one understands the expression as such, the question of coordination between the judgment and the Charter would depend on the interpretation the Charter's preparatory work. However, as seen before, the drafters' intention on the issues of the knowledge of illegality as well as manifest illegality was obscure.

Was the argument one 'moral choice' relevant to the issue of coercion, and the knowledge of illegality and/or manifest illegality? Was 'moral choice' a criterion of immunity or mitigation of punishment?[72] There is no decisive clue in the judgment to answer these questions. Most academic arguments, as already seen, have simply referred to the 'moral choice' test and have not shown any persuasive grounds for their statements. It seems difficult to correctly interpret the expression in question and determine the relationship between the judgment and the Charter's provision.[73]

The Tribunal eventually did not clearly present its view on the questions addressed by the prosecutors and defense counsels during the trial proceeding. The judgment referred to 'moral choice' in the section titled 'The Law of the Charter' and continued to deliver on each defendant. However, the Tribunal did not clarify what the possibility of 'moral choice' concretely meant.

---

[71]Starke associates the issue of 'moral choice' with the mental condition of the accused (J. Starke, *Introduction to International Law*, 10th ed. (London: Butterworths, 1989), 556–7). Descheemaeker stated that the line in question coincided with Section 47 of the German *Military Criminal Code*, which recognized the superior orders defense on the test of the knowledge of illegality (J. Descheemaeker, 'Le Tribunal Militaire International des grands criminels de guerre', *Revue générale de droit international public* 50 (1946): 236, 263). However, the grounds for their arguments have not been indicated.

[72]Those who understand the 'true test' as the test of mitigation of punishment include Maugham, supra n. 24, at 45; W. Harris, *Tyranny on Trial, The Evidence at Nuremberg* (Dallas: Southern Methodist University Press, 1954), 557–8; Woetzel, supra n. 35, at 118–9; V. Morris & M. Scharf, *An Insider's Guide to the International Criminal Tribunal for the Former Yugoslavia, A Documentary History and Analysis*, vol. 1 (New York: Trasnational Publishers, Inc., 1995), 102; K. Ambos, 'Zur Strafbefreienden Wirkung des "Handelns auf Befehl" aus Deutscher und Völkerstrafrechlicher Sicht', *Juristische Rundschau* 6 (1998): 223. Graven also suggested the same kind of view. See J. Graven, 'Principes fondamentaux d'un code repressif des crimes contre la paix et la securite de l'humanite', *Revue de droit international de sciences diplomatiques et politiques* 28 (1950): 374–5. However, neither of them indicate the grounds for their arguments.

[73]Korte understands the ambiguity of the judgment as indicating the willingness of the Allied Powers to punish a wide range of war criminals (M. Korte, *Das Handeln auf Befehl als Strafausschließungsgrund: Die Wirkung des Befehls im Deutschen Recht und im Römischen Statut für den Internationalen Strafgerichtshof* (Baden-Baden: Nomos Verlagsgesellschaft, 2004), 54–6).

At the stage of delivering its judgment on each defendant, the Tribunal mentioned the issue of the superior orders defense in convicting Wilhelm Keitel and Jodl.

Keitel who had been Chief of Staff to the Minister of War was held accountable for being involved in the planning of the illegal wars, the direction of the so-called Commando Order, and having signed the so-called Nacht und Nebel Decree.[74] The Tribunal convicted Keitel on all four counts of crimes against peace, war crimes, crimes against humanity, and conspiracy on these crimes.[75] Jodl who had been Chief of the National Defense Section in the High Command was held responsible for being involved in the planning of the illegal wars, having signed the Commando Order, and planning to eliminate Soviet commissars. He was also convicted on all four of the abovementioned counts.[76]

Both Keitel and Jodl resorted to the superior orders defense. Jodl emphasized that he had been 'a soldier sworn to obedience'.[77] Further, they contended that they had resisted Hitler's orders and had tried to avoid or mitigate the harshness of the criminal conduct but in vain.[78]

The judgment for these two defendants was restricted to stating that mitigation of punishment could not be recognized under Article 8 of the Charter:

> his [Keitel's] defense relies on the fact that he is a soldier, and on the doctrine of 'superior orders', prohibited by Article 8 of the Charter as a defense.
>
> There is nothing in mitigation. Superior orders, even to a soldier, cannot be considered in mitigation where crimes as shocking and extensive have been committed consciously, ruthlessly, and without military excuse or justification.[79]
>
> His [Jodl's] defense, in brief, is the doctrine of 'superior orders', prohibited by Article 8 of the Charter as a defense. There is nothing in mitigation. Participation in such crimes as these has never been required of any soldier and he cannot now shield himself behind a mythical requirement of soldierly obedience at all costs as his excuse for commission of these crimes.[80]

The former quote of the judgment for Keitel expressed that even mitigation of punishment should not be allowed under Article 8 of the Charter if the accused had consciously conducted a criminal act. In this case, the knowledge of illegality was deemed to be a test on deciding on the mitigation of punishment. However, there was no detailed discussion on 'moral choice'.

No further argument was made with respect to the statement on the issue of superior orders in the section of the 'Law of the Charter'.

---

[74] Judgment, IMT, vol. 1, 171, 288–91.

[75] Ibid., 291.

[76] Ibid., 322–5.

[77] Ibid., 322.

[78] Ibid., 289–90, 322–4.

[79] Ibid., 290–1.

[80] Ibid., 325.

3.2.4 Conclusion

Some specific issues had been consistently examined on the superior orders defense during the drafting of the Nuremberg Charter and in the debates between the prosecutors and defense counsels at the Nuremberg Trial. They were problems of coercion, the knowledge of illegality and/or manifest illegality. As seen in Chapter 2, these issues had conventionally been deemed relevant to the problem of the superior orders defense in the United Kingdom, the United States, France, and the Soviet Union. It was only natural that the similar issues were discussed during the judicial proceeding at Nuremberg.

The judgment of the Nuremberg Trial understood that the issue dealt with by Article 8 of the Nuremberg Charter was restricted to the very existence of superior orders, and it confirmed that such a fact should not exempt the accused. It then presented the test of 'moral choice' in dealing with factors incidental to superior orders. However, the notion of 'moral choice' was not clarified. The trial was concluded without resolving the important issue of the superior orders defense.

As seen in this section, various interpretations of the 'moral choice' test were possible. Did the test relate to the issue of coercion, the knowledge of illegality and/ or manifest illegality? Should the accused be exempted if it was judged that 'moral choice' had not been possible, or should only mitigation of punishment be allowed? A combination of these elements would lead to various conclusions on the meaning of the judgment on 'moral choice'. In particular, if one construes that the Tribunal allowed immunity on the ground of coercion, the judgment would consequently contradict the intention of the drafters of the Charter.

Thus, the 'Nuremberg Principle' on the superior orders defense introduced ambiguous factors. The ambiguity of the 'Principle' became even more conspicuous at the Subsequent Proceedings, which were held by the United States and France in their respective occupying zones in Germany.

3.3 The Subsequent Proceedings

The IMT finished the prosecution of major German war criminals. Then, the so-called Subsequent Proceedings were held by the United States and France in their occupying zones in Germany to try other German war criminals.[81]

[81]The studies which examined the Subsequent Proceedings in relation to the superior orders defense include Jescheck, supra n. 35, at 385–99; Dinstein, supra n. 1, at 162–89. With regard to the Subsequent Proceedings in general, see T. Taylor, 'Nuremberg Trials, War Crimes and International Law', *International Conciliation* 450 (1949): 254–6, 272–335. See also O. Kranzbühler, 'Nuremberg as a Legal Problem', in *Nuremberg, German Views of the War Trials*, eds W. Benton & G. Grimm (Dallas: Southern Methodist University Press, 1955), 122–3; Greenspan, supra n. 69, at 496–502; A. Dinstag, '*Fedorenko v. United States*: War Crimes, the Defense of Duress, and American Nationality Law', *Columbia Law Review* 82 (1982): 146–7.

The four Allied Powers divided Germany into four occupying zones and controlled them accordingly. They provided for the Control Council Law No.10 (CCL10) '[i]n order to give effect to the terms of ... the Charter' in those areas.[82] The CCL10 vested each occupying country with the right to prosecute German war criminals in their occupying zones. However, the United Kingdom and the Soviet Union did not directly apply the CCL10 and separately conducted trials of their own.[83] War crimes trials that specifically applied the CCL10 were conducted by the US Military Tribunals and the French Military Government Tribunals set up in the respective occupying zones of Germany.[84] The trials at these tribunals officially applied the Nuremberg Charter through the CCL10. The examination of the proceedings can be deemed to be important in considering the development of the 'Nuremberg Principle', which the Nuremberg Trial indicated.

The consultation of the records of the Military Government Tribunals in the French-occupied zone have been prohibited.[85] This section will mainly deal with the twelve cases which were examined by the US Military Tribunals in its occupying zone. The law reports of the US Military Tribunals recorded one case of the French Military Government Tribunal, which will also be observed.[86]

Article 2(4)b of the CCL10 stipulated on the superior orders defense as follows:

> The fact that any person acted pursuant to the order of his Government or of a superior does not free him from responsibility for a crime, but may be considered in mitigation.[87]

---

[82]Control Council Law No.10, Punishment of Persons Guilty of War Crimes, Crimes against Peace and against Humanity, 1 Trials of War Criminals before the Nuernberg Military Tribunals under Control Council Law No.10 (1949) [hereinafter, NMT], vol. 1, XVI–XIX.

[83]The United Kingdom did not directly execute the CCL No. 10 but conducted war crimes trials under the Royal Warrant. Regarding the said Royal Warrant, see The United Nations War Crimes Commission, *Law Reports of Trials of War Criminals*, vol. 2 (London: HMSO, 1947), 126–9. Regarding the trials conducted by the United Kingdom and the Soviet Union, see Taylor, supra n. 81, at 254–5; Maugham, supra n. 24, at 20–22.

[84]The legal basis of the establishment of these tribunals is explained in The United Nations War Crimes Commission, *Law Reports of Trials of War Criminals*, vol. 3 (London: HMSO, 1948), 113–6, 100–102.

[85]See C. Moisel, 'Résistance und Repressalien, Die Kriegsverbrecherprozesse in der Französischen Zone und in Frankreich', in N. Frei, *Transnationale Vergangenheitspolitik, Der Umgang mit Deutschen Kriegsverbrechern in Europa nach dem Zweiten Weltkrieg* (Göttingen: Wallstein Verlag, 2006), 247–8.

[86]Some cases of the French Permanent Military Tribunals were recorded in the Reports of the United Nations War Crimes Commission. However, these Tribunals were established by the *Ordonnance* of 28 August 1944 and had jurisdiction over war crimes trials in France and its colonies (The United Nations War Crimes Commission, supra n. 84, at, 93). The Permanent Military Tribunals were different from the Military Government Tribunals in the French Zone of Germany, which was established by the *Ordonnance* of 25 November 1945 and the *Ordonnance* of 25 February 1946, of the French Commander -in-Chief (ibid., 93, 100).

[87]Control Council Law No.10, Punishment of Persons Guilty of War Crimes, Crimes against Peace and against Humanity, NMT, vol. 1, XVII.

As already mentioned, the CCL10 was provided in order to put into effect the London Agreement of 1945, which included the Nuremberg Charter.[88] The words of Article 2(4)b of the CCL10 thus resembled those of Article 8 of the Nuremberg Charter. The only difference between them was that the CCL10 did not use the restrictive phrase of the Charter, 'if the Tribunal determines that justice so requires'. However, as seen in the previous section, the IMT, in applying the Nuremberg Charter, did not specify the notion of the 'requirement of justice'. This notion has a general character and does not fully clarify the content of the norm in itself. Further, in any event, the CCL10 recognized the mitigation of punishment. The fact that the CCL10 deleted the phrase in question does not seem to be critical.[89]

The Subsequent Proceedings mainly dealt with lower ranking state organs in contrast to the Trial of the Major War Criminals at Nuremberg. Naturally, in the Subsequent Proceedings, the problem of coercion under superior orders was discussed more actively. However, most of the prosecutors, defense counsels, and judges in discussing the problem did not refer to national laws or international agreements for the prosecution of inferior state organs. The Subsequent Proceedings relied on the CCL10, which was based on the Nuremberg Charter and had been stipulated for its realization.

As will be seen below, a view that, in principle, recognized immunity on the ground of coercion incidental to superior orders came to the fore in the Subsequent Proceedings. It should be noted that a foothold for such a view was Article 8 of the Nuremberg Charter. Such an argument made by the prosecutors, defense counsels, and judges indicated that the understanding that the Nuremberg Charter provided for the principle of absolute responsibility had not been indisputable from the outset.

This section mainly deals with war crimes trials at the Military Tribunals in the US-occupied zone and examines the arguments of the prosecutors and defense counsels, as well as the judgments. Just as in the previous section, debates between the prosecutors and defense counsels will not be directly consulted for the purpose of interpreting the judgments. We will survey them in order to grasp the overall picture of discussions at the Subsequent Proceedings.

3.3.1 The Argument of the Prosecution

Most part of the prosecutors' arguments at the Subsequent Proceedings was basically similar to the arguments presented at the Nuremberg Trial. In the latter, the chief prosecutors of the United Kingdom, France, and the Soviet Union strengthened the manifest illegality of the criminal conduct. Most prosecutors at the Subsequent Proceedings basically followed their view in pointing out that the

---

[88]Ibid., XVI.

[89]See Greenspan, supra n. 69, at 496; Dinstein, supra n. 1, at 163–5.

accused had been aware of the illegality of their conduct. These facts do not necessarily verify how the prosecutors understood the provisions of the Nuremberg Charter and the CCL10 with regard to the knowledge of illegality and/or manifest illegality. Did the prosecutors regard those provisions as denying the superior orders defense only for the cases where the accused was aware of the illegality of his/her conduct, or did they only underline the knowledge of illegality without considering such a classification? These points were ambiguous.

However, what should be noted with regard to the Subsequent Proceedings is that some prosecutors relied on the German national laws in denying the superior orders defense by the accused. They quoted Section 47 of the German *Military Criminal Code* and the judicial precedents of the German Supreme Court, which applied the provisions of the Code for reference.[90] The German *Military Criminal Code* recognized the possibility of immunity in the cases where the accused had not been aware of the illegality of his/her conduct. Thus, it would not be appropriate to deem that the prosecutors only emphasized the accused's knowledge of illegality. It would be more natural to understand that the prosecutors conditionally rejected the superior orders defense on the test of the knowledge of illegality.[91]

Meanwhile, it was a common position adopted by the prosecutors to not allow immunity on the ground of coercion under superior orders. This position was the same as that of the prosecutors at the Nuremberg Trial. Most of the prosecutors argued that only the mitigation of punishment could be allowed under the CCL10 even if it had not been possible for the accused to disobey the superior orders. They then rejected the mitigation of punishment, contending that the accused had voluntarily acted in most cases.[92]

However, there was an exception to such a general view on the issue of coercion, which made the prosecution's position at the Subsequent Proceedings instable. The prosecution's argument at the *Ministries* case is worth noting in this respect. In this case, the prosecution recognized the coercion defense in principle. It then contended the conviction of the accused, arguing that the accused could not effectively appeal to the defense relevant to coercion. The prosecutor, in the section titled 'Superior Orders, the Defense of Alleged Duress, and the Mitigation of Punishment for Crime', explained the conditions for the approval of 'necessity as a defense' as follows:

> we think it important to underline certain fundamental concepts and to note certain elements which must be established by a defendant undertaking the burden of establishing a defense of necessity. Some of these concepts, which are emphasized again and again by

[90] Opening Statement of the Prosecution, The *Einsatzgruppen* case, NMT, vol. 4, 53; Closing Statement of the Prosecution, 13 February 1948, by Brigadier General Telford Taylor, ibid., 376; Extracts from Opening Statement of the Prosecution, The *Hostage* case, NMT, vol. 11, 839–40.

[91] See Dinstein, supra n. 1, at 174–6.

[92] Extracts from the Closing Statement of the Prosecution, The *Medical* case, NMT, vol. 1, 958; Closing Statement of the Prosecution, 13 February 1948, by Brigadier General Telford Taylor, The *Einsatzgruppen* case, NMT, vol. 4, 377; Extracts from the Closing Statement of the Prosecution, The *High Command* case, NMT, vol. 11, 372. See also Extracts from Opening Statement of the Prosecution, The *Hostage* case, ibid., 840.

> the authorities, are the following: the presence of 'irresistible force'; a 'present danger for life and limb'; a 'fear of instant death'; the absence of any opportunity for escape; the imminent injury to the accused must be shown not to be disproportionate to the evil which he furthers under duress. . . . It is not enough that the injury to the accused or the possible methods of escape from coercion involved his loss of professional standing, his loss of property, a substantial reordering of his life and habits, or even his confinement and the loss of substantial personal liberty. The historic law has recognized no such personal injuries as a justification for committing evil or invading the rights of others.[93]

The notions of 'necessity' and defense of 'duress' or 'coercion' do not seem to have been differentiated. This was the case with regard to the entire proceeding of the Nuremberg Trial and the Subsequent Proceedings.[94] The prosecutors pointed out that rules on superior orders could not be distinguished from the defenses of duress and coercion, and that the judgment of the Subsequent Proceedings, which had actually recognized the latter defenses, had connected them with the issue of superior orders.[95] Here, the notion of necessity was examined in connection with superior orders.[96] Such recognition of immunity[97] as a general rule meant that the prosecution denied the principle of absolute responsibility.

The prosecution showed this kind of disorder in the *Ministries* case, the last of the twelve cases that were dealt with by the Military Tribunals in the US-occupied zone. As will be seen later, some tribunals had already delivered judgments that recognized the superior orders defense on the ground of coercion by the time the prosecutor made the closing statement on the *Ministries* case. The instability of the prosecution's argument might have been influenced by such a general trend of the Subsequent Proceedings.

3.3.2 The Argument of the Defense Counsels

3.3.2.1 Applicable Law

With regard to the superior orders defense, some defense counsels first questioned whether or not the application of the Nuremberg Charter and the CCL10 in the Subsequent Proceedings had been appropriate. They contended that it was Section

---

93 Closing Statements for the Prosecution, The *Ministries* case, NMT, vol. 14, 88.

94 See O. Liwerant, 'Les exécutants', in *Droit international penal*, eds H. Ascensio, E. Decaux et A. Pellet (Paris: Éditions a. pedone, 2000), 222.

95 Closing Statements for the Prosecution, The *Ministries* case, NMT, vol. 14, 85–7.

96 The relationship among the defense of necessity, the coercion defense, and the superior orders defense has variously been understood by commentators. In international law, the defenses of necessity and coercion have often been regarded the same (Liwerant, supra n. 94). At the Subsequent Proceedings, the prosecution deemed them to be the same and emphasized that they were closely related to the superior orders defense (Closing Statements for the Prosecution, The *Ministries* case, NMT, vol. 14, 84–8).

97 Regarding the terminology of 'justification', see note 9 of Chapter 2.

47 of the German *Military Criminal Code*, and not Article 8 of the Nuremberg Charter nor Article 2(4)b of the CCL10, that had been effective at the time the accused had conducted criminal acts.[98]

Section 47 of the German *Military Criminal Code* recognized the conditional immunity under the superior orders defense. The section allowed immunity if the accused had not been aware of the illegality of his/her conduct. As was seen in the preparatory work of the Nuremberg Charter, there remained the possibility that the Charter and the CCL10 had adopted the principle of absolute responsibility with regard to the knowledge of illegality. Therefore, it could be expected that the consequence would become considerably different if the tribunals applied the German *Military Criminal Code* in the Subsequent Proceedings.

The defense counsels did not confine themselves to criticizing the retroactive application of the Charter and the CCL10. Some defense counsels contended that the rule that the four Allied Powers provided on the superior orders defense had not been established as an international norm even at the time of the trials. The grounds for such contention were the facts that the Washington Convention of 1922, which denied the superior orders defense, had not been put into effect and that the Versailles Peace Conference of 1919 had not categorically rejected the said defense.[99]

They further emphasized that the national laws of the drafting countries of the Nuremberg Charter were drastically changed just before the end of World War II. The British Manual of Military Law and the US Rules of Land Warfare were revised in 1944. It was seen in the previous chapter that an immunizing function of the superior orders defense was much restricted by the revision. The defense counsels concluded that such revision had been the consequence of political opportunism foreseeing the end of the war.[100]

The defense counsels that asserted the application of the German *Military Criminal Code* emphasized that Section 47 of the Code allowed the superior orders defense on the test of the knowledge of illegality.[101] Otherwise, they supported the said defense by referring to the peculiar mental situation of soldiers in the field and arguing that it was difficult for those soldiers to decide on the illegality of their conduct.[102]

[98]Extracts from the Final Plea for Defendant Fischer, The *Medical* case, NMT, vol. 1, 961–8; Extract from the Closing Statement for Defendant Naumann, The *Einsatzgruppen* case, NMT, vol. 4, 329–34; Closing Statement for the Defendant Pohl, The *Pohl* case, NMT, vol. 5, 914–7; Closing Statements for all Defendants on Fundamental Issues of Law, The *Farben* case, NMT, vol. 8, 902–3; Extract from the Closing Brief for Defendant Hoth, The *High Command* case, NMT, vol. 11, 407; Extracts from Closing Statement for Defendant List, The *Hostage* case, ibid., 1224–5.

[99]Extract from the Closing Statement for Defendant Naumann, The *Einsatzgruppen* case, NMT, vol. 4, 329–31.

[100]Ibid., 332–3; Opening Statement for Defendant List, The *Hostage* case, NMT, vol. 11, 858–62; Extracts from Closing Statement for Defendant List, The *Hostage* case, *ibid.*, 1224–5.

[101]Extracts from the Final Plea for Defendant Fischer, The *Medical* case, NMT, vol. 1, 961–3; Closing Statement for Defendant Pohl, The *Pohl* case, NMT, vol. 5, 914–7.

[102]Opening Statement for Defendant Pook, ibid., 289.

However, unlike at the Nuremberg Trial, the defense counsels did not concentrate on the issue of the knowledge of illegality in supporting the superior orders defense. Further, as seen above, the prosecution's position was not clarified on this issue through the Nuremberg Trial and the Subsequent Proceedings. The prosecutors even implied that they denied the superior orders defense only for the cases of manifest illegality. This approach of the prosecution would have had some influence on the fact that the issue of the knowledge of illegality did not draw much attention of the defense counsels.

3.3.2.2 Coercion

With regard to the superior orders defense, most defense counsels emphasized that the accused had been under some coercion because of superior orders.

The factor of coercion was one of the major issues with regard to the superior orders defense at the Nuremberg Trial. However, the judgment of the trial did not fully respond to the arguments of the prosecutors and defense counsels. The IMT judgment restricted itself to deliver that '[t]he true test, which is found in varying degrees in the criminal law of most nations, is not the existence of the order, but whether moral choice was in fact possible'. The meaning of 'moral choice' was ambiguous.

The positions of the defense counsels at the Subsequent Proceedings varied depending on the interpretation of Article 2(4)b of the CCL10, which was closely related to the Nuremberg Charter. Some defense counsels understood that the CCL10 did not go so far as denying immunity on the ground of coercion and asserted immunity of the accused under the CCL10.[103] For instance, Willi Heim, who defended Paul Blobel in the *Einsatzgruppen* case, seemed to connect the fact of coercion with the possibility of moral choice when he stated:

> In Adolf Hitler's Germany, men who refused obedience were either put in a concentration camp or shot dead, regardless of person and rank, . . . In reality there was no chance to make a choice in accordance with the moral law; this applies also to the defendant Blobel. For either he had to carry out the order or if he refused to do so, he would lose his liberty, or he would even have been shot dead by a summary court martial.[104]

Meanwhile, other defense counsels argued that Article 2(4)b should not be applied to the cases where the defense of necessity mattered.[105] It was explained that the defense of necessity was 'a fundamental principle of the criminal law of all

---

[103] Opening Statement for Defendant Greifelt, The *Einsatzgruppen* case, NMT, vol. 4, 699–700; Closing Statement for Defendant Flick, The *Flick* case, NMT, vol. 6, 1153; Extracts from the Closing Brief for Defendant Lehmann, NMT, vol. 11, 434.

[104] Opening Statement for Defendant Blobel, The *Einsatzgruppen* case, NMT, vol. 4, 87.

[105] Closing Statement for All Defendants on the Evidence on the Charges of Crimes against Peace, The *Farben* case, NMT, vol. 8, 985–6.

civilized nations', the effect of which transcended that of any rules in general. However, as noted before, the preparatory work of the Nuremberg Charter showed that Article 8 of the Charter originally embodied the principle of absolute responsibility. The Charter thus widely denied the superior orders defense by taking into account incidental factors such as coercion. The position of the defense counsels to assert immunity on the ground of coercion thus contradicted the substance of the Nuremberg Charter. This consequence would not have changed whether they contended the application of the CCL10, which reflected the Charter provisions, or denied its application.

Some defense counsels, while supporting immunity on the ground of coercion under superior orders, underlined that the coercion in question had been backed by state power.[106] This argument was the same as that of the defense counsels at the Nuremberg Trial. For instance, Rudolf Dix, who defended Friedrich Flick, pointed out that in the Middle Ages, the scholastics' theory, which was based on the mental order of the Catholic church, legally backed disobedience to the state, whereas there was no supra-national authority that supported the international obligation of disobedience in the modern world:

> These teachings fall upon arid soil as long as firm international institutions have not been created again which give authoritative advice to the individual citizen, conscience stricken in a conflict between international and national duty of obedience and can protect him in his battle against his state. So far there are no such international and supra-national institutions. ... Whoever established legal obligations must protect compliance with them.[107]

In other words, the accused had been put under coercion which had been legal as well as 'physical'.[108]

However, most of the defense counsels did not contend that superior orders should always lead to immunity on the ground of coercion. For instance, the defense counsel in the *Farben* case argued that Article 2(4)b of the CCL10 did not reject the defense of necessity but it was required for the said defense to establish that the accused had acted under 'clear and present danger'.[109] At this point, the position of the defense counsels was different from the principle of automatic immunity that was grounded on the notion of 'legal coercion', although their decision on the existence of 'clear and present danger' was different from that of the judgment in most cases.

---

[106]Final Plea for Defendant Karl Brandt by Dr. Servatius, The *Medical* case, NMT, vol. 2, 128; Closing Statement for Defendant Flick, The *Flick* case, NMT, vol. 6, 1156; Extract from the Closing Brief for Defendant von Kuechler, The *High Command* case, NMT, vol. 11, 399, 427.

[107]Closing Statement for Defendant Flick, The *Flick* case, NMT, vol. 6, 1156.

[108]Ibid., 1153.

[109]Closing Statement for All Defendants on the Evidence on the Charges of Crimes against Peace, The *Farben* case, NMT, vol. 8, 985–6. See also Extracts from the Closing Brief for Defendant Lehmann, The *High Command* case, NMT, vol. 11, 434.

3.3.3 *The Judgment*

3.3.3.1 Immunity on the Ground of Coercion

At the last stage of the Subsequent Proceedings, the prosecutors came to approve the possibility of recognizing the coercion defense in relation to superior orders. The position of the prosecutors appeared to have been influenced by the judgment delivered by the US Military Tribunals by that time. The judgment of the Subsequent Proceedings, notwithstanding the provision of Article 2(4)b of the CCL10, strongly suggested supporting conditional immunity under the superior orders defense on the whole.

The *Medical* case, which was identified at the first stage of the Subsequent Proceedings, mainly dealt with the cruel medical experiments conducted by the medical staff of the Nazi regime and the leaders of the SS (*Schutzstaffel*: Protective Squadron).[110] The judgment delivered that the superior orders defense should not be recognized even if the accused had not had a wide range of discretion regarding their conduct.[111] Even if the accused had not been free to decide on their conduct, 'the fact of such orders could merely be considered, under Control Council Law No.10, as palliating punishment'.[112] However, the judgments following the *Medical* case substantially deviated from the position of this case on the problem of superior orders.

A crucial point was that most of the subsequent judgments suggested the approval of the possibility of immunity on the ground of coercion incidental to superior orders. The judgment of the *Flick* case was one of the examples. In this case, Flick and others, who had been responsible for regulating the entire German industry of iron and steel as well as coal, were indicted on the counts of participating in the slave-labor program of the Nazi regime, plundering public and private property, and persecuting Jews.[113] The judgment emphasized that the accused would have been exposed to serious dangers, including execution, if they disobeyed the plan of the Nazi regime on slave labor.[114] The tribunal then decided that four of the six accused were not guilty on this count, stating that Article 2(4)b of the CCL10 did not reject the defense of necessity.[115]

The judgment of the *Einsatzgruppen* case considered the problem of coercion within the notion of the superior orders defense. The Einsatzgruppen were special task forces, which were organized to exterminate the Jews and gypsies in Eastern Europe as well as Soviet officials. The leaders of the Einsatzgruppen were indicted

---

[110] Indictment, The *Medical* case, NMT, vol. 1, 8–17.

[111] Judgment, The *Medical* case, NMT, vol. 2, 227.

[112] Ibid.

[113] Indictment, The *Flick* case, NMT, vol. 6, 11–25.

[114] Opinion and Judgment, ibid., 1197.

[115] Ibid., 1200–1202. The judgment deemed the defense of necessity to be the same with the defense of coercion.

on three counts of crimes against humanity, war crimes, and membership in criminal organizations.[116] The accused contended that they could not have but obeyed the orders. However, the tribunal rejected this contention, deciding that the accused had not even intended to reduce the effect of the orders.[117]

The judgment of the *Einsatzgruppen* case denied the superior orders defense by the accused in the section titled 'Duress Needed for Plea of Superior Orders'. The tribunal stated that the superior orders defense could not be allowed in cases where the accused had positively obeyed orders and had not carried out their actions under coercion[118]:

> there is no law which requires that an innocent man must forfeit his life or suffer serious harm in order to avoid committing a crime which he condemns. The threat, however, must be imminent, real, and inevitable. No court will punish a man who, with a loaded pistol at his head, is compelled to pull a lethal lever. . . . But . . . When the will of the doer merges with the will of the superior in the execution of the illegal act, the doer may not plead duress under superior orders. . . . In order successfully to plead the defense of superior orders the opposition of the doer must be constant.[119]

The judgment specifically treated the question of immunity on the ground of coercion as that of the superior orders defense. At this point, the *Einsatzgruppen* judgment was different from the *Flick* judgment, which differentiated the superior orders defense from the defense of necessity and treated the problem of coercion in relation to the latter. However, the question of whether to differentiate the superior orders defense from the defense of coercion or necessity or to examine the latter under a unified notion of the superior orders defense would not be essential. In any case, the judgment that suggested the general recognition of the coercion defense in terms of superior orders contradicted the CCL10.

The *Einsatzgruppen* judgment did not allow the superior orders defense of the accused eventually. The tribunal decided that the accused had positively obeyed the orders. Thus, the delivering of the judgment as to the conditions under which the superior orders defense could be allowed would be characterized as *obiter dictum.*[120] In common law, *obiter dictum* is not directly necessary for the judgment to reach its conclusion and does not have a binding effect. Nonetheless, it may influence the following judicial precedents as a 'persuasive' argument.[121] It would not be appropriate to completely deny the significance of the line of the *Einsatzgruppen* judgment on the conditions for the approval of the superior orders defense.

It is also necessary to pay attention to the particular character of the formation of the trials of the Subsequent Proceedings. It was the US Military Tribunals that

---

[116]Amended Indictment, The *Einsatzgruppen* case, NMT, vol. 4, 13–22.

[117]Opinoin and Judgment, The *Einsatzgruppen* case, ibid., 481.

[118]Ibid., 480–83.

[119]Ibid., 480–81.

[120]A. Goodhart, 'Determining the ratio decidendi of a Case', *Yale Law Journal* 60 (1930): 178–80.

[121]B. Garner (ed.), *Black's Law Dictionary*, 8th ed. (St. Paul: West Publishing co., 2004).

treated the *Einsatzgruppen* case as well as the other cases. However, as already noted, these trials were held under the CCL10. This international instrument authorized the relevant countries to conduct war crimes trials in their respective occupying zones and provided for the definition of crimes to be prosecuted, general principles of criminal law, guiding rules on punishment, and other procedural rules. The trial proceedings were held by the national military tribunals of the relevant countries. Although, it may be said that they partially bore an international character in executing the provisions of the CCL10.

It is often pointed out that, also with regard to the judgments of international trials, the legal effect of *obiter dictum* is different from that of *ratio decidendi*.[122] This is an argument that only *ratio decidendi* has a binding effect on the parties of the trials. However, international trials have been expected to bear quasi-legislative functions to some extent, reflecting the facts that the legislative body lacks at the international level. Influential arguments have shown that the difference between *ratio decidendi* and *obiter dictum* remains to be something relative with regard to international trials.[123] The legal effect of *ratio decidendi* and *obiter dictum* would not completely be the same even in international trials. However, it would not be appropriate to *a priori* deny any legal effect of the latter. The same could be said with the Subsequent Proceedings.

Thus, the *obiter dictum* of judgment would not be deemed thoroughly meaningless even in common law. In addition, the Subsequent Proceedings bore some international character, although they were conducted by the military tribunals of the relevant countries. Taking these points into consideration, the *obiter dictum* of the *Einsatzgruppen* judgment would be worth evaluating at least as what 'suggested' that the tribunal approved the coercion defense.

As was shown in the *Flick* and *Einsatzgruppen* cases, the judgments of the Subsequent Proceedings substantially deviated from the provision of their applicable law as the trials proceeded. The judgment of the *Farben* case is particularly noteworthy in this respect. In this case, leaders of the I.G. Farben Industrial Corporation, which had much influence on the German economy, were indicted on the counts of collaborating with the Nazi regime in planning aggressive wars, plundering the occupying area of Germany, exploiting slave labor, and committing mass murder.[124]

The *Farben* judgment connected the issue of coercion incidental to orders with the possibility of moral choice, which the judgment of the Nuremberg Trial mentioned with respect to the superior orders defense. The accused contended

---

[122]For instance, Dissenting Opinion of Judge Read, *Anglo-Iranian Oil Co.Case*, ICJ Rep 1952, 143; Separate Opinion of Judge Gros, *Case Concerning the Barcelona Traction, Light and Power Company, Limited*, ICJ Rep 1970, 280, para. 21.

[123]H. Lauterpacht, *The Development of International Law by the International Court* (London: Stevens & Sons Limited, 1958), 61–2; S. Rosenne, *The Law and Practice of the International Court* (Dordrecht: Martinus Nijhoff Publishers, 1985), 614; M. Shahabuddeen, *Precedent in the World Court* (Cambridge: Cambridge University Press, 1996), 152–60.

[124]Indictment, The *Farben* case, NMT, vol. 7, 10–80.

that he made use of slave labor under coercion and without any intention of criminal conduct.[125] The judgment in the section titled 'The Defense of Necessity' quoted Article 8 of the Nuremberg Charter together with the notion of moral choice in the judgment of the Nuremberg Trial and dismissed the argument of the accused:

> Thus the IMT recognized that while an order emanating from a superior officer or from the government is not, of itself, a justification for the violation of an international law (though it may be considered in mitigation), nevertheless, such an order is a complete defense where it is given under such circumstances as to afford the one receiving it of no other moral choice than to comply therewith. As applied to the facts here, we do not think there can be much uncertainty as to what the words 'moral choice' mean. . . . Nor are we without persuasive precedents as to the proper application of the rule of necessity in the field of the law with which we are here concerned.[126]

The *Farben* judgment construed that the judgment of the Nuremberg Trial had approved immunity on the ground of coercion. As already discussed, it would be appropriate to understand that Article 8 of the Nuremberg Charter adopted the principle of absolute responsibility in terms of coercion. Thus, the *Farben* judgment seemed to denote an inappropriate interpretation of the Charter.

The dissenting opinion of the *Farben* judgment sounded more persuasive in light of the original meaning of the Nuremberg Charter. Judge Paul Hebert, in his dissenting opinion, pointed out that the accused had voluntarily made use of slave labor and that moral choice had been possible for him. He decided that the defense of necessity, which the majority had mentioned, could not be established. As far as this decision is concerned, his opinion was the same with that of the majority that denied the defense of necessity as to the case in question. The point was that judge Hebert eventually denied the defense of necessity in a general way in regarding the said defense as contradicting the Nuremberg Charter:

> The defense of necessity as accepted by the majority would, in my opinion, lead logically to the conclusion that Hitler alone was responsible for the major war crimes and crimes against humanity committed during the Nazi regime. If the defense of superior orders or coercion, as directed in the Charter of the IMT, was not recognized in the case of the principal defendants tried by that Tribunal as applied to defendants who were subject to strict military discipline and subject to the most severe penalties for failure to carry out the criminal plans decreed and evolved by Hitler, it becomes difficult to ascertain how any such defense can be admitted in the case of the present defendants. The IMT judgment embraces no doctrinal defense of necessity by governmental coercion. That decision, it seems to me, constitutes complete negation of any such theory.[127]

Judge Herbert's view appeared appropriate in understanding the Nuremberg Charter as having denied the coercion defense in terms of superior orders. However, as already seen, some important issues remained open with the IMT judgment. It is

---

[125]Opinion and Judgment, The *Farben* case, NMT, vol. 8, 1174.

[126]Ibid., 1176. The judgment regarded the defense of necessity as the same with the defense of coercion, which comprised superior orders defense.

[127]Dissenting Opinion of Judge Hebert on the Charges of Slave Labor, The *Farben* case, ibid., 1310.

difficult to decide whether or not the IMT judgment strictly followed Article 8 of the Nuremberg Charter. With regard to the judgment of the Subsequent Proceedings, we should focus on the very fact that Judge Hebert's view turned out to be in the minority. The majority of the judgments suggested the possibility of immunity on the ground of coercion incidental to superior orders.

Only the judgments of the *Medical* and *Hostage* cases appeared to sustain the original idea of the Nuremberg Charter. In the *Hostage* case, the tribunal judged on the persecution and the murder of civilians in occupied areas by troops of the German armed forces, the plundering in those areas, the persecution of prisoners of war, and so forth.[128] The persecution of civilians included orders to execute a hundred hostages as retaliation for each German soldier killed.[129] The judgment rejected the superior orders defense by the accused even while considering a possible consequence of disobedience:

> We concede the serious consequences of the choice [between lawless punishment by government and lawful punishment under the law of nations] especially by an officer in the army of a dictator. But the rule [to approve immunity solely on the test of the knowledge of illegality] becomes one of necessity, for otherwise the opposing army would in many cases have no protection at all against criminal excesses ordered by superiors.[130]

This judgment resembled, in approving the knowledge of illegality as an immunizing factor, that of the *Einsatzgruppen* case, which considered such knowledge with relation to moral choice. On the other hand, they differed on whether or not the superior orders defense should be admitted in considering the possibility that the accused would have been executed as a consequence of disobedience. The *Hostage* judgment followed the principle of absolute responsibility in this context as had been indicated by the Nuremberg Charter.

Such a position appeared to be in minority in the Subsequent Proceedings. The judgments of five of the twelve cases that the US Military Tribunals treated[131] and one of the judgments delivered by the French Military Government Tribunal[132] did approve – although in their *obiter dictum* – the coercion defense in terms of superior orders. Furthermore, the *Flick* judgment of the US Military Tribunal specifically allowed immunity of the accused on the ground of coercion. Academic arguments that deem that the judgments of the Subsequent Proceedings recognized the

---

[128]Indictment, Including Appendix Listing Positions of the Defendants, The *Hostage* case, NMT, vol. 11, 764–81.

[129]Ibid., 766.

[130]Judgment, The *Hostage* case, NMT, vol. 11, 1237.

[131]The judgments of *Einsatzgruppen* and *Farben* that were examined in this section, the judgments of *Krupp* and *High Command* that will be introduced below, and the *Ministries* judgment. In the trial of the *Ministries* case, state secretaries and other high-ranking officials of Nazi Germany were tried for the counts of the planning and waging of aggressive wars, persecution of civilian populations, plunder and spoliation, and so on (Indictment, The *Ministries* case, NMT, vol. 12, 13–63).

[132]Judgment on Appeal, The *Roechling* case, NMT, vol. 14, 1104–5.

coercion defense[133] would be said to have reflected the general trend of the Subsequent Proceedings sketched above.

3.3.3.2 Variation of Detailed Rules and the Principle of Conditional Immunity

Meanwhile, the details of the majority view on superior orders in the Subsequent Proceedings were not necessarily unified. For instance, the *Farben* judgment related the possibility of moral choice mainly with the factor of coercion. In contrast, the *Einsatzgruppen* judgment connected moral choice with the two problems of coercion and the knowledge of illegality.[134]

Some of the judgments that recognized or suggested to recognize immunity on the ground of coercion treated this issue independent from the superior orders defense. The judgment of *Krupp* set a section titled 'Necessity as a Defense' and clearly explained some conditions for its establishment.[135] The *High Command* judgment denied the superior orders defense as 'absurdity' in light of the CCL10. The judgment then implied the possibility of additionally recognizing the defense of coercion or necessity for the same situations.[136] This approach is reminiscent of the academic arguments in France, which separated the issue of coercion from that of superior orders and treated the former as a general defense. Before the end of World War II, the issue of superior orders was mainly discussed in France as the question of whether or not Article 64 of the French *Penal Code* should be applied. This approach was also adopted in later international judicial precedents as well as the ICC Statute.

However, a significant fact was that the judgments of the Subsequent Proceedings deviated from the Nuremberg Charter, though most of the relevant lines of which were *obiter dictum*. The majority of the judgments of the Subsequent Proceedings substantially suggested immunization on the ground of coercion incidental to superior orders, irrespective of the construction of theory that each judgment presented. The *Krupp* and *High Command* judgments separated the defense of necessity from the superior orders defense. Nonetheless, the respective situations that were examined as necessity in these two cases were relevant to

---

133 Dinstag, supra n. 81, at 146, note 85; Dinstein, supra n. 1, at 180–81.

134 Opinion and Judgment, The *Einsatzgruppen* case, NMT, vol. 4, 470–83.

135 Judgment, The *Krupp* case, NMT, vol. 9, 1435–48. In the case of *Krupp*, officials of Fried Krupp, Essen, the principal German maker of armament and the producer of iron and coal, were tried for the counts of participating in aggressive wars, persecution of civilian population, plunder and spoliation in the invaded countries, and so on (Indictment, ibid., 7–51).

136 Judgment, The *High Command* case, NMT, vol. 11, 507–15. In the case of *High Command*, generals, lieutenant generals, and an admiral of Nazi Germany were tried on the counts of the participation in aggressive wars, summary execution of Soviet political commissars, murder of Allied troops on so-called commando missions, persecution of civilians, and so on (Indictment, The *High Command* case, NMT, vol. 10, 10–55).

superior orders.[137] Thus, the majority of the judgments of the Subsequent Proceedings showed such a tendency, even more conspicuously compared to the IMT judgment, as breaking away from the Nuremberg Charter and the CCL10 that had introduced the principle of absolute responsibility.

Such a development seems to have reflected a difference between the respective backgrounds of the Nuremberg Trial and the Subsequent Proceedings to some extent.

First, there was a difference on personal jurisdiction. The Subsequent Proceedings tried those who had not been prosecuted at the IMT. However, as was seen before, the CCL10 that was directly applied at the Subsequent Proceedings was provided in order to execute the provisions of the Nuremberg Charter. Therefore, the personal jurisdiction of the respective trials should not have been discriminated. Still, the Subsequent Proceedings actually tried a wide range of the accused including under secretaries, lay judges, and deputy members of a family enterprise, whereas the IMT restrictively dealt with cases involving high-ranking state officials such as ministers and commanders in chief. It would be natural that the issue of coercion incidental to superior orders was examined more intensively in the Subsequent Proceedings.

Further, a difference of the time in which those proceedings were completed might have influenced the positions of the respective tribunals. The Nuremberg Trial concluded in October 1946. The Subsequent Proceedings were completed in April 1949, that is, nearly 4 years after the surrender of Germany.

It should be noted here that the German Reipzig Trials ended up in a defective manner, reflecting a change in situations after World War I. The Allied Powers were discontent with the Reipzig Trials held by the German Supreme Court and expressed their intention to conduct other trials of German war criminals on their own. However, the Reipzig Trials themselves were fairly behind schedule. Positive arguments for war crimes trials had considerably been weakened by the time the Allied Powers consulted to bring about a change in their policy. Eventually, renewed trials were not realized.

The Allied Powers expressed a change in policy in January 1922 in disapproval of the consequence of the Reipzig Trials.[138] About two and a half years had passed since the conclusion of the Versailles Treaty in June 1919. By that time, the Allied Powers had already lost enthusiasm in conducting trials by themselves. The final judgment of the Subsequent Proceedings was delivered nearly 4 years after the conclusion of World War II.[139] In light of the precedents of the Reipzig Trials, it would be natural to understand that the judgments of the Subsequent Proceedings were delivered in a different atmosphere from that of the IMT judgment.

[137]Judgment, The *Krupp* case, NMT, vol. 9, 1435; Judgment, The *High Command* case, NMT, vol. 11, 507–9.

[138]*Journal du droit international* (1921): 1077–8; 'Vermischtes, Deutsche Juristen!', *Deutsche Juristen - Zeitung* (1922): 106–7.

[139]The judgments which recognized the defense of coercion were concentrated from late 1948 to the beginning of 1949.

In particular, with regard to the Subsequent Proceedings, the whole proceedings completed in 1949 when the German Federal Republic (West Germany) was established. The United States, the United Kingdom, and France, in a new international era of the radicalized Cold War, came to focus on the solidarity of Western countries.[140] The United States established the War Crimes Modification Board in 1949 and initiated a reexamination of the judgments of war crimes trials.[141] Those who had been convicted in the Subsequent Proceedings were also reexamined by the United States High Commissioner.[142] Out of about a hundred who had been convicted in the Subsequent Proceedings, nearly 80 were allowed for mitigation of punishment or parole by 1951 under the decision of the High Commissioner.[143] The West Allied countries decided to set up the Interim Mixed Parole and Clemency Board with the restoration of German sovereignty and the Mixed Parole and Clemency Board later in 1955. With the examination of the Board, those who had been serving their sentences under the jurisdiction of the United States, the United Kingdom, and France in German territory had all been released by 1958.[144]

Meanwhile, the judgments of the Subsequent Proceedings that suggested the approval of immunity on the ground of coercion under superior orders raised some conditions for immunity. For instance, the *Einsatzgruppen* judgment delivered that a threat incidental to orders must be 'imminent, real, and inevitable' in order to establish the superior orders defense.[145] The judgment also stated that a peril brought about by obedience should not be disproportionately larger than that caused by disobedience.[146] The *Krupp*[147] and *High Command*[148] judgments presented the same conditions. Further, these judgments required that the coercion be to such a degree that the accused be deprived of his/her free will[149] and that the repulsion of the accused against orders be consistent.[150]

The French Military Government Tribunal in the French-occupied zone in Germany supported these judgments of the US Military Tribunals. The *Roechling* judgment of the French Tribunal is an example. In the *Roechling* case, the directors of the Roechling firm, a large steal and coal enterprise, were indicted on the counts

---

[140]With regard to the arguments inside the US government on the problem of German war crimes, see T. Schwartz, *America's Germany, John J. McCloy and the Federal Republic of Germany* (Cambridge, Mass.: Harvard University Press, 1991), 156–75; P. Mauguire, *Law and War, An American Story* (New York: Columbia University Press, 2000), 235–82.

[141]Schwartz, supra n. 140, at 160–61.

[142]*Ibid.*

[143]*Ibid.*, 168.

[144]*Ibid.*, 173–4; Mauguire, supra n. 140, at 250–82.

[145]Opinion and Judgment, The *Einsatzgruppen* case, NMT, vol. 4, 480.

[146]Ibid., 471.

[147]Judgment, The *Krupp* case, NMT, vol. 9, 1443.

[148]Judgment, The *High Command* case, NMT, vol. 11, 509.

[149]Judgment, The *Krupp* case, NMT, vol. 9, 1439; Judgment, The *High Command* case, NMT, vol. 11, 509.

[150]Opinion and Judgment, The *Einsatzgruppen* case, NMT, vol. 4, 481.

of participating in the planning of aggressive wars, plundering German-occupied areas, exploiting slave labor in those areas, and so forth.[151] The judgment approved the defense of necessity in *obiter dictum*, quoting the *Krupp* judgment of the US Military Tribunal as well as the national judicial precedents in France:

> the existence of necessity is admitted, as a defense under all modern legislation only if the compulsion coincides with the punishable act and if its effects are such that the person claiming this defense is not able to resist in consideration of his (or her) age and sex.[152]

Although the judgments of the Subsequent Proceedings took the issue of coercion seriously, they did not support automatic immunity by the superior orders defense and denied the issue of coercion to be dealt with abstractedly. The judgments that recognized possible immunity on the ground of coercion as a basic rule eventually rejected immunity of the accused in many cases as a consequence of examining various conditions.[153] The only judgment that recognized immunity in conclusion was that in the *Flick* case.

3.3.4 Conclusion

The judicial proceedings under the Nuremberg Charter, which were composed of the Nuremberg Trial and the Subsequent Proceedings, did not work out a conclusive solution for the problem of the superior orders defense. The international rule-making was in a chaotic situation on this problem before World War II. Under such circumstances, the judicial proceedings under the Nuremberg Charter can be evaluated to have shown a certain direction. They consistently presented an idea that the fact of superior orders should not unconditionally immunize the accused. However, the things were different with the issues of the knowledge of illegality and/or manifest illegality, and coercion, which had conventionally been discussed with regard to the national laws of the drafting countries of the Nuremberg Charter and in the Reipzig Trials.

The drafters of the Nuremberg Charter understood Article 8 of this instrument as denying the possibility of immunity even if the fact of coercion would have been taken into consideration. This is clear from the preparatory work of the Charter. In the Nuremberg Trial, the prosecutors' views were unified at least on the point that the Charter had not allowed immunity on the ground of coercion in the case of manifest illegality. However, the judgment in denying immunity on the mere fact of superior orders newly presented the possibility of moral choice as a 'true test'. The

[151]Indictment, The *Roechling* case, NMT, vol. 14, 1061–75.

[152]Judgment on Appeal, The *Roechling* case, ibid., 1104–5. The defense of necessity is deemed the same with the coercion defense.

[153]Opinion and Judgment, The *Einsatzgruppen* case, NMT, vol. 4, 481–3, 488; Opinion and Judgment, The *Farben* case, NMT, vol. 8, 1179; Judgment, The *Krupp* case, NMT, vol. 9, 1438–48; Judgment, The *High Command* case, NMT, vol. 11, 509; Judgment, The *Ministries* case, NMT, vol. 14, 339; Judgment on Appeal, The *Roechling* case, ibid., 1104–5.

notion of moral choice was not made clear. Moreover, there was no answer to the question of whether the accused could be immunized on the test of moral choice or only the mitigation of punishment could be allowed.

The vague expression of the IMT judgment on the superior orders defense caused serious confusion in the Subsequent Proceedings. The applicable law of the Subsequent Proceedings was the CCL10, which was closely related to the Nuremberg Charter. On the superior orders defense, Article 2(4)b, which reflected the relevant Charter provision, was applied. However, even the argument of the prosecution fell into disorder with respect to the interpretation of Article 2(4)b – a view which recognized immunity on the ground of coercion incidental to superior orders contrasted with the majority that denied such immunity.

The majority of the judgments of the Subsequent Proceedings suggested recognizing immunity on the ground of coercion in terms of superior orders. In some cases, it was expressed that the CCL10 did not reject the defenses of necessity or coercion, although it excluded the superior orders defense. However, it would be appropriate to understand that the CCL10, which was provided to realize the Charter provisions, supported the absolute responsibility with regard to coercion. The 'Nuremberg Principle' on the superior orders defense had already revealed its unstableness by the time the IMT put forth the notion of moral choice. The 'principle' took on even more serious vulnerability by the fact that many judgments of the Subsequent Proceedings suggested to break away from the principle of absolute responsibility.

Meanwhile, the discussion on the knowledge of illegality and/or manifest illegality did not show such conspicuous turbulence in a series of the trials under the Nuremberg Charter. In the first place, the understanding of the drafters of the Charter was not clear on these issues. Then, the IMT did not clarify its position on these problems and they were not paid much attention during the Subsequent Proceedings. Eventually, the judgments such as in the *Einsatzgruppenn* and *Hostages* cases showed a position to allow immunization on the test of the knowledge of illegality. However, it is not possible to determine how such a position relates to the provision of the Nuremberg Charter. The original meaning of the Charter itself cannot be specified on the issues of the knowledge of illegality and/or manifest illegality.

If one takes the 'Nuremberg Principle' on the superior orders defense as a simple denial of automatic immunity, the 'Principle' was consistently held throughout the judicial proceedings under the Nuremberg Charter. However, the realm of debates on the superior orders defense was actually much wider. In the drafting of Article 8, the delegates of the four Allied Powers intended to introduce absolute responsibility at least in terms of coercion. Those delegates thus meant a revision, at the international level, of the principle of conditional immunity that had been held back in their own countries. Nonetheless, the principle of absolute responsibility was eventually adjusted or amended at the stage of the trials.

The factor of coercion, which is to be considered in deciding on immunity or the mitigation of punishment, bears peculiar characteristics if it is consulted in the context of superior orders. This is the point that some defense counsels contended at the Nuremberg Trial and the Subsequent Proceedings. The orders of the government or superiors are legally binding and are grounded on state power at least in the respective national legal systems. Physical and/or mental coercion comes to additionally be attended with such legal coercion in case of superior orders.

The defense counsels also argued that international institutions had not been developed fully enough to reject immunity on the ground of legal coercion by national society. There had been no supranational organ that could protect individuals who resisted coercion by national legal systems. Therefore, they contended that it was not appropriate to discuss international criminal responsibility of individuals who had not resisted superior orders.

The Nuremberg Charter widely opened a way to pursue the international criminal responsibility of state organs in denying automatic immunity by the mere fact of orders. In light of the chaotic international legal situations before the establishment of the Nuremberg Charter, the denial of automatic immunity would have been very much influential to the subsequent international rule-making. However, an idea of 'international criminal responsibility of state organs', which the Charter intended to reinforce, was pressed to be adjusted at the stage of its application. That was the adjustment by limiting responsibility on the ground of such factors as coercion incidental to orders. The major reason presented for this adjustment was contradiction or a gap between the idea of international criminal responsibility of state organs and a lack of international institution to practically guarantee this idea. It may be said that a tension between international and national legal systems was strongly noticed at the stage of trials that examined concrete cases.

The trials held by the Allied Powers under the Nuremberg Charter presented the principle not to recognize automatic immunity under the superior orders defense. However, they confined themselves to presenting this principle. A question of conditional immunity was thus entrusted to the following international rule-making as a remaining problem.

3.4 The Tokyo Trial

The Tokyo Trial[154] was held to try Japanese major war criminals. The trial was conducted under the authority of the Supreme Commander for the Allied Powers, Douglas MacArthur, who oversaw the occupation of postwar Japan.[155] The Tokyo

[154]The proceedings of the Trial are recorded in R. Pritchard & S. Zaide (annot. comp. ed.), *The Tokyo War Crimes Trial*, 22 vols (New York: Garland Pub., 1981); *Kyokutō Kokusaigunjisaiban Kankei Shiryōshūsei: Kokushikan Daigaku Fuzoku Toshokan Shozō: Eibun Sokkiroku (Compiled Documents on the International Military Trial for the Far East: Kokushikan University Library: Shorthand Notes in English)* [microfilm] (Tokyo: Kashiwa Shobō, 1994). They are also recorded in Japanese in *Kyokutō Kokusaigunjisaiban Sokkiroku (Shorthand Notes of the International Military Trial of the Far East)* (Tokyo: Yūshōdōshoten, 1968), 10 vols.

[155]Pritchard & Zaide, supra n. 154, vol. 20, at 48, 418–9.

Trial was different from the Nuremberg Trial in that its constitution, jurisdiction, and functions were approved by the Supreme Commander for the Allied Powers.[156] The IMT was jointly set up by the United States, the United Kingdom, France, and the Soviet Union. Nonetheless, the Charters of the International Military Tribunal for the Far East (IMTFE) and the IMT were 'in all material respects ... are identical'.[157] The judgment of the Tokyo Trial denoted that 'this Tribunal prefers to express its unqualified adherence to the relevant opinions of the Nuremberg Tribunal'.[158]

Article 6 of the Tokyo Charter, which provided on the superior orders defense as follows, was modeled on Article 8 of the Nuremberg Charter:

> Responsibility of Accused. Neither the official position, at any time, of an accused, nor the fact that an accused acted pursuant to order of his government or of a superior shall, of itself, be sufficient to free such accused from responsibility for any crime with which he is charged, but such circumstances may be considered in mitigation of punishment if the Tribunal determines that justice so requires.[159]

This provision also treated the issue of the official position that the Nuremberg Charter provided in its Article 7. The content of the charters basically accorded with each other in these points.[160]

With regard to the superior orders defense, Article 6 of the Tokyo Charter provided that the fact that the accused acted pursuant to order did not 'of itself' have an effect of immunization. This is different from Article 8 of the Nuremberg Charter, which did not make use of such a restrictive phrase. It might be construed on this point that Article 6 of the Tokyo Charter consciously excluded the principle of absolute responsibility.[161] However, with respect to Article 6, it should be noted, as will be seen below, that the prosecution expressed contradictory views with regard to the possibility of immunity on the test of manifest illegality during the Tokyo Trial. The prosecution played a key role at the drafting of the Tokyo Charter.[162] In light of the fact that the argument of the prosecution was not

---

[156] *Ibid.*, 48, 419.

[157] *Ibid.*, 48, 439.

[158] *Ibid.*

[159] Pre-Trial Documents, General Headquarters Supreme Commander for the Allied Powers, Charter of the International Military Tribunal for the Far East, in Pritchard & Zaide, supra n. 154, vol. 1, at 3.

[160] The similarity between Article 6 of the Tokyo Charter and Article 8 of the Nuremberg Charter has often been pointed out. For instance, see United Nations War Crimes Commission, supra n. 2, at, 282–3; Bassiouni, supra n. 69, at, 473. As the studies which closely examine Article 6 of the Tokyo Charter, see Dinstein, supra n. 1, at 156–9; Y. Kita, 'Sensōhanzaininsaiban to Jōkanmeirei no Kōben – Tōkyō Saiban no Baai – (Trials of War Criminals and Superior Orders Defense – The Case of Tokyo Trial –)', *Nihon Hōgaku* 59, no. 2 (1993): 205–44.

[161] Dinstein, supra n. 1, at 157.

[162] S. Horwitz, *The Tokyo Trial* (New York: Carnegie Endowment for International Peace, 1950), 483.

consistent during the trial, it would be questionable to determine that Article 6 of the Tokyo Charter consciously removed the principle of absolute responsibility.

The interpretation of the phrase 'of itself' should have been significant especially for the defense, which would have influenced the possibility of the immunity of the accused. Nonetheless, Article 6 of the Tokyo Charter was not examined in detail by the defense counsels, nor was Article 8 of the Nuremberg Charter and the judgment of the Nuremberg Trial. In particular, at the stage of individual defenses of each accused, the notion of the superior orders defense was hardly referred to.[163] This was in contrast with the case of the Nuremberg Trial.

As Röling, who served as a judge at the Tokyo Trial, stated, it was unthinkable of the accused to involve the Tennō (Japanese Emperor) in the judicial proceeding, whereas the responsibility of the Führer was a significant issue at the Nuremberg Trial.[164] On the defense's side, it had been proposed prior to the trial to avoid the prosecution of the Tennō and to prioritize the defense of the state over that of individuals.[165] However, with regard to the latter proposal, there was criticism even among the defense counsels that it would infringe on the fundamental rights of individual defendants.[166] The views were not unified among defense counsels with regard to this problem.

The defense took up the issue of the superior orders defense in its summations at the final stages. However, individual references to the said defense during the individual defenses were few. These facts could be thought to have reflected the case that there had not been a unified view with regard to this problem on the side of the defense.

3.4.1 The Argument of the Defense Counsels and the Prosecution

The defense positively discussed the superior orders defense only in its summations at the final stages. The defense counsel Hyōichirō Kusano mentioned the said defense in arguing individual responsibility.

Kusano first referred to 'the principle of criminal responsibility, which requires the existence, at the time of commission of an alleged offense, of a possibility of expecting the offender not to commit such an act'.[167] He drew attention to Article 35 of the concurrent Japanese *Criminal Code*, which stipulated '[n]o act is punishable, which is done in accordance with the provisions of law or regulations or in

---

[163]The defense counsels, in their summations at the final stages, referred to the issue of superior orders as a ground for immunization (Pritchard & Zaide, supra n. 154, vol. 18, at 43, 399–420, 738–44). However, there were no arguments on the theory of the superior orders defense.

[164]B. Röling (ed. by A. Cassese), *The Tokyo Trial and Beyond, Reflections of a Peacemonger* (Cambridge: Polity Press, 1993), 107.

[165]T. Sumimoto, *Senryō Hiroku (Ge) (Secret Notes on the Occupation (The Second Part))* (Tokyo: Mainichi Shinbunsha, 1952), 166.

[166]*Ibid.*

[167]Pritchard & Zaide, supra n. 154, vol. 19, at 47, 548–9.

pursuance of a legitimate business',[168] as an example for this principle. Then, he expressed his view that 'the impossibility of expecting him to act otherwise [to disobey orders] will exempt him from any wickedness or blameworthiness and hence from any criminal responsibility'.[169] In stating so, he also cited Article 21 of the Chinese *Criminal Code* at the time, which decided on the responsibility of subordinates on the test of the knowledge of illegality as well as Article 114 of the French *Penal Code* that provided for the exemption (immunity) of subordinates who had obeyed orders.[170] Thus, Kusano connected the issue of the superior orders defense with that of 'the principle of impossibility of expectation (*Nichtzumute[sic] barkeit*)'[171] and contended that the said defense should have been recognized to bear certain effect. In light of the fact that the Japanese criminal law has been much influenced by the German criminal law, it was natural that the defense counsel relied on the principle of impossibility of expectation and not on the notion of 'defense'.[172] Still, his argument also seemed relevant to the fact that the defendants had adopted a common approach to avoid the prosecution of the Tennō. If the defendants mainly discussed the superior orders defense, the responsibility of superiors who had given orders would come to the forefront as a consequence of denying the subordinates' responsibility. If one relied on the principle of the impossibility of expectation, consultation would be restricted to the responsibility of subordinates who had obeyed orders. The responsibility of superiors would not be derived directly from the principle of impossibility of expectation and the prosecution of the Tennō could be avoided for the moment.

Meanwhile, before the summations by the defense, the prosecution classified the accused into the following three categories and explained the ground of individual responsibility for each of them:

(1) [t]hose defendants who had the ultimate duty or responsibility for policy formulation fixed by the law of Japan;
(2) those defendants, who although they do not have the ultimate duty or responsibility, had the duty or responsibility for policy formulation in a subordinate or intermediate capacity fixed by the law of Japan; and
(3) those defendants, who although they had no duty or responsibility fixed by the law of Japan, have by their acts and statements placed themselves on the policy-making level and are therefore chargeable with responsibility in fact.[173]

The second category was relevant to the superior orders defense. The prosecution argued that modern political thinking overlooked the importance of these intermediate people. They contended that '[i]t is these subordinate officials who ordinarily formulate government policy in the first instance'[174]:

---

[168] *Ibid.*, 47, 552.

[169] *Ibid.*, 47, 556.

[170] *Ibid.*, 47, 552–4.

[171] *Ibid.*, 47, 557.

[172] *Ibid.*, 47, 557.

[173] Pritchard & Zaide, supra n. 154, vol. 16, at 40, 542–3.

[174] *Ibid.*, 40, 547–8.

> A person with ultimate responsibility has multifarious duties covering a wide field and he must rely upon his subordinates. . . . Even under the most technical view, these persons are instigators and accomplices in the establishment of the policy. The only way a person having intermediate responsibility can escape criminal liability for an act which is an international crime is to show that in the particular instance he had nothing to do with the specific act or that the policy adopted was in fact opposed by him and contrary to that which he counselled.[175]

Thus, the prosecution asserted the responsibility of the accused in arguing that 'subordinate officials' had not substantially maintained a subordinate character. This view of the prosecution conflicted with that of the defense counsels on the characterization of those who belonged to the second category presented above.

In answering the argument of the prosecution, Kusano raised Articles 1 and 2 of the Japanese *Regulations for the Duty of Government Official* that described the status of the accused and presented a legal ground for their obligation to obey:

> Article 1. Government officials shall, pledging their allegiance and assiduous services to His Majesty the Emperor and the Emperor's Government, obey laws and orders and discharge their respective duties.
>
> Article 2. Government officials shall, with respect to their duties, observe the orders of their superior officials to whom they are assigned, provided however that they may express their opinions to such orders.[176]

Then he emphasized that soldiers had been under the vigorous duty to observe superior orders and that disobedience to orders had severely been punished as the crime of defiance under the *Army Criminal Code* and the *Navy Criminal Code*.[177] Thus, the defense construed that the state organs that the prosecution included in the second category had substantially been subordinate. The defense refuted that such accused could not have been expected to disobey superior orders.

In answering the defense, the prosecution stated that 'superior orders are not recognized as a defense in international law'[178] and contended that the Tokyo Charter only recognized the mitigation of punishment. The prosecution cited the theory presented by Oppenheim:

> The fact that a rule of warfare has been violated in pursuance of an order of the belligerent government or of an individual belligerent commander does not deprive the act in question of its character as a war crime; neither does it, in principle, confer upon the perpetrator immunity from punishment by the injured belligerent.[179]

The accused would exceptionally be immunized only in the cases where the illegality of the criminal conduct had not been manifest or that the laws of war in question had been ambiguous. This is a quotation from the sixth edition of Oppenheim's *International Law*. As seen in Chapter 2, this argument was presented after

---

[175]*Ibid.*, 40, 548.

[176]Pritchard & Zaide, supra n. 154, vol.19, at 47, 559–60.

[177]*Ibid.*, 47, 560.

[178]*Ibid.*, 48, 372.

[179]*Ibid.*

the outbreak of war and it replaced automatic immunity that had been expressed up to its fifth edition of 1935. Nonetheless, it should be noted that even a severe view on the superior orders defense in the sixth edition still suggested immunity on the test of manifest illegality. The prosecution itself confirmed this point in its statement. The reply of the prosecution that quoted Oppenheim's argument and expressed that the superior orders defense could not be allowed under international law would not be said to have been accurate.

The defense relied on the principle of the impossibility of expectation and asserted the immunity of the accused. The prosecution did not mention this theory and kept emphasizing that the Tokyo Charter denied the superior orders defense. Did the prosecution connect the principle of the impossibility of expectation with that of the superior orders defense and then deny them as a whole, or did the prosecution just ignore the argument on the principle of the impossibility of expectation presented by the defense? These points were not clear. In any event, it was at least certain that they expressed the conflicting views with regard to the possibility of immunity on the ground of coercion.

3.4.2 The Judgment

The IMTFE in its judgment denoted that it completely followed the judgment of the Nuremberg Trial on the issue of the superior orders defense:

> 'The Charter specifically provides ... "the fact that a defendant acted pursuant to order of his Government or of a superior shall not free him from responsibility but may be considered in mitigation of punishment." This provision is in conformity with the laws of all nations... The true test which is found in varying degrees in the criminal law of most nations is not the existence of the order but whether moral choice was in fact possible'.
>
> With the foregoing opinions of the Nuremberg Tribunal and the reasoning by which they are reached this Tribunal is in complete accord.[180]

Thus, neither did the judgment show its interpretation on the IMT's judgment, particularly on the phrase 'moral choice' nor did the IMTFE consult Article 6 of the Tokyo Charter in detail. By showing its full compliance to the IMT's judgment, the IMTFE's judgment could be said to have also succeeded its ambiguity. Did international law allow conditional immunity under the superior orders defense, or could the accused only mitigate his/her punishment even after considering any factors relevant to superior orders? The Tokyo Trial ended up without showing its original view on these fundamental questions.

Five judges presented their individual opinions in addition to the judgment at the Tokyo Trial. With respect to the superior orders defense, these judges did not protest against the majority view. Judge Radhabinod Pal presented his individual opinion over 1200 pages which dissented from the majority view. However, with

[180] Pritchard & Zaide, supra n. 154, vol. 20, at 48, 438–9.

regard to the superior orders defense, he only cited the editions of the British Manual of Military Law and the US Rules of Land Warfare that preceded the revision before the end of World War II and recognized automatic immunity under the said defense.[181] Judge Pal did not specifically elaborate on these instruments.

Judge Röling strengthened in his dissenting opinion that soldiers could not be punished just because they had participated in war in obedience to orders of the government.[182] However, what he underlined was the peril that was to be caused by the influence of soldiers on the policymaking of state. He did not argue on the superior orders defense with regard to illegal acts in general that included crimes against peace.

3.4.3 *Conclusion*

At the Tokyo Trial, various views were presented on the superior orders defense at the summations by the prosecution and the defense, and the reply by the prosecution to the defense summations. However, the trial concluded without resolving these conflicting views. The judgment restricted itself to agreeing with the IMT judgment on the issue of the superior orders defense.

It seems that such an outcome of the trial was much influenced by the fact that the accused, especially from the military sections, had shared a policy of never jeopardizing the imperial household and prioritizing the defense of the state over that of individuals. The superior orders defense was seldom referred to by the accused during the trial. With regard to the said defense, the Tokyo Trial could not be deemed to have added something particular to the development of the 'Nuremberg Principle'.

3.5 The 'Nuremberg Principle' and the Theory of Superior Orders Defense

3.5.1 *Theoretical Ambiguity of the 'Nuremberg Principle'*

What is the theoretical consequence of the denial of the superior orders defense? This question was not fully addressed during the Nuremberg Trial. The motive for drafting Article 8 of the Nuremberg Charter was well illustrated in Jackson's report to the US president, which was written during the London Conference. In this

---

[181]The Dissenting Opinion of the Member for India (Rab[sic]habinod B. Pal), in Pritchard & Zaide, supra n. 154, vol. 21, at 1146–7.

[182]The Separate Opinion of the Member for the Netherlands (Bernard Victor Röling), in *ibid.*, 179–81.

report, Jackson underlined that the combination of the superior orders defense and immunity of a head of state would lead to a denial of any individual responsibility.[183] Article 8 was thus proposed to remove obstacles for the punishment of war crimes, leaving aside theories of criminal responsibility.

Almost the same could be said with concurrent academic arguments mainly in the United States, the United Kingdom, France, and the Soviet Union, which were involved in the drafting of the Nuremberg Charter. Those who denied the superior orders defense either partially or generally and contended either conditional immunity or absolute responsibility constructed their arguments abstractedly, or from the viewpoint of policy. For instance, Clifford Bartlett stated, '[t]he great principle of natural justice, which while casting its cloak of immunity over the officer for acts committed while in the line of his duty, does not strip him from the consequences of wanton, cruel, and unnecessary crime'.[184] Hugh Bellot also expressed that a declaration to punish war criminals whether or not acting under orders 'would be in consonance with the principles of International Law and the spirit of justice'.[185] Further, as already noted, Oppenheim's *International Law* from its sixth edition onward contended that automatic immunity by superior orders cannot be regarded 'as expressing a sound legal principle'.[186] On the other hand, from the more practical viewpoint as in the case of Jackson, some commentators criticized the superior orders defense as leading to the impossibility of the execution of the laws of war.[187]

3.5.2 Theories of Superior Orders Defense

To begin with, various explanations have been given for the ground for recognizing superior orders as a defense. There has not been any unified theory established with regard to this point. Roughly speaking, theoretical grounds for the superior orders

[183]Report to the President by Mr. Justice Jackson, June 6, 1945, in *Jackson Report*, 47.

[184]H. Bartlett, 'Liability for Official War Crimes', *Law Quarterly Review* 35 (1919): 191.

[185]H. Bellot, 'War Crimes: Their Prevention and Punishment', *Transactions of Grotius Society* 2 (1917): 49.

[186]Oppenheim, supra n. 21 (1940), at 453–4; L. Oppenheim, *International Law, Revised 6th ed. by H. Lauterpacht, vol. 2, Disputes, War and Neutrality* (London: Longmans, Green & Co., Oppenheim, 1944), 452.

[187]Bellot, supra n. 185, at 46; G. Finch, 'Superior Orders and War Crimes', *American Journal of International Law* 15 (1921): 445; J. Berger, 'The Legal Nature of War Crimes and the Problem of Superior Command', *American Political Science Review* 38 (1944): 1207; P. Coste-Floret, 'La répression de crimes de guerre et le fait justificatif tiré de l'ordre supérieur', *Recueil dalloz de doctrine de jurisprudence et de legislation – Chronique* (1945): 21. Also, Lauterpacht criticized the superior orders defense in using the expression, 'perversion of justice' (H. Lauterpacht, 'The Law of Nations and the Punishment of War Crimes', *British Yearbook of International Law* 21 (1994): 73) and Glueck questioned the recognition of the said defense for enemy combatants (S. Glueck, *War Criminals, Their Prosecution & Punishment* (New York: Alfred A. Knopf, 1944), 157).

defense have been argued in the following three variations: (1) an argument based on the theory of the immunity of state acts, (2) an argument that underlines the absolute character of military discipline, and (3) an argument that focuses on real coercion brought about by superior orders, and the knowledge of illegality and/or manifest illegality of the criminal conduct.

3.5.2.1 Theory of the Immunity of State Acts

Commentators such as Quincy Wright understood the superior orders defense as one aspect of the notion of the 'act of state'. Wright denied the punishment of war crimes committed by enemy state organs on the basis of an idea of the immunity of state acts. He stated, '[e]fforts to hold individuals liable before an international tribunal for such acts when committed under orders or subsequent acceptance by the government seems contrary to the principle of independence of states as it would be destructive of discipline'.[188] A similar view was held by Hans Kelsen; he contended that war crimes as state acts could not be punished by hostile countries without specific treaties that authorized such prosecution, except for the cases of espionage and war treason.[189] Shinobu also expressed that any act conducted under superior orders was a state act and individuals who executed the orders should not be punished.[190] Thus, if one connects the superior orders defense with the theory of the immunity of state acts, the said defense should always bear a function of automatic immunity.

3.5.2.2 Absolute Character of Military Discipline

Some commentators who asserted automatic immunity emphasized the absolute character of military discipline, either together with the theory of the immunity of state acts or independently from this theory. Wright, as quoted, pointed out the specific character of military discipline besides the theory of the immunity of state acts and contended automatic immunity under the superior orders defense.[191] On the other hand, Graham Bower only underlined the absolute character of military discipline. He stated, 'no army or navy could exist if every subordinate were

---

[188] Q. Wright, 'The Outlawry of War', *American Journal of International Law* 19 (1925): 79.

[189] H. Kelsen, 'Collective and Individual Responsibility in International Law with Particular Regard to the Punishment of War Criminals', *California Law Review* 31 (1943): 530–71; H. Kelsen, 'Collective and Individual Responsibility for Acts of State in International Law', *Jewish Yearbook of International Law* (1948): 226–39. Kelsen differentiated war crimes committed under the orders of governments from those as private acts. He denied the punishment by adversaries only for the former.

[190] J. Shinobu, *Senjikokusaihō Kōgi (Lectures on International Laws of War)*, vol. 3 (Tokyo: Maruzen, 1941), 406.

[191] Wright, supra n. 188, at 79.

permitted or required to constitute himself a judge of the legality or morality of the orders received from his superiors'.[192]

These commentators can be said to have emphasized military discipline from the viewpoint of military or state interest. Meanwhile, military discipline was otherwise understood as placing soldiers under coercion. This is what the US national courts underlined in dealing with the issue of the superior orders defense.[193] At the Nuremberg Trial, defense counsels such as Merkel and Jahrreiss abstractedly recognized the factor of coercion. They asserted the immunity of the accused in arguing that superior orders usually evoked the state of strong coercion regardless of individual circumstances.[194] With regard to the trials of high-ranking officials, it would be expected, as was pointed out during the trials carried out under the Nuremberg Charter, that there existed some discretion on the part of subordinates who received orders. However, those defense counsels related the absolute character of military discipline with fictitious notion of coercion and asserted automatic immunity by the superior orders defense.

Oppenheim's position in his *International Law* up to its fifth edition resembled the arguments of Merkel and others at the Nuremberg Trial. Oppenheim presented the notion of legal compulsion. He then acknowledged automatic immunity under the superior orders defense without consulting whether actual coercion was at work in respective cases.[195] Just with the emphasis that soldiers were under coercion in national legal systems, he contended that superior orders were always accompanied by such coercion that should immunize the soldiers who had conducted whatever criminal act.

3.5.2.3 Actual Coercion, and the Knowledge of Illegality and/or Manifest Illegality

Not all commentators who understood the issue of the superior orders defense as that of coercion recognized automatic immunity by a mere fact of orders. With regard to the academic arguments that have been investigated here, the majority recognized immunity on the condition that actual coercion had existed. This is a position supporting the principle of conditional immunity.

Lauterpacht, for instance, supported conditional immunity. He understood the problem of the superior orders defense as what reflected a tension between 'the dictates of absolute discipline and efficiency in what is essentially an instrumentality of power and the equally inescapable subjection of that instrument of power to

[192] G. Bower, 'The Laws of War: Prisoners of War and Reprisals', *Transaction of Grotius Society* 1 (1916): 25.

[193] See Sect. 2.1. On this point, Poljokan referred to the interest of the army or state as well as the coercion under which subordinates are placed (I. Poljokan, *La responsabilité pour les crimes et délits de guerre* (Paris: Jouve et c^{ie}, Éditeurs, 1923), 154–65).

[194] See Sects. 3.2 and 3.3.

[195] See Sect. 2.1.

the authority of the law'. He then deemed the said defense to be that of coercion in part. However, his conclusion was not that of automatic immunity.[196] Bartlett, in identifying the superior orders defense with that of duress/compulsion, also argued that subordinates could not be immunized on the ground of orders if they had not been faced with 'urgent or immediate' danger.[197] Renault,[198] Frederick Pollock,[199] Clyde Eagleton,[200] Jacob Berger,[201] Cost-Floret,[202] and other commentators expressed similar views. They supported immunity just on the condition that actual coercion had existed in respective cases. The arguments expressed by the defense counsels as well as some judgments at the Subsequent Proceedings were also similar to these views.

There were many commentators who attached importance to the knowledge of illegality and/or manifest illegality, either in addition to coercion or independently. As seen in Chapter 2, British and US judicial precedents until World War II and the Reipzig Trials conducted by the German Supreme Court held conditional immunity on the ground of these factors. This was an idea to recognize immunity in the cases where the accused had not been aware of the illegality of the conduct in question or that the illegality of the conduct had not been manifest. The defense counsels contended in the same way at the Nuremberg Trial. With regard to academic arguments, a treatise of Winthrop and the sixth and subsequent editions of Oppenheim's *International Law* approved of immunity in cases where the illegality of the criminal conduct had not been manifest.[203] Further, most of those who recognized immunity on the ground of coercion as mentioned above additionally supported immunization because of a lack of the knowledge of illegality and/or a lack of manifest illegality.[204]

There have been some arguments to deem the idea that allowed immunity on the test of coercion, and the knowledge of illegality and/or manifest illegality, to have relied on the test of *mens rea* of crime or the general principle of criminal law.[205] However, such an understanding would not be said to be appropriate.

---

[196]Lauterpacht, supra n. 187, at 71–3.

[197]Bartlett, supra n. 184, at 191.

[198]L. Renault, 'De l'application du droit pénal aux faits de guerre', *Revue générale de droit international public* 25 (1918): 27.

[199]F. Pollock, 'The Work of the League of Nations', *Law Quarterly Review* 138 (1919): 197–8.

[200]C. Eagleton, 'Punishment of War Criminals by the United Nations', *American Journal of International Law* 37 (1943): 497.

[201]Berger, supra n. 187, at 1207–8.

[202]Coste-Floret, supra n. 187, at 21.

[203]W. Winthrop, *Military Law and Precendents, 2nd ed.* (Washington, DC: GPO, 1920), 296–7; Oppenheim, supra n. 21 (1940), at, 453–4; *id.*, supra n.186 (1944), at, 452–3.

[204]Renault, supra n. 198, at 27; F. Pollock, 'The Work of the League of Nations' *Law Quarterly Review* (1919): 197; Eagleton, supra n. 200, at 497; Berger, supra n. 187, at 1207–8; Lauterpacht, supra n. 187, at 73.

[205]Dinstein, supra n. 1, at 87–90; Lauterpacht, supra n. 187, at 73.

Mens rea is a terminology of common law. Some of those who sort out the problem by using this notion construe that the existence of factors such as coercion means a lack of *mens rea* and immunity of the accused. However, even if the criminal act was conducted under coercion, *mens rea* is not denied. It is explained in common law that, in the case of coercion, *mens rea* still existed but the intent of the accused had been overwhelmed by the threatening of others.[206]

Further, if one regards conditional immunity as the consequence of applying the general principle of criminal law, the same rule should be applied for the cases of superior orders and the others that are irrelevant to orders likewise. However, a lack of manifest illegality of the criminal conduct is not usually deemed to be a test for immunity of the accused. Moreover, at least from the viewpoint of common law, which does not recognize a mistake of law as a defense in principle,[207] immunity on the ground of a lack of the knowledge of illegality would need to be categorized as a peculiar rule on superior orders. In common law, such conditional immunity under the superior orders defense cannot be deemed to be a result of applying a general principle of criminal law.

If the knowledge of illegality and/or manifest illegality should be the tests for immunization with regard to superior orders, it would be necessary, especially for commentators of common law countries, to emphasize the peculiar character of the cases of superior orders. It would be possible to underline the significance of military discipline from the viewpoint of state interest. It would also be thinkable to recognize a combination of coercion – whether or not the coercion is strong enough – caused by military discipline and the factors of a lack of the knowledge of illegality and/or a lack of manifest illegality as bringing about a multiplier effect.

Meanwhile, only a limited number of commentators specifically approved absolute responsibility.[208] Commentators such as Finch[209] and Bellot[210] denied automatic immunity but did not clarify whether to support conditional immunity or absolute responsibility. Mérignhac[211] and some others clearly denied immunity on the ground of coercion but did not mention the issues of the knowledge of illegality and/or manifest illegality.

---

[206]M. Allen, *Textbook on Criminal Law*, 8th ed. (Oxford; New York: Oxford University Press, 2005), 159–60; A. Bowers, 'A Concession to Humanity in the Killing of Innocents – Validating the Defences of Duress and Superior Orders in International Law' *Windsor Review of Legal and Social Issues* 15 (2003): 38–40.

[207]See note 13 of Chapter 2.

[208]For instance, see Glueck, supra n. 187, at 156–7.

[209]Finch, supra n. 187, at 445.

[210]Bellot, supra n. 185, at 49.

[211]A. Mérignhac, 'De la sanction des infractions au droit des gens commises, au cours de la guerre européenne, par les empires du centre', *Revue générale de droit international public* 24 (1917): 49–53.

3.5.3 The Meaning of the 'Nuremberg Principle'

Thus, arguments on the theoretical grounds of the superior orders defense had been significantly varied. In addition, as already noted, it was not clear which theory the IMT intended to disapprove. Nonetheless, the Nuremberg Trial at least consistently denied automatic immunity under the superior orders defense. This could be said to have objectively meant a complete rejection of the views that connected the superior orders defense with the theory of the immunity of state acts and that regarded military discipline as absolute.

Article 8 of the Nuremberg Charter was, in the first place, an important provision that allowed the international criminal law to 'pierce' national sovereignty as Jackson noted in his report. It clarified that the control of international criminal law should reach to state acts. The idea that deemed military discipline to be absolute was also dismissed.

Second, Article 8 denied the idea to immunize the accused on the ground of an abstract notion of coercion without examining concrete cases. Military discipline puts subordinates who receive orders under strong coercion in most cases. However, the peril that those subordinates would face could possibly be neither grave nor imminent. This is what the judgments of the Subsequent Proceedings confirmed. In the process of applying international criminal law, the prosecution of state organs at the center of power, that is, the prosecution of those who have comparatively large discretionary power has been focused in particular. If so, it would be all the more necessary to prudently examine the factor of coercion incidental to orders.

Then, what can be said about the remaining problems of conditional immunity? Should the accused be immunized in cases where actual coercion to a certain degree accompanied superior orders, or that the execution of orders was the consequence of a lack of the knowledge of illegality and/or a lack of manifest illegality? As we have seen in this chapter, the trials conducted under the Nuremberg Charter did not deliver a specific answer to these questions as a whole. In particular, on the problem of coercion, the unstableness of the 'Nuremberg Principle' was conspicuous.

With respect to the debates on the problem of coercion, conflict of views later surfaced in the judgment of the ICTY regarding common law versus continental law. Common law does not allow the coercion defense in the case of serious crimes such as murder, whereas continental law generally recognizes the possibility of immunization by the coercion defense. However, at the stage of the trials under the Nuremberg Charter, such a structure of debates had not yet been brought about in clear relief. During the drafting of the Nuremberg Charter, the British delegate Fyfe presented his view to allow only the mitigation of punishment even in cases where the accused had been threatened to conduct the criminal act. At the trial, the defense counsels asserted immunity on the ground of coercion. This conflict of views could actually be understood as that between common law and continental law. However, it should be noted that it was the US Military Tribunals that recognized immunity on the ground of coercion in the Subsequent Proceedings.[212] The structure of debates on conditional immunity under the Nuremberg Charter was rather complicated in comparison with the following development of the debates.

Thus, the 'Nuremberg Principle' on the superior orders defense eventually denied the theory of the immunity of state acts and the absolute character of military discipline. Meanwhile, a series of judicial proceedings completed with no conclusion on the issues of actual coercion, and the knowledge of illegality and/or manifest illegality. What kind of evaluation has been given to this manner of presenting the 'principle' in the following international rule-making and judicial precedents? We will look at this point in the next chapter.

[212]Greenspan points out that British criminal law does not recognize the killing of innocent persons on behalf of his/her own life and criticizes the judgments of the US military tribunals (Greenspan, supra n. 69, at 499–500).

Chapter 4
After the Trials Under the Nuremberg Charter

Abstract The international rule-making after the Nuremberg Trial basically succeeded the specific rule presented by the 'Nuremberg Principle' as well as its unstableness – the problem of conditional responsibility. The conflict characterizing the discussions has also been reflected on some relevant judicial precedents after the Nuremberg Trial. There has not been any unified position on the question of conditional responsibility, especially on the issue of coercion, in international practice. In contrast, academic arguments after the Nuremberg Trial have generally supported conditional responsibility. Most of them have recognized immunity on the tests of the knowledge of illegality and/or manifest illegality, whereas those who have approved the factor of coercion as a ground for immunity have been comparatively limited.

4.1 International Rule-Making

A series of judicial proceedings under the Nuremberg Charter strongly influenced the subsequent rule-making process in international criminal law. The establishment of a general rule on the superior orders defense has been one of the major subjects in the drafting of some treaties after the Nuremberg Trial. However, as seen in the previous chapter, the Nuremberg Charter and the trials conducted under the Charter did not present a clear and consistent view on conditions or tests for denying the superior orders defense.

Attempts to establish a general rule on the superior orders defense have been shown in the drafting process of the Genocide Convention, Geneva Conventions of 1949, Additional Protocol I, and the Draft Code of Crimes against the Peace and Security of Mankind. As will be seen below, these instruments either do not provide for the superior orders defense or remain ambiguous on this issue. The ICC Statue, which was concluded at the end of the twentieth century, moved forward with the process of clarifying rules on superior orders. However, the relationship between the rules of the ICC Statute and general international rules is still unknown. In the following sections, we will consult the drafting process of these international instruments and the problems that are yet to be solved.

H. Satō, *The Execution of Illegal Orders and International Criminal Responsibility*,
DOI 10.1007/978-3-642-16753-9_4,

4.1.1 *Preparatory Work of Treaties and Superior Orders Defense*

4.1.1.1 Genocide Convention and Superior Orders Defense

It was at the drafting of the Genocide Convention that the problem of the superior orders defense was first undertaken by the major drafting process of international criminal law after the Nuremberg Trial.[1] The Economic and Social Council of the United Nations set up the Ad Hoc Committee on Genocide through its 1948 resolution and examined a draft Convention on the Crime of Genocide submitted by the Committee. Article 5 of the draft of the Committee provided for personal jurisdiction of the convention and read, '[t]hose committing genocide or any of the other acts enumerated in Article IV shall be punished, whether they are heads of State, public officials or private individuals'.[2]

With regard to the issue of superior orders, the delegate of the Soviet Union presented its proposal on Article 5. He contended that a sentence that reads as '[c]ommand of the law or superior orders shall not justify genocide' should be added to this article.[3] The Soviet delegate explained that if one denied the principle shown in the Soviet proposal, the provision was to be understood to declare in advance that every individual who could assert orders of law or superiors would be immunized.[4] The delegate contended, 'no person for any reason could free himself from the responsibility for the crime'.[5] This is the position supporting the principle of absolute responsibility. However, the Soviet proposal was objected to by the Venezuelan delegate from the viewpoint of consistency with its national law. Further, the Lebanese delegate objected by arguing that a peculiar intention of a doer was necessary for the establishment of the crime of genocide. Eventually, the Committee rejected the Soviet proposal by two votes to four, with one abstention.[6]

[1]The studies which examine the preparatory work of the Genocide Convention in relation to the superior orders defense include Y. Dinstein, *The Defence of 'Obedience to Superior Orders' in International Law* (Leyden: A.W. Sijthoff, 1965), 217–23. See also S. Adachi, 'Kokusaihōjō no Meirei to Fukujū no Kankei (The Relationship between Orders in International Law and Obedience)', Bōeidaigakkō Kiyō 24 (1972): 334; H. Levie, 'The Rise and Fall of an Internationally Codified Denial of the Defense of Superior Orders', *Revue de droit militaire et de droit de la guerre* 30 (1991): 199; M. Bassiouni, *Crimes against Humanity in International Criminal Law, 2nd revised ed.* (The Hague: Kluwer Law International, 1999), 477–8.

[2]Report to the Economic and Social Council on the Meetings of the Committee Held at Lake Success, New York, From 5 April to 10 May 1948, UN Doc. ECOSOC OR, 3rd Year, 7th Session, Supplement No. 6 (E/794), 9.

[3]Ibid.

[4]Ibid; UN Doc. Ad Hoc Committee on Genocide, Summary Record of the 18th Meeting (E/AC.25/SR.18), 4.

[5]Ibid., 6.

[6]UN Doc. Report to the Economic and Social Council, supra n. 2, at 9; UN Doc. Ad Hoc Committee on Genocide, supra n. 4, at 6, 9.

The Soviet delegate presented the same proposal when the United Nations General Assembly examined the draft convention on genocide.[7] There was a lively discussion at the Sixth Committee of the General Assembly on this proposal. Objections against the Soviet proposal were mainly based on the argument that it conflicted with the national laws of various countries[8] and that an intention of a doer was not taken into consideration.[9] For instance, according to the Venezuelan delegate, the Venezuelan criminal law stipulated that only superiors who had given orders would bear responsibility and that its constitutional law provided for unconditional obedience in the army, a denial of which would lead to disorder of discipline.[10] Further, the Iranian delegate, from the same point of view, expressed that it would be appropriate to apply the respective national laws.[11] With regard to the issue of an intention of criminal conduct, the Greek delegate objected to the Soviet view. He emphasized that an intention was an important element of genocide and that the IMT considered whether or not the accused had been free to conduct the acts in interpreting Article 8 of the Nuremberg Charter.[12] The US delegate also expressed that if one adopted the Soviet proposal, a judge would be forced to convict an innocent person. He then contended that the problem should be left to judges to decide in the respective cases.[13]

In answering these objections, the Soviet delegate and those who supported the Soviet proposal first underlined that a denial of the superior orders defense was the principle presented by Article 8 of the Nuremberg Charter.[14] Then, they contended that international law should be given priority over national laws if there were any conflicts between them.[15] On the other hand, with respect to the problem of an intention, there seemed to be no substantial difference between the Soviet contention and the objections against it. For instance, the Polish delegate who supported the Soviet view pointed out that the Soviet proposal did not reject immunity on the ground of the impossibility of disobedience or of coercion.[16] Further, the Czechoslovakian delegate agreed with the Soviet proposal, arguing that the problem of an intention would be decided under the judges' discretion.[17] Speaking after these delegates, the Soviet delegate mentioned that his proposal had been misunderstood

[7] UN Doc. GAOR, 3rd Session, Part I, 6th Committee, 301–2.

[8] The views of the delegates of Belgium (ibid., 302), Venezuela (ibid., 306), Dominican Republic (ibid., 308), Peru (ibid., 309), Iran (ibid., 310).

[9] The views of the delegates of Greece (ibid., 306–7), United States (ibid., 307), Iran (ibid., 311).

[10] Ibid., 306.

[11] Ibid., 310.

[12] Ibid., 306–7.

[13] Ibid., 307.

[14] See the statements of the delegates of the Soviet Union (ibid., 302), France (ibid., 305), Czechoslovakia (ibid., 308), Poland (ibid., 311).

[15] For instance, the statement of the delegate of Egypt (ibid., 307).

[16] Ibid., 311.

[17] Ibid., 308.

and explained that an intention was a constituent element of genocide so that an innocent person should never be deemed responsible for it.[18]

Nonetheless, there were no revisions in the draft provision on the issue of intention. Further, there were no concessions with regard to the problem of conflict with national laws. In such circumstances, the Soviet proposal was put to vote and was rejected by 28 to 15 votes, with six abstentions.[19] At the voting, the delegates of France, the United States, and some others added an explanation that a final solution to the problem should be entrusted to the ILC.[20]

It can be said that during the drafting of the Genocide Convention, there emerged an almost unified view that the superior orders defense should not be denied in ignoring the factor of an intention as well as coercion. Conflict of views developed, apart from the principle of absolute responsibility, between those who regarded a denial of the superior orders defense as harmful to national legal order and those who denied automatic immunity but left open the possibility of immunity. That was conflict between the principles of automatic immunity and conditional immunity.

4.1.1.2 Geneva Conventions and the Additional Protocol I

A view that it had been too early to provide for an international rule on the superior orders defense remained to be the majority at the international rule-making after the conclusion of the Genocide Convention. At the drafting of the Geneva Conventions of 1949, the International Committee of the Red Cross (ICRC) proposed a draft provision embodying conditional immunity on the test of the knowledge of illegality.[21] However, it was dismissed at the diplomatic conference.[22] Although a record of the diplomatic conference was a restricted one, it is noted that the state parties could not achieve a consensus on the superior orders defense and decided to entrust the decision to judges who would apply their national laws in respective cases.[23]

[18]Ibid., 312–3.

[19]Ibid., 313.

[20]Ibid., 314.

[21]Remarques et propositions du comité international de la Croix-Rouge, Document destiné aux gouvernements invités par le conseil fédéral suisse à la conférene diplomatique de Genève (21 avril 1949) (Genève, 1949), 19, 34, 68, 88.

[22]Commentary, III Geneva Convention Relative to the Treatment of Prisoners of War (Geneva, International Committee of the Red Cross, 1960), 622.

[23]Final Record of the Diplomatic Conference of Geneva of 1949, vol. II Section B, 115. With regard to the preparatory work of the Geneva Conventions, see also J. Graven, 'Principes fondamentaux d'un code repressif des crimes contre la paix et la securite de l'humanite', Revue de droit international de sciences diplomatiques et politiques 28 (1950): 376; G. Draper, *The Red Cross Conventions* (London: Stevens & Sons Limited, 1958), 21–2; Dinstein, supra n. 1, at 223–5; Levie, supra n. 1, at 199–200.

It was also the case with the drafting of the Additional Protocol I.[24] The ICRC presented its own draft at the diplomatic conference, which provided for the superior orders defense in Article 77 as follows:

1. No person shall be punished for refusing to obey an order of his government or of a superior which, if carried out, would constitute a grave breach of the provisions of the Conventions or of the present Protocol.
2. The fact of having acted pursuant to an order of his government or of a superior does not absolve an accused person from penal responsibility if it be established that, in the circumstances at the time, he should have reasonably known that he was committing a grave breach of the Conventions or of the present Protocol and that he had the possibility of refusing to obey the order.[25]

This draft provision held conditional immunity similar to the ICRC proposal at the drafting of the Geneva Conventions of 1949. Draft Article 77 took into consideration both the knowledge of illegality and coercion under which the accused had been placed. However, at the Committee I of the Diplomatic Conference that consulted this proposal, various conflicting arguments were made with regard to the treatment of these factors incidental to superior orders.

The problem was the phrase, 'if . . . he had the possibility of refusing to obey the order' of Article 77 (2) of the ICRC draft. There was an argument when the Belgian delegate evaluated that this draft provision paid attention to the 'threatening' brought about by superior orders.[26] The Australian delegate proposed the deletion of the phrase, which, in his argument, allowed immunity too broadly.[27] On the contrary, the delegates of Nigeria,[28] India,[29] Pakistan,[30] and others criticized that the ICRC proposal was too severe from the viewpoint of military discipline. Meanwhile, the US delegate contended that it was not necessary to provide for the defenses of self-defense, duress, mistake of fact, and so forth, and proposed a deletion of the phrase 'and that he had the possibility of refusing to obey the order', which he deemed to be ambiguous.[31]

---

[24]With regard to the arguments on the superior orders defense at the drafting of the Additional Protocol I, see Levie, supra n. 1, at 200–203.

[25]International Committee of the Red Cross, Draft Additional Protocols to the Geneva Conventions of August 12, 1949, in Official Records of the Diplomatic Conference on the Reaffirmation and Development of International Humanitarian Law Applicable in Armed Conflicts, Geneva (1974–1977) [hereinafter, Official Records] (Bern, 1978), vol. 1, Part 3, at 25.

[26]Official Records, vol. 9, at 132–3. See also the statements of the delegates of Libyan Arab Republic (ibid., 137) and Argentina (ibid., 142).

[27]Amendments to Draft Additional Protocol I and Annex, Official Records, vol. 3, Part 1, at 331.

[28]Official Records, vol. 9, at 132.

[29]Ibid., 143.

[30]Ibid., 146.

[31]Ibid., 129; Amendments to Draft Additional Protocol I and Annex, Official Records, vol. 3, Part 1, at 332.

A final draft of Article 77(2) was adopted by 40 votes to nine, with 28 abstentions. It was difficult to deem it fully representing the position of the Committee as a whole:

> The mere fact of having acted pursuant to an order of an authority or a superior does not absolve an accused person from penal responsibility, if it be established that in the circumstances at the time he knew or should have known that he was committing a grave breach of the Conventions or of this Protocol. It may, however, be taken into account in mitigation of punishment.[32]

The word 'mere' in the phrase, '[t]he mere fact of having acted pursuant to an order of an authority or a superior' were added by the delegate of the Netherlands.[33] Draft Article 77 presented by the Working Group A after the discussion at the Committee I provided that '[t]he fact of having acted [wilfully] pursuant to an order of an authority or a superior does not absolve an accused person from penal responsibility, if...', showing the possibility to use the word 'wilfully'.[34] With regard to this point, the delegate of the Netherlands proposed to use the word 'mere' instead of 'wilfully', which was adopted as the proposal of the Committee I. The French delegate explained at the voting that he interpreted the insertion of the word 'mere' as approving the grounds of immunity such as necessity that criminal law usually provided.[35] However, many delegates disapproved this proposal, which took into consideration the factors of the knowledge of illegality and coercion. They objected to the proposal or abstained from voting, deeming it to be in conflict with national legal orders and military discipline.[36]

There was no further discussion at the Plenary Meetings, and Draft Article 77 was rejected by 36 votes to 25, with 25 abstentions.[37] The reason for the objections and the abstentions was that, as was the case with the voting at the Committee I, the draft article would threaten national legal orders and military discipline.[38]

Thus, the Additional Protocol I was concluded without a provision on the superior orders defense. In the first place, there was a conflict of view on whether or not the superior orders defense should be denied as a principle. Some delegates who objected to the draft articles or abstained from voting emphasized national legal orders and military discipline. They were reluctant to even recognize conditional immunity. It can be said that the minimum idea, that is, the idea to deny

[32] Report of Working Group A, Official Records, vol. 10, at 212. See also Official Records, vol. 9, at 389–92.

[33] Ibid., 389–90.

[34] Report of Working Group A, Official Records, vol. 10, at 211–2.

[35] Official Records, vol. 9, at 402.

[36] See the statements of the delegates of Zaire (ibid., 405–6), Oman (ibid., 406), Syrian Arab Republic (ibid., 408), United Arab Emirates (ibid., 410), Republic of Korea (ibid., 411), Kuwait (ibid., 413), Democratic Yemen (ibid., 414).

[37] Official Records, vol. 6, at 307–8.

[38] See the statements of the delegates of Syrian Arab Republic (ibid., 308–9), Democratic Yemen (ibid., 331–2), Sudan(ibid., 339).

automatic immunity under the superior orders defense, which had been consistently upheld throughout the trials under the Nuremberg Charter, was disputed there.

Meanwhile, among those who denied automatic immunity, various arguments were shown with regard to the question of how to deal with the factors of the knowledge of illegality, coercion, and so forth, which had been incidental to superior orders. Some detailed discussions developed at the drafting of the Additional Protocol I as compared to the case of the Genocide Convention, especially with respect to the issue of coercion. As a result, it appears that severer conflict of views surfaced at the drafting of the Additional Protocol. Still, it would be thought that such a conflict had potentially existed either at the drafting of the Genocide Convention.

It is to be noted that some delegates who asserted automatic immunity under the superior orders defense in referring to national legal orders and military discipline did not simply pursue the priority of national laws and military discipline. For instance, during the drafting of the Additional Protocol I, the Jordanian delegate pointed out that Article 77 related to the problem of protecting subordinates who had rejected obedience.[39] The delegate of the Syrian–Arab Republic stated that it was not possible to support the Draft Article under the circumstances in which the decision on responsibility was entrusted to the authority of national law.[40]

Thus, they drew attention to the problem related to the application and enforcement of international law and was caused by structural relationship between international and national legal orders. This was a practical problem with regard to the obstacles that would surface when one intended to accomplish international legal orders. Such arguments resembled those of some defending counsels at the Nuremberg Trial and the Subsequent Proceedings. However, what the delegates of Jordan and the Syrian–Arab Republic contended was not conditional immunity that the majority of the defending counsels upheld at those trials. The delegates went so far as to contend automatic immunity under the superior orders defense. Such contention that refused the minimum principle held under the Nuremberg Charter was not supported any longer in the work of the ILC and in the drafting of the ICC Statute, as will be seen next.

4.1.2 Codification Process at the ILC

Apart from the above international rule-making, the ILC from the beginning proceeded with the formulation of international rules that the Nuremberg Charter and the Nuremberg Trial indicated. The Commission thus presented the Nürnberg Principles to the General Assembly of the United Nations.

---

39 Official Records, vol. 9, at 142.

40 Official Records, vol. 6, at 309.

These principles were further generalized as the work on the Draft Code of Crimes against the Peace and Security of Mankind. However, similar to the cases of the drafting of the treaties observed above, the problem of the superior orders defense has not thoroughly been resolved at the ILC.[41]

4.1.2.1 Formulation of the Nürnberg Principles

The United Nations General Assembly in its 1947 resolution directed the ILC to '[f]ormulate the principles of international law recognized in the Charter of the Nürnberg Tribunal and in the judgment of the Tribunal'.[42] At the request of the ILC, the Special Rapporteur, Jean Spiropoulos, reported on the Nürnberg Principles in 1950. He proposed the following rule on the superior orders defense as the Fourth Principle:

> The fact that a person acted pursuant to order of his Government or of a superior does not free him from responsibility under international law. It may, however, be considered in mitigation of punishment, if justice so requires.[43]

As the Special Rapporteur stated in the commentary, the proposed principle was basically modeled on Article 8 of the Nuremberg Charter, with some difference in expression.[44] On the possibility of moral choice denoted by the judgment of the Nuremberg Trial, the Special Rapporteur understood it not as a test of immunization but as 'the criterion for the determination of the degree of responsibility'.[45]

The Special Rapporteur's interpretation on the possibility of moral choice was different from that of some judgments of the Subsequent Proceedings. As was seen in Section 3 of the previous chapter, there were some judgments at the Subsequent Proceedings that connected the possibility of moral choice with the knowledge of illegality or coercion and then recognized a room for immunization on these grounds. The Special Rapporteur did not take such a position, construing that the Nuremberg Charter and the IMT judgment had only approved the mitigation of punishment on the superior orders defense.

However, the ILC got embroiled in a dispute especially with this Fourth Principle. From the very beginning, there was a criticism that the draft principle, which did not allow immunity, was contrary to the legal notion, for instance, of necessity.[46]

---

[41]The studies which examine the Nürnberg Principles and the Draft Code of Crimes against the Peace and Security of Mankind in relation to the superior orders defense include T. Okuhara, 'Kokusairengō to Sensōhanzai (The United Nations and War Crimes)', in *Kokusairengō no Kihonmondai (Fundamental Issues of the United Nations)* , ed. T. Kamiya (Tokyo: Sakai Shoten, 1973), 279–320. See also Adachi, supra n. 1, at 335–6.

[42]GA Res. 177(II).

[43]Yearbook of International Law Commission [hereinafter, YILC] (1950), vol. 2, at 192.

[44]Ibid.

[45]Ibid., 193.

[46]YILC (1950), vol. 1, at 42.

The discussion further developed into that of the mission of the ILC. What the General Assembly directed was a formulation of international rules that the Nuremberg Charter and the IMT judgment showed. However, if those rules could not be deemed to be principles of international law, what should the ILC, which was entrusted with 'formulation', do with them?

There were two opposing views at the ILC. On the one hand, there was an argument that the ILC should limit itself to a mere formulation, whether or not the content of the rules would be appropriate.[47] The other argument was that the ILC should not present such principles as the Commission itself could not hold as appropriate.[48]

The ILC eventually arrived at a compromise, adopting a proposal of the member of the Commission, James Brierly, to loosen the content of Article 8 of the Nuremberg Charter by attaching greater importance to the judgment of the Nuremberg Trial.[49] The Commission construed that the IMT exceptionally recognized immunity in light of the fact that the IMT judgment made the possibility of moral choice a true test of deciding criminal responsibility.[50] According to Brierly, the possibility of moral choice would be decided by examining whether or not the accused had been sane or he/she had been under coercion at the time of the criminal conduct.[51]

Thus, the ILC adopted the Fourth Principle without deviating from the rule which it thought had been presented by the Nuremberg Charter and the IMT judgment, and in a manner to be able to keep up with a strong criticism that it would be inappropriate not to recognize the superior orders defense in all cases:

> The fact that a person acted pursuant to order of his Government or of a superior does not relieve him from responsibility under international law, provided a moral choice was in fact possible to him.[52]

The Commission in its commentary explained that this principle was based on Article 8 of the Nuremberg Charter as interpreted by the IMT judgment.

This formulation was different from the draft Nürnberg Principle proposed by the Special Rapporteur. However, it actually was in accord with the Special Rapporteur's own idea. In addition to the report on the Nürnberg Principles, Spiropoulos also presented a report on the Draft Code of Offences (Crimes) against the Peace and Security of Mankind in 1950 at the request of the ILC. In the latter, he criticized the position that he thought the Nuremberg Charter and the IMT judgment put forth as contrary to 'public opinion'. It was Spiropoulos' idea to approve the possibility of immunity under the superior orders defense.

---

47 Ibid., 44, 45, 46, 47.

48 Ibid., 42–3, 44, 45, 47.

49 Ibid., 47.

50 Ibid., 43, 45.

51 Ibid., 288.

52 YILC (1950), vol. 2, at 375.

4.1.2.2 Draft Code of Crimes against the Peace and Security of Mankind

Superior Orders Defense and 'Moral Choice'

The United Nations General Assembly in its Resolution 177(II) of 1947 directed the ILC to work on the Draft Code of Offences (Crimes) against the Peace and Security of Mankind in addition to the formulation of the Nürnberg Principles.[53] The ILC again designated Spiropoulos as the Special Rapporteur and requested him to work on the Draft Code as general rules, which comprehended the Nürnberg Principles.

As already noted, the provision of the draft on the superior orders defense that the Special Rapporteur presented was different from what he understood as the relevant Nürnberg Principle. Spiropoulos, in examining the British Manual of Military Law and US Rules of Land Warfare before the establishment of the Nuremberg Charter, argued that there had not been any consensus on whether or not a fact of superior orders could be a defense.[54] He then analyzed that a central issue on the superior orders defense was a pressure that had been put on the persons who had received orders. His conclusion was that the IMT judgment, which had not allowed immunity on the ground of superior orders, would be right from 'a purely dogmatical point of view', although 'public opinion' would hardly approve such a rigid rule.[55]

The ILC eventually did not hold an idea that the IMT judgment supported absolute responsibility. Consequently, the Commission could unify its view in accordance with the position of the Special Rapporteur of his own. That was the view that the IMT judgment approved the possibility of immunity under the superior orders defense by showing the moral choice test. The ILC concluded to provisionally adopt this Nürnberg Principle as part of the Draft Code.[56]

The examination of the Draft Code was temporarily suspended in 1954 because the problem of the definition of aggression had not been settled at the General Assembly. Until then, the ILC had basically maintained its position on the superior orders defense that it expressed in 1950. In 1951, the Commission, following the Second Report of Special Rapporteur,[57] proposed a draft article on the said defense, which was almost the same as the Fourth Principle of the Nürnberg Principles adopted in 1950.[58] The commentary explained that the proposed article reflected the IMT judgment and related moral choice with the possibility of acting against orders.[59]

---

[53]GA Res. 177 (II).

[54]YILC (1950), vol. 2, at 270–72.

[55]Ibid., 272.

[56]Ibid., 380.

[57]YILC (1951), vol. 2, at 60.

[58]'The fact that a person charged with an offence defined in this Code acted pursuant to order of his government or of a superior does not relieve him from responsibility, provided a moral choice was in fact possible to him' (ibid., 137).

[59]Ibid.

There was criticism on the draft article that the notion of moral choice was ambiguous.[60] The ILC corresponded to this criticism in its 1954 report by presenting the more concrete expression 'if, in the circumstances at the time, it was possible for him not to comply with that order'.[61] This amendment only clarified the explanation that the ILC had already made on moral choice. The content of the draft article was not substantially changed.[62]

Error and Coercion

The General Assembly adopted a resolution on the definition of aggression in 1974. In response to this, the ILC reopened discussion on the Draft Code of Offences (Crimes) against the Peace and Security of Mankind in the 1980s. However, there was no change on the fundamental view of the Commission on the superior orders defense, at this stage either.

Newly designated Special Rapporteur Doudou Thiam treated the problem of the '[p]rinciples relating to the determination and extent of responsibility' in his Fourth Report of 1986. He tried to add a more detailed and comprehensive investigation on the factors that could be the ground of immunity in terms of superior orders. As was seen above, the ILC Report of 1954 proposed a decision on the problem of immunity by making use of the test, 'if, in the circumstances at the time, it was possible for him not to comply with that order'. In contrast, Thiam showed the concrete factors as error and coercion.[63] He proposed to recognize them as immunizing grounds with regard to the superior orders defense.

What Thiam called 'error' meant a lack of manifest illegality or of the knowledge of illegality on the part of a doer of criminal conduct. In the previous chapter, we saw that during the Nuremberg Trial and the Subsequent Proceedings, the prosecution and defense mainly debated on the knowledge of illegality and/or manifest illegality, and coercion, in relation to the superior orders defense. In light of this fact, it would be said to have only been natural that Thiam made such a proposal in the Fourth Report.

On the issue of coercion, Thiam interpreted that the IMT judgment, by presenting the moral choice test, denied the responsibility of the accused who had not been free to act and loosened the content of Article 8 of the Nuremberg Charter.[64] However, he reserved that there could not be any immunization in the case of crimes against humanity, such as genocide and apartheid. On the issue of error, he consulted the judgments of the US Military Tribunals as well as some other

[60]The criticism of the delegates of the UK and Egypt (YILC (1954), vol. 2, at 120).

[61]Ibid., 150.

[62]In 1954, there were no detailed examinations at the Sixth Committee on the draft article presented by the ILC (GAOR, 9th Session (1954), 125–7, 129–33, 135–6, 137–44).

[63]YILC (1986), vol. 2, no. 1, at 77–9.

[64]Ibid., 77–8.

precedents and argued that it was not easy to find out relevant international rules; however, he still expressed his position to approve immunity on the ground of error.[65] Eventually, the draft article that Thiam presented in 1986 only referred to the factor of coercion as the draft article that was adopted in 1954 by the ILC. The Thiam's draft read, '[t]he order of a Government or of a superior does not relieve the perpetrator of criminal responsibility, unless he acted under the threat of a grave, imminent and irremediable peril'.[66]

The Special Rapporteur thus tried to deepen the argument on the superior orders defense. However, there seldom were discussions on this topic at the ILC in 1986[67] and 1987.[68] The Drafting Committee also did not fully consider the issue of the superior orders defense.[69] The Report of the ILC of 1987 did not propose relevant draft articles.[70]

Thiam's proposal to specifically consult the issues of error and coercion was modestly reflected in the work of the ILC in 1991. In the same year, the Drafting Committee presented its draft, which read that immunity could not be recognized 'if, in the circumstances at the time, it was possible for him not to comply with that order'.[71] This draft followed the content of the ILC Report of 1954. The ILC adopted Draft Article 11 in the First Reading, which completely followed the proposal of the Drafting Committee.[72] A commentary to the article stated that 'a genuine possibility of not carrying out the order' would not be recognized 'in cases of irresistible moral or physical coercion, state of necessity and obvious and acceptable error'.[73] Thus, although the draft did not apparently answer the questions raised by the Special Rapporteur, it substantially supported his argument as far as one consulted the commentary attached by the ILC.

In this restrictive way, the ILC presented its position to suggest immunization on the ground of error and coercion by the First Reading. However, in the subsequent reports of the ILC, the same position was not necessarily held in a specific manner.

---

[65]Ibid., 79.

[66]Ibid., 83.

[67]YILC (1986), vol. 1, at 135–56. At the 6th Committee in the same year, the delegates of Brazil and Argentina pointed out that the issue of the superior orders defense was included in that of the coercion (UN Doc. A/C.6/41/SR.39, at 11; UN Doc. A/C.6/41/SR.41, at 3), and the Soviet delegate stated that the superior orders defense should not be allowed (UN Doc. A/C.6/41/SR.42, at 15). However, there were no other detailed arguments. There were no specific comments on the superior orders defense in the Committee after 1986.

[68]There were criticism that the notion of 'moral choice' was ambiguous (YILC (1987), vol. 1, at 10, 17, 33) and that the defense of error or coercion should not be recognized for serious crimes (ibid., 51, 58).

[69]YILC (1987), vol. 1, at 226.

[70]YILC (1987), vol. 2, no. 2, at 13–17.

[71]YILC (1991), vol. 1, at 191.

[72]Ibid., 240.

[73]A/46/10, at 257.

There was no decisive criticism to Draft Article 11 which was adopted at the First Reading. Further, at the Commission in 1994, there were only some comments that pointed out the ambiguity of the wordings 'if, in the circumstances at the time, it was possible for him not to comply with that order'.[74] However, Draft Article 11 that was presented by the Drafting Committee in 1995 did not leave any room for immunity:

> The fact that an individual charged with a crime against the peace and security of mankind acted pursuant to an order of a Government or a superior does not relieve him of criminal responsibility, (but may be considered in mitigation of punishment if justice so requires).[75]

The chairman of the Drafting Committee explained that the phrase in question was deleted as it might cause improper interpretation and that the relevant problems should be treated in terms of general defenses.[76] Meanwhile, the substantive provision of Draft Article 14, which provided for general defenses, had not yet been prepared.[77] There was no telling whether or not immunity should be allowed in terms of superior orders.

It was soon after the establishment of the ICTY in 1993 and the ICTR in 1994 that this proposal of the Drafting Committee was presented; the statutes of both international tribunals deny the superior orders defense in Article 7 and 6, respectively.[78] These two articles only recognize the mitigation of punishment. This does not necessarily mean that the two tribunals thoroughly deny immunity on the ground of, for example, coercion incidental to superior orders. As will be seen below, the ICTY discussed the factor of coercion incidental to orders separately from the superior orders defense. Still, it is certain that the statutes of the two international tribunals deny the superior orders defense in principle, leaving open a question of whether the tribunals have a wide or narrow understanding of the notion of superior orders. A change in the manner of prescription at the Drafting Committee can be said, as the commentary of the Committee itself referred to the problem of conformity with the ICTY Statute,[79] to have been influenced by the establishment of the two tribunals.

The final draft of the Drafting Committee of 1996 almost reproduced its draft of 1995 on the issue of the superior orders defense.[80] The former drew attention to the

---

[74]YILC (1994), vol. 1, at 111, 143.

[75]YILC (1995), vol. 1, at 197.

[76]Ibid., 202.

[77]Ibid., 197.

[78]UN Doc. S/25704 (1993); SC Res. 955 (1994).

[79]YILC (1995), vol. 1, 202.

[80]'The fact that an individual charged with a crime against the peace and security of mankind acted pursuant to an order of a Government or a superior does not relieve him of criminal responsibility, but may be considered in mitigation of punishment if justice so requires (YILC (1996), vol. 1, at 32)'.

commentary attached to the latter.[81] Consequently, the final draft succeeded the manner to rely, with regard to the problem of immunity under superior orders, on the draft article that provided for general defenses. However, Draft Article 13 that treated general defenses was still not furnished with discrete content and only mentioned the 'general principles of law'.[82]

It was pointed out at the ILC that it would be difficult to prepare concrete provisions on general defenses without any collaboration with criminal lawyers, that it would be appropriate to entrust respective courts to decide on these issues, and that there had been various views on the evaluation of defenses regarding the criminal conduct in question.[83] The final draft did not correspond to the questions raised by Thiam, but there was no argument at the ILC on this point.[84] After the conclusion of the Second Reading, the ILC adopted the final draft of the Drafting Committee as it was.[85]

Thus, the ILC initially interpreted the Nuremberg Charter as recognizing conditional immunity. Further, the Commission clarified its position to support conditional immunity as a principle of international law. However, as international rule-making on international criminal law stagnated in the mid-1950s, the discussion on the superior orders defense also came to be halfhearted.

From the 1990s onward, that is, as the ICTY and the ICTR started functioning, a more detailed discussion was required on various topics of international criminal law. The ILC began to treat not only the superior orders defense but also other general defenses of criminal law at this stage. However, the discussion at the Commission did not fully correspond to the change in situations since the 1990s. With regard to the superior orders defense, the issues of error and coercion were newly categorized as those of general defenses. The ILC has been suspending its proposition on these issues.

The final draft article on the superior orders defense restricts itself to deny automatic immunity. It does not add anything to Article 8 of the Nuremberg Charter at least superficially. Nonetheless, it would be worth noting that the ILC has always been conscious of the possibility of immunity on the ground of a lack of the knowledge of illegality and coercion in relation to the superior orders defense. At this point, the work of the ILC would be evaluated as distinguished from the preparatory work of the Nuremberg Charter.

[81]Ibid., 48.

[82]Ibid., 33.

[83]Ibid., 59–60.

[84]Ibid., 48.

[85]Ibid., 151–2.

4.1.3 Statutes of the International Criminal Tribunals

4.1.3.1 Statutes of ICTY and ICTR

In the 1990s, the United Nations Security Council established two ad hoc international criminal tribunals – the ICTY and the ICTR – under Chapter 7 of the United Nations Charter. This action strongly influenced the adoption of the ICC Statute at the end of the twentieth century.

With regard to the two international tribunals established by the Security Council, their basic legal instruments were prepared by the reports of the United Nations Secretary General which were then approved by the Security Council. As they were not adopted at diplomatic conferences, it is difficult to consult the respective drafting processes. This section will be limited to introducing the relevant provisions of those instruments. With respect to the ICTY, the tribunal has already delivered a judgment on the superior orders defense, which we will separately examine later.

Statute of ICTY

The ICTY is an ad hoc tribunal whose establishment was determined by Security Council Resolution 808 in 1993. It was the first tribunal that was set up under the auspices of the international society as a whole. The ground for establishing such a judicial organ would be arguable as the Security Council is basically a political organ and has been composed of a restricted number of countries. Nonetheless, the Security Council represents the United Nations as a universal international organization. Moreover, the competence that the Security Council holds under Chapter 7 of the United Nations Charter is fairly wide and the establishment of tribunals itself has not been decisively questioned. Whether or not the establishment of ad hoc tribunals by the Security Council is the best as international judicial activity, the ICTY would be evaluated as furnished with universality as well as certain legitimacy at least in a procedural aspect.

The Security Council recognized the widespread violations of international humanitarian law in the territory of the former Yugoslavia as a threat to international peace and security, and decided to set up an international tribunal aiming at restoring and maintaining peace in the area. The Statute of the International Tribunal presented by the Secretary General was approved by Security Council Resolution 827. The Tribunal started its operation soon.

With regard to the superior orders defense, Article 7(4) of the ICTY Statute provides as follows:

> The fact that an accused person acted pursuant to an order of a Government or of a superior shall not relieve him of criminal responsibility, but may be considered in mitigation of punishment if the International Tribunal determines that justice so requires.[86]

[86]UN Doc. S/25704, at 15.

This provision was modeled on Article 8 of the Nuremberg Charter. As a result, its construction is also the same as Article 4 of the Draft Code of Crimes against the Peace and Security of Mankind adopted by the ILC in 1996. However, the Draft Code means to apply its Article 13, which provides for general defenses to the cases of superior orders. This point remains ambiguous with the ICTY Statute.

The commentary to Article 7 of the ICTY Statute confirms that the fact of superior orders shall be considered only in the mitigation of punishment 'should the International Tribunal determine that justice so requires' Automatic immunity by the mere fact of orders is clearly disapproved here. The commentary then continues to state '[f]or example', and explains that the fact of orders may be considered 'in connection with other defences such as coercion or lack of moral choice'.[87] Does the commentary mean to deny automatic immunity under the superior orders defense but provide room for conditional immunity? The point is whether the expression following the words 'for example' mean to recognize immunity if the superior orders were accompanied by factors such as coercion.[88] This problem of Article 7(4) will focus on the judgment of *Prosecutor v. Drazen Erdemović* of the ICTY, which will be seen later.

Meanwhile, Article 7(4) of the ICTY Statute does not refer to the issues of the knowledge of illegality and/or manifest illegality. The international trials for the former Yugoslavia, different from the Nuremberg Trial, do not limit their personal jurisdiction to high-ranking state officials. Besides, its material jurisdiction includes not only genocide and other crimes against humanity but also violations of the laws or customs of war, the manifest illegality of which has often been debatable. In such conditions, the ICTY Statute that denies the superior orders defense without considering the issue of the knowledge of illegality could be said to have adopted severe rules in light of the arguments at the ILC, which have been seen above.

Statute of ICTR

The ICTR is another ad hoc tribunal established by the Security Council resolution.

The Security Council recognized the 'systematic, widespread and flagrant violations of international humanitarian law' as a threat to international peace and security and decided to set up an international tribunal to punish those who were responsible for those violations. The Statute of the Rwanda Tribunal was established by Security Council Resolution 955 in 1994. Soon after that, the ICTR started operating.

---

[87]Ibid.

[88]See V. Morris & M. Scharf, *An Insider's Guide to the International Criminal Tribunal for the Former Yugoslavia, A Documentary History and Analysis*, vol. 1 (New York: Trasnational Publishers, Inc., 1995), 105–7.

The ICTR Statute provides for the superior orders defense in Article 6(4) with nearly the same expression with Article 7(4) of the ICTY Statute:

> The fact that an accused person acted pursuant to an order of a government or of a superior shall not relieve him or her of criminal responsibility, but may be considered in mitigation of punishment if the International Tribunal for Rwanda determines that justice so requires.[89]

As the ICTY Statute, this provision does not specifically indicate what legal implications the factor of coercion, in addition to the mere fact of superior orders, would have. It is necessary to look at the precedents of the ICTR on this point, but the Tribunal still has not dealt with this issue in concrete cases.

The ICTR Statute restricts its material jurisdiction to genocide, crimes against humanity, and violations of Article 3 common to the Geneva Conventions and of Additional Protocol II. They are the criminal conduct of manifest illegality, so that the issues of the knowledge of illegality and/or manifest illegality would not matter under the statute.

4.1.3.2 Rome Statute of ICC

Manifest Illegality and Coercion

The ILC has been positively involved in the establishment of an international criminal court from the beginning. The Commission concluded in 1950 that the setting up of such a court was desirable in accordance with the Special Rapporteur's report.[90] As already noted, the work on the Draft Code of Offences (Crimes) against the Peace and Security of Mankind was suspended because the agenda of the definition of aggression piled up. However, as the United Nations General Assembly adopted the resolution on the definition of aggression, it directed the ILC by its resolution of 1981 to reopen the working on the Draft Code. In 1983, the ILC again proposed a question of an international criminal court to the General Assembly.[91]

As the Security Council established the ICTY and ICTR in the 1990s, the United Nations started to intensively deal with the issue of international criminal jurisdiction.[92] The General Assembly requested the ILC 'to address the question of

---

[89] SC Res. 955.

[90] YILC (1950), vol. 2, at 379.

[91] YILC (1983), vol. 2, no. 2, at 16.

[92] Contemporary academic arguments include B. Graefrath, 'Universal Criminal Jurisdiction and an International Criminal Court', *European Journal of International Law* 1 (1990): 67–88; J. Crawford, 'Prospects for an International Criminal Court', *Current Legal Problems* 48 (1995): 303–26; J. Dugard, 'Obstacles in the Way of an International Criminal Court', *Cambridge Law Journal* 56 (1997): 329–42. The studies which examine the ICC Statute in relation to the superior orders defense include J. Grayson, 'The Defence of Superior Orders in the International Criminal Court', *Nordic Journal of International Law* 64 (1995): 243–60; P. Gaeta, 'The Defence of Superior Orders: The Statute of the International Criminal Court Versus Customary International Law', *European Journal of International Law* 10 (1999): 172–91; O. Triffterer (ed.),

establishing an international criminal court or other international criminal trial mechanism'.[93] Further, in 1992, the General Assembly urged to prioritize on the drafting of a statute of an international criminal court, among other issues on the Draft Code.[94] Responding to this, the ILC presented the Draft Statute for an International Criminal Court in 1994 and proposed to hold an international conference of plenipotentiaries in order to conclude a treaty.[95]

The draft ICC Statute did not deal with substantive rules on international criminal law at the beginning. Rules on the superior orders defense and other general defenses were deemed to have remained as an agenda of the Draft Code of Crimes against the Peace and Security of Mankind.[96] However, the Preparatory Committee on the Establishment of an International Criminal Court, which was involved in preparing a diplomatic conference based on the work of the ILC proposed to change a course of action in its 1996 report. The Preparatory Committee pointed out that it was the majority view to include 'the fundamental principles of criminal law' into the statute from the viewpoint of the principle of legality. Then, it contended to deal with 'all general elements of crimes and the basic principles of liability and defence' in the instrument.[97] The Committee's proposition on the general principles of criminal law remained to be preliminary at this stage. With regard to the superior orders defense, it restricted itself to calling attention not to mingle the said defense with the notions of necessity and duress.[98]

In order to consult various proposals from state parties, the informal groups were set under the Preparatory Committee. These groups made a provisional report on each provision of the statute. The report proposed two ideas on the issue of the superior orders defense. The first proposal was as follows:

1. The fact that a person acted pursuant to an order of a Government or of a superior, (whether military or political) shall not relieve the person of criminal responsibility (if the order appears to be manifestly unlawful)(and the person has a greater risk to himself or herself no alternative but to obey, or has no other moral choice)[sic].
2. Where the person has acted pursuant to an order of a government or of a superior in the circumstances as described in paragraph 1, the sentence may be reduced having regard to the circumstances (this fact may be considered in mitigation of punishment if the court determines that justice so requires).[99]

Commentary on the Rome Statute of the International Criminal Court, Observer's Notes, Article by Article (Baden-Baden: Nomos Verlagsgesellschaft, 1999), 573–88.

[93]GA Res. 44/39.

[94]GA Res. 47/33.

[95]GAOR, 49th Session, Supplement No. 10 (UN Doc. A/49/10), 43.

[96]Ibid, 182–8.

[97]Report of the Preparatory Committee on the Establishment of an International Criminal Court, vol. 1 (Proceedings of the Preparatory Committee during March – April and August 1996), GAOR, 51st Session, Supplement No.22 (UN Doc. A/51/22), 41.

[98]Ibid., 47.

[99]Report of the Preparatory Committee on the Establishment of an International Criminal Court, vol. 2 (Compilation of Proposals), GAOR 51st Session, Supplement No. 22A (UN Doc. A/51/22), 102.

This proposal implied to consider the issues of manifest illegality and the possibility of moral choice in terms of superior orders. It reflected the idea that had been supported by the ILC at least until its 1991 report.

The second proposal of the informal group meant to make some difference on the possibility of immunity according to each category of crimes.[100] It denied automatic immunity under the superior orders defense with regard to genocide, crimes against humanity, and the crime of aggression. On the other hand, it recognized possible immunity on the test of manifest illegality with regard to serious violations of the laws and customs of war and grave breaches of the Geneva Conventions.

Superior Orders Defense and General Rules on Defenses

Thus, with regard to the drafting of the ICC Statute, too, the issues of manifest illegality and coercion had been considered in terms of the superior orders defense until 1996. However, the report of the Preparatory Committee in 1997[101] and the report of the Inter-seasonal Meeting in 1998[102] deleted the section on the moral choice test that had been provided in the report of the Preparatory Committee in 1996. The former two reports implied to recognize immunity just in relation to the tests of the knowledge of illegality and/or manifest illegality. The Draft Statute for the International Criminal Court adopted at the Preparatory Committee before the diplomatic conference also followed those drafts issued on and after 1997. Article 32 of the Draft Statute thus only referred to the knowledge of illegality and/or manifest illegality.[103]

Nonetheless, it should be noted here that those proposals since 1997 were all equipped with another provision dealing with general defenses. For instance, the draft of the Preparatory Committee in 1998 recognized immunity on the ground of a mental disease, self-defense, necessity, and so forth, besides superior orders (Article 31). There was shown an idea to deal with the issue of coercion in a provision on general defenses and not to provide for particular rules in the case of superior orders. It resembled the academic arguments developed in prewar France as well as the position that was presented by the judgments of the Subsequent Proceedings.

As was seen before, the ILC presented the Draft Code in 1996, which denies immunity under the superior orders defense but prepares other provisions on general defenses. Such a structure of the Draft Code is different from its previous

---

[100]Ibid.

[101]Decisions Taken by the Preparatory Committee at its Session Held from 1 to 12 December 1997, in *International Criminal Court: Compilation of United Nations Documents and Draft ICC Statute before the Diplomatic Conference*, ed. M. Bassiouni (No Peace without Justice, 1998), 274.

[102]*Ibid.*, 182.

[103]Draft Statute for the International Criminal Court, UN Doc. A/Conf.183/2/Add.1, at 59.

versions in providing for the issue of coercion incidental to orders separately from the superior orders defense. The change in the construction of provisions of the Draft ICC Statute that were relevant to the superior orders defense can be said to have almost concurred with the same kind of change of the ILC Draft Code.

The United Nations Diplomatic Conference of Plenipotentiaries on the Establishment of an International Criminal Court approved this basic structure of the draft provisions presented by the Preparatory Committee. During the Diplomatic Conference held in Rome from June to July 1998, discussions were mainly held at 'informal' and 'off-the-record' meetings in order to facilitate the smooth adjustment of views. Consequently, the arguments at the conference were not thoroughly recorded. [104] We will then look at the reports of the Working Groups set up for respective topics of the conference.

The Diplomatic Conference proceeded with the reports of the Working Groups which reflected the arguments of the unofficial meetings and were presented to the Committee of the Whole. The Working Group on General Principles of Criminal Law presented Draft Article 32, which was titled 'Superior Orders and Prescription of Law':

1. The fact that a crime referred to in article 5 has been committed pursuant to an order of a Government or of a superior, whether military or civilian, shall not relieve the perpetrator of criminal responsibility unless:
   a. The person was under a legal obligation to obey orders of the Government or the superior in question; and
   b. The person did not know that the order was unlawful; and
   c. The order was not manifestly unlawful.
2. For the purpose of this article, orders to commit genocide or crimes against humanity are manifestly unlawful.[105]

There was no reference to the issue of coercion. A lack of the knowledge of illegality and a lack of manifest illegality were raised as principal grounds for immunity. However, the draft of the Working Group also treated the issues of 'duress' together with a mistake of fact, a mental disease, intoxication, and self-defense as immunizing grounds.[106] The word 'duress' has since been consistently used and was adopted in the final ICC Statute. This is a notion that was explained to have unified 'necessity' and 'duress/coercion' that had been differentiated until the 1996 report by the Preparatory Committee.[107]

[104]A. Cassese, 'The Statute of the International Criminal Court: Some Preliminary Reflections', *European Journal of International Law* 10 (1999): 145.

[105]Report of the Working Group on General Principles of Criminal Law, UN Doc. A/CONF.183/C.1/WGGP/L.4/Add.1, at 5–6.

[106]Ibid., 4–5.

[107]Report of the Preparatory Committee on the Establishment of an International Criminal Court, vol. 2 (Compilation of Proposals), GAOR 51st Session, Supplement No. 22A (UN Doc. A/51/22), 100–101; Triffterer, supra n. 92, at 550–51.

The Committee as a Whole finally approved the draft of the Working Group, which was examined by the Drafting Committee.[108] Article 33 of the ICC Statute as adopted in Rome is almost the same with Draft Article 32 of the Working Group.[109]

Article 33 clearly recognizes immunity mainly on the tests of the knowledge of illegality and manifest illegality with regard to the superior orders defense. Meanwhile, Articles 31 and 32 deal with the issue of duress together with mental disease, intoxication, self-defense, and a mistake of fact as the grounds of immunization, just as the drafts of the Preparatory Committee and the Working Group did. However, a condition of proportionality is required for the establishment of the defense of duress, under which a doer of criminal conduct should 'not intend to cause a greater harm than the one sought to be avoided'.[110]

Thus, the ICC Statute provides for the issue of coercion in its provisions which deal with general defenses, and recognizes only a lack of the knowledge of illegality together with a lack of manifest illegality as immunizing grounds in terms of the superior orders defense. What should be noted is that the statute generally disapproves a mistake of law as a defense in Article 32. The article explains a mistake of law as a mistake 'as to whether a particular type of conduct is a crime within the jurisdiction of the Court'. This is a problem of the knowledge of illegality on the side of a doer of criminal conduct. It is thus limited to the case of superior orders that a mistake of law is admitted as an immunizing ground. It is also only for the case of superior orders that manifest illegality is to be a test of immunization.

These rules on the superior orders defense correspond to those that were presented by the judicial precedents of British and US national courts before World War II. In common law, a mistake of law cannot be recognized as a defense for serious crimes. Nonetheless, those courts supported immunity on the ground of

---

[108] P. Saland, 'International Criminal Law Principles', in *The International Criminal Court, The Making of the Rome Statute*, ed. R. Lee (The Hague: Kluwer Law International, 1999), 211–2. The Drafting Committee was not assigned the substantive consultation of respective topics (Report of the Drafting Committee to the Committee of the Whole, UN Doc. A/CONF.183/C.1/L.83, at 6).

[109] 'Article 33 Superior Orders and Prescription of Law

1. The fact that a crime within the jurisdiction of the Court has been committed by a person pursuant to an order of a Government or of a superior, whether military or civilian, shall not relieve that person of criminal responsibility unless:

(a) The person was under a legal obligation to obey orders of the Government or the superior in question;

(b) The person did not know that the order was unlawful; and

(c) The order was not manifestly unlawful.

2. For the purpose of this article, orders to commit genocide or crimes against humanity are manifestly unlawful (Rome Statute for the International Criminal Court, UN Doc. A/CONF.183/9, at 26)'.

[110] Regarding this point, see A. Bowers, 'A Concession to Humanity in the Killing of Innocents – Validating the Defences of Duress and Superior Orders in International Law' *Windsor Review of Legal and Social Issues* 15 (2003): 61–4.

a lack of the knowledge of illegality in the case that superior orders mattered. For instance, the *Smith* judgment of the United Kingdom emphasized the importance of military discipline and delivered that it would not be proper for soldiers to judge on the legality of orders on their own, although unconditional obedience would also be problematic.[111] Meanwhile, the judgment of *McCall v. McDowell et al.* of the US national court pointed out that military discipline set soldiers who received orders under coercion.

A reason for introducing special rules on the knowledge of illegality and manifest illegality only for the case of superior orders was not shown during the drafting of the ICC Statute. Why should a lack of the knowledge of illegality and a lack of manifest illegality be recognized as grounds for immunity just in terms of the superior orders defense? It would be necessary to deepen discussions on this point as well as the problem of a mistake of law in general.[112] In relation to the superior orders defense, the abovementioned national precedents might well be consulted in considering the problem.

The ICC Statute was adopted through the discussions surveyed above. Then, in what manner and to what extent will this instrument be accepted by the international society? Within what realm will the ICC effectively operate? The development of its operation cannot be fully predicted.

With regard to the relationship between the ICC Statute and customary international law, the statute itself pays attention to the possibility that customary international law would independently develop outside of it. On this point, it is worth noting that Article 10 of the ICC Statute stipulates that '[n]othing in this Part shall be interpreted as limiting or prejudicing in any way existing or developing rules of international law for purposes other than this Statute'.

Such a position of the ICC Statute has been reflected to some legislative measures of state parties. In particular, with respect to the general principles of criminal law, it seems to be avoided to accept the rules of the ICC Statute just as they are into national laws. For example, the 2001 *International Criminal Court Act* of the United Kingdom accepts the definitions of crimes of the ICC Statute but does not stipulate the general principles of criminal law. The 2000 *Crimes against Humanity and War Crimes Act* of Canada defines crimes in a slightly different way from the ICC Statute and does not accept general principles of criminal law provided by the statute. The *Act of 19 June 2003 Containing Rules Concerning Serious Violations of International Humanitarian Law (International Crimes Act)* of the Netherlands follows the

---

[111]Renault also raised the absolute character of military discipline as the ground for recognizing the superior orders defense on the test of the knowledge of illegality (L. Renault, 'De l'application du droit pénal aux faits de guerre', *Revue générale de droit international public* 25 (1918): 27).

[112]The assumption that a mistake of law cannot generally be recognized as the ground for immunization, especially outside of the ICC, would also be questioned. As already noted, the ambiguity of the laws of war that Oppenheim's *International Law* pointed out is not the problem restricted to the case of superior orders.

ICC Statute only with some rules on general principles of criminal law, such as that of the superior orders defense and command responsibility.

The position of Article 33 of the ICC Statute in customary international law would be said to be much influenced by the future operation of the ICC. It seems too early to evaluate its character as a general international rule at the present.

4.1.4 Conclusion

International rule-making on the superior orders defense seems to have attained a certain goal after a long period of confusion at the moment that the ICC Statute was concluded. However, it seems necessary to spare some more time to appraise the provision of the ICC Statute as a general rule of international law

During the drafting of the Genocide Convention and Additional Protocol I, there were opposing views first on whether or not automatic immunity should be recognized under the superior orders defense. Then, among those who denied automatic immunity, various views were further expressed with regard to the problems of the knowledge of illegality and coercion, that is, the problems of conditional immunity.

The ILC from the outset expressed its understanding that the Nuremberg Charter and Nuremberg Trial established some important rules in international criminal law. However, it could not put forth specific rules on the superior orders defense in its work of the Draft Code of Crimes against the Peace and Security of Mankind.

The ILC seriously considered the notion of moral choice that was presented by the IMT judgment. The Commission conditionally allowed the superior orders defense on the ground of this notion. It was in contrast to the drafting of the two international instruments mentioned above in which some delegates contended that even conditional immunity was too severe and asserted automatic immunity. However, the notion of moral choice could not easily be clarified by the ILC.

There was constant criticism at the ILC that the notion of moral choice was ambiguous. Nonetheless, the intention of the Special Rapporteur to specify the conditions of immunity was not reflected in the Draft Code. Draft Article 5, finally adopted in 1996, only provides that the fact of orders may be considered in the mitigation of punishment 'if justice so requires'. Meanwhile, Draft Article 14, which provides for 'Defences', only refers to 'the general principles of law' on the grounds of immunity and remains to shelve consideration of individual problems.

Different from these international rule-making processes, the ICC Statute would be said to have tentatively established a comprehensive rule on the superior orders defense. The Statute in Article 33 recognized the superior orders defense on the ground of a lack of the knowledge of illegality and a lack of manifest illegality. Further, on the issue of coercion, Article 31 provides for it as one of the general grounds for immunity. Nonetheless, it would not be appropriate to declare at the moment that these rules of the ICC Statute represent the general rules of international law.

Thus, in international rule-making after the trials under the Nuremberg Charter, two problems have hindered the establishment of rules on the superior orders defense: the position that denies the principle that was clearly presented at Nuremberg and the conflict of views on the remaining issues left ambiguous at those trials. The former, that is, the assertion of automatic immunity no longer surfaced at the work of the ILC as well as the drafting of the ICC Statute. However, the latter problem on conditional immunity has always been a major issue in a series of drafting processes of international instruments.

To begin with, the 'Nuremberg Principle' itself on the superior orders defense involved unstable factors. It originally meant absolute responsibility at least in terms of coercion but leaned to conditional immunity during the trials. In the international rule-making after the trials under the Nuremberg Charter, it may be said that such unstableness inherent in the 'Nuremberg Principle' has surfaced all over again.

However, such a character of the 'Nuremberg Principle' has not been reproduced exactly as it was. A swaying that appeared throughout the drafting of the Nuremberg Charter, the Nuremberg Trial, and the Subsequent Proceedings was that from absolute responsibility to conditional immunity. In contrast, in the subsequent international rule-making, the position of absolute responsibility has hardly come to the forefront. The detailed rules on conditional immunity have been consistently discussed.

At the drafting of the Genocide Convention, the Soviet delegate completely denied the superior orders defense initially. However, toward the end of the conference, he came to follow the others' arguments that construed his position as having supported conditional immunity. In the subsequent drafting processes of international instruments, the drafts that adopted conditional immunity in principle have usually been presented. In addition, such drafts have not been decisively criticized.

International rule-making after the trials under the Nuremberg Charter and the Subsequent Proceedings has basically succeeded the confusion that surfaced at those trials. However, the swaying of arguments that reappeared has not been so wide as compared to the case of those trials.

As discussed before, the change in the arguments that appeared under the Nuremberg Charter could be thought to have reflected a difference in the backgrounds of and prerequisites for the respective judicial fora. First, the Subsequent Proceedings indirectly applied the Nuremberg Charter, but they actually tried much inferior state organs as compared to the Nuremberg Trial. It was only natural that the issue of coercion was focused more in the Subsequent Proceedings. Second, the Subsequent Proceedings concluded almost 4 years after the end of World War II, whereas the Nuremberg Trial concluded about a year and a half after the war. With time, the Allied Powers became less enthusiastic for war crimes trials and its major interest moved to the reconstruction of international relations and economy. What appeared on the debates on the superior orders defense in those circumstances was the shift from absolute responsibility to conditional immunity.

From the Nuremberg Trial to the Subsequent Proceedings, the backgrounds of the trials thus significantly changed. The circumstances that have surrounded the rule-making process after the trials under the Nuremberg Charter are similar to those of the Subsequent Proceedings in every aspect. The expansion of personal jurisdiction and relative cool-down of international environment, which was observed at the Subsequent Proceedings, has accompanied the following international rule-making in a developed way.

The ILC, at the beginning of its work, summed up the war crimes trials after World War II by formulating the Nürnberg Principles. However, in the subsequent work on the Draft Code of Crimes against the Peace and Security of Mankind, it was aimed to provide for rules that should be generally applied. It was also the case with the drafting of the Geneva Conventions and Additional Protocol I. The personal jurisdiction of these instruments are not restricted to major war criminals and other high-ranking officials but reach every kind of war criminals, including soldiers at the front. It would be even more needed to squarely examine the problems of coercion, and the knowledge of illegality and/or manifest illegality, than the case of the Subsequent Proceedings.

In addition, international rule-making after the trials under the Nuremberg Charter has not been conducted as postwar administrative measures. What has been tackled is the establishment of rules that should generally be applied at the international society. Such legislative work, which does not restrict its personal jurisdiction in advance, would be expected to be even more objective compared to the case of the Subsequent Proceedings.

It would not directly be concluded that such resemblance between the backgrounds of international rule-making after the trials under the Nuremberg Charter and those of the Subsequent Proceedings prescribes the character of the former. Nonetheless, it is the case that the swaying of views in postwar rule-making has been narrowed in a manner close to that of the Subsequent Proceedings. This could be thought to have something to do with the fact that they resemble each other in their expansion of personal jurisdiction and estrangement from peculiar atmosphere just after the war.

4.2 Judicial Precedents

As seen in the previous section, a comprehensive agreement has not been reached on the superior orders defense in the rule-making process after the trials under the Nuremberg Charter. What has restrictively been contented is that automatic immunity cannot be allowed by the said defense. This situation of international consensus has influenced some national and international trials held after Nuremberg.

With respect to military trials, the judgments of trials are often not publicized or the reasons of the judgments are not given; therefore, it is difficult to generally survey the national judicial precedents that dealt with the issue of international rules on the superior orders defense. Further, at the international level, criminal proceedings by international tribunals had not been conducted after the trials under the Nuremberg Charter until the 1990s, and there has been only one international judicial precedent which directly treated this issue up to the present. However, it would be said that a variety of views on the superior orders defense in international law have already been reflected in some national or international judicial precedents which have drawn wide attention in the international society.

In this section, we will first look at the retroactive trials of Nazi war criminals which have been focused as war crimes trials in national courts. Then, the *Erdemović* judgment of the ICTY – only one international judicial precedent after the trials under the Nuremberg Charter that conducted an in-depth examination of the superior orders defense – will be seen. It is aimed at surveying the present situation of relevant precedents by comparing the views of those judicial organs.

With regard to the war crimes trials that were held by military tribunals or other judicial organs of the Allied Powers before or after the Nuremberg Trial, the report of the United Nations War Crimes Commission introduced their outline.[113] Quite a few Allies stipulated special national laws for war crimes prosecution. These national laws followed Article 8 of the Nuremberg Charter in basically denying the superior orders defense.[114] However, as far as one looks at the judicial precedents taken up in the report, most of the legal theories adopted by respective tribunals relied not on international law but on national criminal laws or provisions of the manuals of national military law.[115] This would be said to have reflected the fact that international rules on the superior orders defense had been ambiguous during the war.

4.2.1 National Cases

Nearly in concurrence with the trials under the Nuremberg Charter, the Allied Powers started war crimes trials at their national military tribunals or other judicial organs of their own countries. However, as East-West tensions were growing after the war and the position of West Germany in international relations was changing, those countries became less enthusiastic about continuing on with war crimes prosecution.[116]

In the 1980s, this situation changed once more. As the East-West relationship had improved to some extent, many official documents in the jurisdiction of the

[113] United Nations War Crimes Commission, *Law Reports of Trials of War Criminals* (London: HMSO, 1947–9), vols 1–15.

[114] *Ibid*, vol. 5, at 19–22.

[115] *Ibid.*, vol. 1, at 44,; *ibid.*, vol. 3, at 54–5; *ibid.*, vol. 13, at 114–7. However, many of the judgments of those tribunals did not specifically indicate the reasons for the decision. With regard to this point, see *ibid.*, vol. 15, at x–xi.

[116] See M. Lippman, 'The Pursuit of Nazi War Criminals in the United States and in Other Anglo-American Legal Systems', *California Western International Law Journal* 29 (1998): 15; F. Weinschenk, 'The Murderers among Them'– German Justice and the Nazis', *Hofstra Law & Policy Symposium* 3 (1999): 140–41.

East countries became accessible.[117] Then, it was newly informed that a considerable number of former Nazi war criminals had been entering West countries. The prosecution of Nazi war crimes was thus focused once more in some former Allies. The countries that took new legislative measures for the prosecution of Nazi war criminals included Canada, Australia, the United Kingdom, and France.[118] In Canada and Australia, the respective national courts showed their views on international rules on the superior orders defense at the stage of the application of their national laws at issue. These national precedents will be examined together with the well-known Israeli case in the 1960s.

4.2.1.1 Israel

The trial of Adolf Eichmann held in Israel in 1961 is one of the most famous cases of the trials of Nazi war criminals that have been grounded on newly provided national laws a long period after the end of World War II.[119] As head of the Gestapo Department, Eichmann directed the mass murder of Jews, the so-called final solution of the Jewish problem. [120] In 1960, he was abducted from Argentina by Israeli agents.[121] He was then prosecuted under the *Nazi and Nazi Collaborators (Punishment) Law* of 1950.

At Eichmann's trial, the question of conformity of the said Israeli law with international law was mainly argued. The issues of retroactive penal legislation, extraterritorial jurisdiction, the theory of the immunity of state acts, and several procedural problems were concretely discussed.[122] With regard to the superior orders defense, the Supreme Court of Israel argued this problem in terms of the theory of the immunity of state acts. The court delivered that Sections 8 and 11 of the *Nazi and Nazi Collaborators (Punishment) Law*, which denied the said defense, conformed to the 'Nuremberg Principle'.[123] This view of the court was based on its

---

[117]Lippman, supra n. 116, at 99.

[118]The prosecution of Nazi war criminals has widely been conducted in Germany, and more than 91,000 had been tried in West Germany by 1988 (*Le Monde*, 1 January 1988, at 3). However, the tribunals in West Germany applied German *Criminal Code* of 1871 and excluded the application of the Nuremberg Charter as well as the other relevant treaties concluded after World War II (Weinschenk, supra n. 116, at 144).

[119]With regard to the case of *Eichmann*, see M. Lippman, 'Genocide: The Trial of Adolf Eichmann and the Quest for Global Justice', *Buffalo Human Rights Law Review* 8 (2002): 45–120; D. Lasok, 'The Eichmann Trial', *International and Comparative Law Quarterly* 11 (1962): 355–74.

[120]'Summary', *Attorney-General of the Government of Israel v. Adolf Eichmann, International Law Reports* 36 (1968): 8.

[121]See *ibid.*, 5–7 for the details.

[122]Judgment (Supreme Court, 29 May 1962), *Attorney-General of the Government of Israel v. Adolf Eichmann,* supra n. 120, at 277–342.

[123]*Ibid.*, 313–9.

understanding that the Israeli law and the Nuremberg Charter both denied the superior orders defense for crimes of manifest illegality.

Meanwhile, on the problem of coercion incidental to superior orders, the judgment confined itself to pointing out that Section 11 of the Israeli law denied the coercion defense.[124] The Supreme Court delivered that there was room to construe that the IMT judgment had acknowledged the defense of 'constraint' or 'necessity'.[125] The court grounded its argument on the fact that the IMT judgment had presented the test of moral choice. However, the court did no more than imply such a possibility and avoided to show its conclusion on the IMT judgment. A further discussion on this problem might have led to the argument that the Israeli law conflicted with international rules. It could be said that the Supreme Court did not need to be particular about such a discussion.

4.2.1.2 Australia

In Australia, with a radio program that spotted the fact that many war criminals of World War II had entered the country, there was renewed focus on the issue of war crimes prosecution.[126] On the request of the Special Minister of State, the *Review of Material Relating to the Entry of Suspected War Criminals into Australia (Menzies Report)* was presented in 1987.[127] The report confirmed that a large number of suspects of serious war crimes had entered Australia after the end of the war. Corresponding to this report, the *War Crimes Amendment Act*, 1988,[128] was stipulated. This law provides for the prosecution of war crimes that were committed in Europe from 1 September 1939 to 8 May 1945. With respect to this Australian law, the issue of retroactive legislation, in particular, was discussed intensively.[129]

The first trial under the *War Crimes Amendment Act* was the *Polyukhovich* case. Ivan Polyukhovich was prosecuted on the counts of involvement in the mass murder of Jews in Ukraine during World War II.[130] At this trial, the problems of extraterritorial jurisdiction and retroactive legislation were mainly debated. In the

[124] *Ibid.*, 318.

[125] *Ibid.*

[126] Department of the Special Minister of State, *Review of Material Relating to the Entry of Suspected War Criminals into Australia* (Australian Government Publishing Service, 1987), 7.

[127] *Ibid.*

[128] *Acts of the Parliament – Commonwealth of Australia, 1989*, vol. 1, at 135.

[129] See J. Wagner, 'U.S. Prosecution of Past and Future War Criminals and Criminals against Humanity: Proposals for Reform Based on the Canadian and Australian Experience', *Virginia Journal of International Law* 29 (1989): 921–2.

[130] Regarding the case of *Polyukhovich*, see G. Triggs, 'Australia's War Crimes Trials: All Pity Choked', in T. McCormack & G. Simpson, *The Law of War Crimes, National and International Approaches* (Boston: Kluwer Law International, 1997), 130–32; Lippman, supra n. 116, at 40–44.

judgment of the High Court of Australia on this case, some judges referred to the superior orders defense in international law in the context of the problem of extraterritorial jurisdiction. Those judges respectively approved the legality of Section 16 of the *War Crimes Amendment Act*, which denies the superior orders defense. However, the grounds for their argument considerably varied.

There was an argument among the majority, including Toohey J., that Section 16 of the Act is generally in conformity with international rules.[131] Toohey J. construed that the said section did not provide for rules on the coercion defense. In contrast, Deane J. argued that Section 16 of the Act is different from relevant international rules.[132] Deane J. understood that international law during World War II had recognized the superior orders defense under certain conditions. Yet, he approved the legality of the Act by explaining that the Act newly stipulated common law crimes and its provision did not need to be in conformity with international law.[133]

The position of Brennan J. who objected to the majority on the problem of extraterritorial jurisdiction was not drastically different from those of other three judges on the superior orders defense. The argument of Brennan J. was similar to that of Deane J. in that they did not exclude the possibility that international law during the war had conditionally recognized the superior orders defense.[134] However, Brennan J. emphasized that international rules on the subject were ambiguous during the war. Thus, it became unnecessary for him to decide on the conformity of Section 16 of the Act with concurrent international rules.[135]

In the *Polyukhovich* case, various views were presented on the relationship between the *War Crimes Amendment Act* and international law. Those views shared a basic position of not denying the possibility of conditional immunity on the superior orders defense in international law during World War II. Even the dissenting opinion of Brennan J. was not the exception. However, Toohey J. and Brennan J. remained passive on this point as they underlined that international law during the war had been ambiguous. In addition, while Brennan J. mentioned a lack of manifest illegality and of *mens rea* (subjective element of crime) as what might be deemed to be immunizing factors, the other judges did not refer to these issues.

The judgment of the *Polyukhovich* case did not deny conditional immunity on the superior orders defense in international law during World War II. However, it did not present a unified and specific conclusion on this defense.

---

[131] *Polyukhovich v. The Commonwealth of Australia and Another* (High Court of Australia), (1991) 172 *Commonwealth Law Reports* 501, 682–4.

[132] *Ibid.*, 628.

[133] *Ibid.*, 628.

[134] *Ibid.*, 580–84.

[135] *Ibid.*, 584.

4.2.1.3 Canada

In Canada, with the incident in which a German suspect of war crimes who had been naturalized as a Canadian citizen was extradited to West Germany, a lively discussion went up on the prosecution of war criminals by Canadian judicial organs.[136] The Canadian government set up the Deschênes Commission of Inquiry on War Criminals in 1985.[137] In response to the report of the Commission, An *Act to Amend the Criminal Code, the Immigration Act, 1976 and the Citizenship Act*[138] was stipulated in 1987. The Act provides for the prosecution of persons who committed war crimes or crimes against humanity outside Canada. The first case of the application of the law of 1987 was the trial of *Finta.*[139] During the proceeding, the legality of the law of 1987 was discussed in relation to the problem of retroactive legislation on the pretrial motions at the Ontario High Court of Justice and the cross-appeal at the Supreme Court.[140]

Finta was indicted for crimes against humanity and war crimes with regard to his involvement in the persecution of Jews in Hungary during World War II.[141] He was charged with 'unlawful confinement, robbery, kidnapping and manslaughter', but he denied his responsibility in asserting that he had been ordered by the German SS.[142] At the trial, the jury decided that Finta was not guilty. The prosecution appealed to the Ontario Court of Appeal and the Supreme Court in disputing this decision of the jury.

The prosecution questioned whether the trial judge had appropriately directed the jury in making legal arguments relevant to the case.[143] The issue of international rules on the superior orders defense was discussed with regard to this question.

The prosecution argued that the superior orders defense was not allowed for crimes against humanity and war crimes under international law. It further questioned whether the definition of the superior orders defense given by the judge of the first chamber was appropriate.[144] The Supreme Court surveyed academic arguments and international as well as national judicial precedents until World

---

[136]L. Green, 'Canadian Law, War Crimes and Crimes against Humanity', *British Yearbook of International Law* 59 (1988): 220–21; Lippman, supra n. 116, at 20–22.

[137]Regarding the activities of the Commission, see Green, supra n. 136, at 221–7; Wagner, supra n. 129, at 927–30.

[138]*Statutes of Canada, 1987*, vol. 1, at 1105.

[139]Regarding the case of *Finta*, see I. Cotler, 'International Decision – *Regina v. Finta*', *American Journal of International Law* 90 (1996): 460–76; Lippman, supra n. 116, at 27–32.

[140]*R. v. Finta* (Ontario High Court of Justice), *Dominion Law Reports* 61 (1989): 85–126; *R. v. Finta* (Supreme Court of Canada), [1994] 1 S.C.R. 701, 863–77. Besides the problem of retroactive legislation, such issues as the extra-territorial jurisdiction, the definition of the crime, and the procedural rules were also discussed.

[141]*R. v. Finta* (Ontario High Court of Justice), 85, 91–2.

[142]*R. v. Finta* (Supreme Court of Canada), 793.

[143]Ibid., 704–5.

[144]Ibid., 826–7.

War II and decided that the said defense was allowed for crimes against humanity and war crimes, thus dismissing the contention of the prosecution.[145]

With regard to detailed rules on the superior orders defense, the court consulted academic discussions and state practice and then delivered that conditional immunity could be recognized on the test of manifest illegality.[146] The court went on to denote that immunity on the ground of coercion or necessity could also be recognized with regard to the superior orders defense as the IMT had presented the test of moral choice.[147] This is a position that even if the illegality of criminal conduct was manifest, immunity under the superior orders defense may be recognized in the case that moral choice was not possible for the doer of the conduct because of coercion.

The Supreme Court of Canada thus held in the *Finta* case that conditional immunity under the superior orders defense was recognized in international law. The judgment clearly expressed its position on the problems that had been shelved in international rule-making up to that time. At this point, the *Finta* judgment contrasts with the *Polyukhovich* judgment which did not show a unified and conclusive decision on whether or not immunity should be approved. Furthermore, the judgment of the Supreme Court of Canada was more enterprising as compared to the other relevant precedents in that it concretely raised the immunizing factors such as manifest illegality and coercion.

The *Finta* judgment specifically expressed its position on the question of conditional immunity that has not been resolved since the Nuremberg Trial. Since then, the judgment has been evaluated as an important judicial precedent in international criminal law. However, this does not necessarily mean that the *Finta* judgment has directly been reflected in the subsequent judicial precedents as a leading case. In fact, the ICTY judgment, which we will discuss next, delivered a very opposite decision to that of *Finta* on the question of coercion incidental to superior orders.

4.2.2 The Erdemović *Judgment of ICTY Appeals Chamber*

4.2.2.1 The Majority View and 'Policy Consideration'

The appellant Dražen Erdemović, having been transferred from the Federal Republic of Yugoslavia, was indicted at the ICTY on the count of participating in the execution of around 1,200 unarmed Muslims.[148] On the guilty plea by the accused, the Trial Chamber convicted him with a 10-year imprisonment on the count of

---

[145] Ibid., 828–43.

[146] Ibid., 828–36.

[147] Ibid., 836–8.

[148] Judgment, *Prosecutor v. Dražen Erdemović*, IT-96-22-A (7 October 1997), 2–4.

crimes against humanity. Erdemović appealed and asked for a revision of this judgment.[149]

The appellant demanded immunity or mitigation of punishment on the ground that, among others, the Trial Chamber committed errors of fact by failing to give due consideration to the fact that the appellant had conducted the acts under 'duress' or to the mental condition of the appellant.[150] The prosecution responded that the Trial Chamber had a wide range of discretion on its assessment of the evidence and emphasized that the appellant had had moral choice at the time of the criminal conduct. The prosecution contended that a 10-year prison sentence was not inappropriate.[151]

The Appeals Chamber eventually remitted the case to the Trial Chamber. The reasons for the remittance were that the appellant had not understood that he would lose his right to be tried as a consequence of his guilty plea and that he would receive a severer sentence by admitting to have committed crimes against humanity rather than war crimes.[152] However, the examination of the Appeals Chamber was not restricted to whether or not the appellant had understood the consequence of his guilty plea. The Appeals Chamber further examined the problem of whether the guilty plea of the appellant had been decisive from an objective point of view.

In entering a guilty plea, Erdemović stated that he had been under duress at the time of his criminal conduct. If duress could be admitted as a complete defense, his guilty plea at the Trial Chamber could substantially involve a contention of not guilty irrelevant to his own intention. In other words, Erdemović's guilty plea would be construed as comprising indefinite factors.[153] However, the Appeals Chamber judged that duress, which the appellant had contended at his guilty plea, could not be a complete defense. The court then delivered that the guilty plea had been unequivocal.[154] This is the point to be noted in relation to the debates on the superior orders defense.

The judgment defined the superior orders defense as separate from the defense of duress. It then showed its view that obedience to superior orders was only the fact that should be consulted in considering the defense of duress or mistake of fact.[155] This position was different from that of Article 8 of the Nuremberg Charter. As was seen in the previous chapter, the Nuremberg Charter provided the principle of absolute responsibility under the superior orders defense, denying immunity while considering the factors of coercion and possibly the knowledge of illegality and/or manifest illegality. However, it would not substantially be different whether

[149]Ibid., 2.

[150]Ibid., 9–11.

[151]Ibid., 11–13.

[152]Ibid., 16–8; Joint Separate Opinion of Judge McDonald and Judge Vohrah, ibid., 10–22, 76.

[153]Judgment, ibid., 15.

[154]Ibid., 16. The judgment refers to the Joint Separate Opinion of Judge McDonald and Judge Vorah (ibid., 22–76) on this point.

[155]Ibid., 25.

one discusses cumulative facts of superior orders and coercion as a problem of the coercion defense or of the superior orders defense. In any event, it is the coercion incidental to superior orders that is to be examined. The question of which defenses should be connected with the examination of the fact of coercion would be converged on the definition of the term the 'superior orders defense' and not more than that.

The judgment decided that customary international law had not been established with regard to whether or not duress could be a complete defense for the case of killing innocent people.[156] The test of moral choice presented by the IMT judgment was deemed to be ambiguous. The Appeals Chamber also evaluated the *Einsatzgruppen* judgment of the US Military Tribunal which recognized the coercion defense as groundless. The point was that the US Military Tribunal had applied US national laws in judging the case.[157] Further, the 'general principles of law recognized by civilised nations' could not be found on this issue.[158] The majority of the Appeals Chamber eventually focused on two factors: the role of international criminal law as a norm and the specific character of the crime in question.

The United Kingdom and other countries which inherited the common law tradition, widely denied the defense of duress on the ground of practical 'policy consideration' for the regulation of crimes.[159] As the International Tribunal treated the most heinous crimes as war crimes and crimes against humanity committed during armed conflicts, it was natural not to recognize the defense of duress.[160] This was the argument of the majority of the Appeals Chamber. Thus, the judgment attached importance to policy consideration and tried to fill the gap in relevant international rules. According to the judgment, the policy consideration of the tribunal relates to its concern 'to facilitate the development and effectiveness of international humanitarian law and to promote its aims and application by recognising the normative effect which criminal law should have upon those subject to them'.[161]

The majority expected such a criticism that crimes such as murder had not necessarily occurred much more outside of common law jurisdictions. In answering such

---

[156]Ibid., 29–38. The judgment also refers to the Separate and Dissenting Opinion of Judge Li (ibid., 2) on this point (Judgment, ibid., 16).

[157]Joint Separate Opinion of Judge McDonald and Judge Vohrah, ibid., 30–38. However, as was seen in Sect. 3.3, the US military tribunals specifically applied the Nuremberg Charter *via* the CCL No. 10. If those tribunals referred to US national laws in their judgments, it would be appropriate to construe that they were consulted only in a complementary manner.

[158]Ibid., 38–63; Separate and Dissenting Opinion of Judge Li, ibid., 2–3.

[159]Joint Separate Opinion of Judge McDonald and Judge Vohrah, ibid., 64–7. Regarding this point, Judge Stephen argued that the principles of the common law have not denied the defense of duress for the case of 'either death for one or death for both', that is, the case where the accused has no moral choice (Separate and Dissenting Opinion of Judge Stephen, ibid., at 12–30).

[160]Judgment, ibid., 16; Joint Separate Opinion of Judge McDonald and Judge Vohrah, ibid., 65–6.

[161]Ibid., 66.

criticism, the majority held a joint separate opinion of Judge Gabrielle McDonald and Judge Lal Vohrah who pointed out the specific character of armed conflicts at the international level:

> We are concerned primarily with armed conflict in which civilian lives, the lives of the most vulnerable, are at great risk. Historical records, past and recent, concerned with armed conflict give countless examples of threats being brought to bear upon combatants by their superiors when confronted with any show of reluctance or refusal on the part of the combatants to carry out orders to perform acts which are in clear breach of international humanitarian law. It cannot be denied that in an armed conflict, the frequency of situations in which persons are forced under duress to commit crimes and the magnitude of the crimes they are forced to commit are far greater than in any peacetime domestic environment.[162]

Thus, the judgment clearly expressed its idea to rely on policy consideration. What the majority emphasized on discussing policy consideration was the close relationship between law and social policy. Stating that '[i]t would be naive to believe that international law operates and develops wholly divorced from considerations of social and economic policy', the majority quoted the following arguments of Rosalyn Higgins:

> Reference to the 'correct legal view' or 'rules' can never avoid the element of choice (though it can seek to disguise it), nor can it provide guidance to the preferable decision. In making this choice one must inevitably have consideration for the humanitarian, moral, and social purposes of the law ... Where there is ambiguity or uncertainty, the policy-directed choice can properly be made.[163]

Higgins' *Problems and Process: International Law and How We Use It*, which the majority relied on, construes law as a 'continuing process of authoritative decisions' that should flexibly correspond to the ever-changing political world.[164] What should be attended to in understanding international law as a 'process' is values and aims behind the law. The realization of such values and aims is recognized as key for the interpretation of concurrent rules of international law.[165]

However, a slack interpretation of law in light of the values and aims would bring about various conclusions. The 'aim' of international criminal law, which the majority showed, was 'to facilitate the development and effectiveness of international humanitarian law and to promote its aims and application' by recognizing its normative effect. Then, what is the measure to attain such an aim? The answer would not be led as simply as the judgment did. We will return to this point later.

---

[162]Ibid., 66–7.

[163]Ibid., 68.

[164]R. Higgins, *Problems and Process: International Law and How We Use It* (Oxford: Clarendon Press, 1994), 2.

[165]*Ibid.*, 1–12.

4.2.2.2 Dissenting Opinion of Judge Cassese

It was the Presiding Judge, Antonio Cassese, who severely criticized the majority's idea to rely on policy consideration, which was mainly based on the notion of common law.[166] His dissenting opinion rejected the policy consideration of the majority as 'extraneous to the task of our Tribunal'.[167] Judge Cassese stated as follows on the function of the International Tribunal:

> This International Tribunal is called upon to apply international law, in particular our Statute and principles and rules of international humanitarian law and international criminal law. Our International Tribunal is a court of law; it is bound only by international law. It should therefore refrain from engaging in meta-legal analyses. In addition, it should refrain from relying exclusively on notions, policy considerations or the philosophical underpinnings of common-law countries, while disregarding those of civil-law countries or other systems of law. What is even more important, a policy-oriented approach in the area of criminal law runs contrary to the fundamental customary principle *nullum crimen sine lege*. On the strength of international principles and rules my conclusions on duress differ widely from those of the majority of the Appeals Chamber.[168]

This criticism has been shared among many commentators who analyzed the *Erdemović* judgment of the Appeals Chamber. For instance, Mohamed Shahabuddeen pointed out that the ICTY Statute implies that the tribunal shall apply customary international law and general principles of law, so that the application of policy consideration transcended the competence of the tribunal.[169] David Turns criticized that the judgment showed a partial inclination to common law and its reasoning was too sweeping.[170]

By examining the 'principles and rules of international humanitarian law and international criminal law', Judge Cassese concluded that duress could be a defense under severe conditions in international criminal law.[171] He argued that the special rules of customary international law had not been developed on this problem with regard to war crimes and crimes against humanity such that 'the general rule on duress' should be applied for the case.[172] He raised the following conditions under which the defense of duress could be established: (1) there was an immediate threat

---

[166] Separate and Dissenting Opinion of Judge Cassese, *Prosecutor v. Dražen Erdemović*, IT-96-22-A (7 October 1997).

[167] Ibid., 13.

[168] Ibid., 13–14.

[169] M. Shahabuddeen, 'Duress in International Humanitarian Law', in C. Barea et al., *Liber Amicorum 'In Memoriam' of Judge José María Ruda* (The Hague; London: Kluwer Law International, 2000), 565–6.

[170] D. Turns, 'The International Criminal Tribunal for the Former Yugoslavia: The *Erdemović* Case', *International and Comparative Law Quarterly* 47 (1998): 471–2.

[171] Separate and Dissenting Opinion of Judge Cassese, *Prosecutor v. Dražen Erdemović*, IT-96-22-A (7 October 1997), 14.

[172] Ibid.

of serious harm to life or limb, (2) there was no means to avert such evil, (3) the crime was not disproportionate to such evil, and (4) the accused did not voluntarily bring about the situation leading to duress.[173] The condition of proportionality would not usually be fulfilled for crimes as murder, but the defense might be established in taking into consideration some exceptional circumstances.[174] On the ground of these arguments, Judge Cassese contended to remit the case and direct the Trial Chamber to enter a not-guilty plea.[175]

'The general rule on duress' that Judge Cassese mentioned was guided from national judicial precedents of continental law countries such as Italy and Germany.[176] He, on the other hand, pointed out that some national precedents of common law countries stood in opposition to it.[177] If so, it would be problematic to deem the trend shown in some judicial precedents of continental law countries to be the 'customary rule of international law on duress'[178] or 'a general rule on duress'.[179]

In addition, the notion of policy consideration that Judge Cassese regarded as questionable relates to the problem of recognizing or understanding international law. Commentators who pursue the strict application of the principle of specificity in international criminal law would exclude the notion of policy consideration from the viewpoint of strict legality,[180] which consists of the prohibition of *ex post facto* law, the prohibition of analogies, and so forth. On the other hand, those who attach greater importance to the fact that international criminal law has been underdeveloped and ambiguous in considerable parts would not *a priori* deny the usefulness of the notion of policy consideration. Actually, the principle of specificity in international criminal law has been laxer than that of the national laws of continental law countries, which allows the application of customary international law and general principles of law.[181] If the notion of policy consideration – however arguable it would be – has been functioning in the criminal laws of common law countries, it

---

[173]Ibid., 16.

[174]Ibid., 14. See also R. Merkel, 'Gründe für den Ausschluss der Strafbarkeit im Völkerstrafrecht', *Zeitschrift für die Gesamte Strafrechtswissenschaft* 114 (2002): 448–54. Meanwhile, there is also criticism which deems it problematic to apply the principle of proportionality to the case where the lives of both the accused and the victims matter. See Bowers, supra n. 110, at 31–72.

[175]Separate and Dissenting Opinion of Judge Cassese, *Prosecutor v. Dražen Erdemović*, IT-96-22-A (1997), 14.

[176]Ibid., 30–44.

[177]Ibid., 19–30, 45.

[178]Ibid., 49.

[179]Ibid., 45–6.

[180]A. Cassese, *International Criminal Law*, 2nd ed. (Oxford; New York: Oxford University Press, 2008), 36–41.

[181]M. Bassiouni, 'Universal Jurisdiction for International Crimes: Historical Perspectives and Contemporary Practice', *Virginia Journal of International Law* 42 (2001): 105; Cassese, supra n. 180, at 41–3.

would not be so easy to categorically deny the possibility of its application at the international level.

4.2.2.3 International Rule-Making and the Judgment

Nonetheless, even if one supports the position to rely on policy consideration, the argument of the majority still appears to be problematic. The majority underlined the general aim of the tribunal to regulate heinous crimes and to facilitate the development of international humanitarian law and concretely delivered its judgment on the fundamental principles of criminal law. Actually, there have not been specific international rules on the coercion defense. However, it is also the case that the possibility of conditional immunity on the ground of coercion has consistently been attended to throughout the discussions on the superior orders defense up to the present. Whether or not to rely on policy consideration, it would not be appropriate to completely defy this fact.

The Appeals Chamber delivered its judgment on the *Erdemović* case in 1997. It may not be proper, in trying to evaluate the judgment, to refer to the ICC Statute of 1998 which recognizes the defense of duress in principle. However, it was also confirmed in the previous sections that there emerged the swaying from absolute responsibility to conditional immunity at the trials under the Nuremberg Charter and that such confusion has consistently been reflected on the following international rule-making. Furthermore, at the national level, there has appeared a well-known national precedent which specifically approved conditional immunity. These facts as such seem to be enough to impair the persuasiveness of the *Erdemović* judgment.

The Appeals Chamber thoroughly denied the possibility of immunity by the defense of duress only by referring to the general guidepost of 'the development and effectiveness of international humanitarian law'. If the majority minded the implication of the unstableness which has surfaced over the provision of the Nuremberg Charter, the reasoning at the Appeals Chamber would not have been made so simple.

The fact that the accused had been involved in the illegal execution of more than a thousand civilians[182] might have more than completely excluded the effect of the defense of duress. Nonetheless, such a decision itself would be made on the individual examination of respective cases. It is different from denying the defense of duress generally for crimes of killing civilians.

The superior orders defense had, before the establishment of the Nuremberg Charter, been recognized under some conditions in the national legal systems of most of the countries that drafted the Charter. These drafting countries did not take note of this fact and tried to introduce the principle of absolute responsibility at the

---

[182]The appellant was judged responsible for the execution of 10–100 of those civilians (*Prosecutor v. Dražen Erdemović*, Judgment, IT-96-22-A (7 October 1997), 7).

London Conference. The principal driving force was a sense of crisis that a combination of the superior orders defense and the theory of the immunity of state acts would make war crimes trials impossible. This sense that was expressed, for instance, by the US delegate Jackson during the London Conference was shared by many academic arguments at the time. They relied on the abstract notions of the 'great principle of natural justice', 'spirit of justice', and 'sound legal principle', or confined themselves to emphasizing an overriding necessity to avoid the impossibility of trials. These arguments could be said to have reflected the impact that had been given by the two world wars.

The Appeals Chamber of the ICTY consciously separated the superior orders defense from the defense of duress. Consequently, it did not make an argument in a manner to automatically deny the latter by denying the former. The ICTY's view was different from that of the drafting countries of the Nuremberg Charter at this point. However, the Appeals Chamber did not pay attention to the position that the issue of duress (coercion) had held in the debates on the superior orders defense. Its judgment relied on policy consideration guided from the aim of the tribunal to develop the international humanitarian law and generally denied immunity on the ground of duress for the conduct in question. In light of the fact that academic arguments after the Nuremberg Trial also have not been conclusive on the issue of coercion in terms of superior orders as will be seen next, the hasty look of the judgment would appear even more conspicuously.

What can commonly be observed on the drafting process of Article 8 of the Nuremberg Charter and the *Erdemović* judgment of the ICTY Appeals Chamber is a lack of concrete theory on individual criminal responsibility. In respective cases, the consideration for the necessity of punishment or the general notion of 'the development and effectiveness of international humanitarian law' came to the forefront. The measures of realizing these notions would be varied depending on the discussants. The best way of their realization could not automatically be guided by themselves. Nonetheless, the drafters of the Nuremberg Charter intended to introduce absolute responsibility without consulting the concrete theories of criminal law. The ICTY judgment denied the defense of duress in a similar manner.

Why did the delegates of the Allied Powers and the judges of the ICTY make such a decision? The Nuremberg Trial had an aspect of 'victor's justice' as often said. In contrast, the ICTY, which was established by the Security Council resolution to try international crimes during civil war, does not have such a character. The proceedings at the ICTY have, at least formally, been conducted from a neutral point of view as has been the case with international rule-making held around the United Nations.

However, what should be noted is that the ad hoc tribunals established by the Security Council resolutions had been operating to contribute to settle the ongoing disputes. At this point, the background of those tribunals was considerably different from that of postwar international rule-making. In particular, with regard to the case of the former Yugoslavia, it has often been criticized that the actions taken by the United Nations were one step behind. The expectation for the operations of the International Tribunal, including its function to counterbalance such a criticism, was even more enhanced.[183] It may be said that the IMT and ICTY possess the same kind of features in that they were urged to deal with serious international crimes that had actually been committed. It might be said that this feature would have much influenced the judgments of those institutions.

The debates on the superior orders defense have thrown into relief a tension between international and national legal orders as well as various problems relevant to such a tension. Since the end of World War II, the international society has always 'hesitated' to adopt the principle of absolute responsibility. The fact would not bring about a specific answer to the problem of the superior orders defense. However, it could be thought to have certain significance as the case relevant to the law.

The ICTY judgment intended to defy this case for the sake of 'the development and effectiveness of international humanitarian law'. What is to be reminded here is that the drafting countries of the Nuremberg Charter tried to introduce the principle of absolute responsibility without reflecting on the trend of the national legal systems of their own countries. It might be said that the ICTY judgment bears in common its peculiar character with such decision of the drafters of the Nuremberg Charter in some important aspects.

4.3 Academic Arguments

As seen above, the legal consequence of the superior orders defense cannot be specified by examining international rule-making after the trials under the Nuremberg Charter as well as some national judicial precedents that applied international law on this issue. Still, at least conditional immunity has always been discussed as one of the possibilities. The judgment of the ICTY Appeals Chamber that denied conditional immunity has been an exception in these circumstances.

The principle of conditional immunity has more positively been held in academic arguments after the Nuremberg Trial.

Until the Nuremberg Trial, some influential commentators such as Wright and Kelsen supported automatic immunity under the superior orders defense. However, such an argument has seldom been seen after the Nuremberg Trial.[184] The principle of the 'denial of automatic immunity', which was specifically presented at the Nuremberg Trial, can be said to have received a stable evaluation both in state practice and academic arguments as a whole.

---

[183]See McCormack & Simpson, supra n. 130, at 24; R. Brooks, 'Law in the Heart of Darkness: Atrocity & Duress', *Virginia Journal of International Law* 43 (2003): 883–5.

[184]For instance, Schick recognized automatic immunity on the ground of the theory of the 'immunity of state acts' (F. Schick, 'War Criminals and the Law of the United Nations', *University of Toronto Law Journal* 7 (1947–8): 45–51). See also P. Boissier, *Völkerrecht und Militärbefehl* (Stuttgart: K. F. Koehler Verlag Stuttgart, 1953), 30–52.

Meanwhile, there have been few commentators who clearly support the principle of absolute responsibility, which denies immunity even in considering any factors incidental to superior orders such as coercion, the knowledge of illegality and/or manifest illegality, and the possibility of moral choice. For example, Rosa Brooks states regarding the *Erdemović* judgment of the ICTY Appeals Chamber that 'when push comes to shove there seems to be an "absolute moral postulate["] that says that killing innocent people in order to save one[']s own life is always wrong' and denies the defense of duress.[185] There have been some other articles indicating that 'the superior orders defense cannot be recognized'. However, they do not necessarily specify the realm of their discussion such that it is not clear whether they only deny automatic immunity or also conditional immunity.[186] In addition, some commentators such as Arthur Goodhart and Whitney Harris used the expression that the superior orders defense is 'not recognised' or that 'individuals may be held accountable' for crimes executing superior orders and yet substantially held conditional immunity by showing some conditions for the recognition of the said defense.[187]

The principle of conditional immunity has specifically been held by many commentators after the Nuremberg Trial as well as before it. Most of these commentators recognize the knowledge of illegality and/or manifest illegality as the tests of immunization. They deem that a lack of the knowledge of illegality and/or a lack of manifest illegality disapprove the subjective elements of crime and consequently deny the establishment of crime.

For instance, James Insco argues that the accused does not have *mens rea* necessary for the establishment of crime if the illegality was not manifest. He states that if one makes manifest illegality a test of immunization, a balance between 'the supremacy of the law' and 'military discipline' would be kept.[188] Ian D. Brownlee argues that such an understanding is most appropriate considering the interests of justice both for soldiers and the civil society.[189] The position of John Starke is also in accord with these arguments, which holds that a problem of subjective elements

---

[185]Brooks does not refer to the issue of the knowledge of illegality nor manifest illegality as she does not generally discuss the superior orders defense. Brooks, supra n. 183, at 880, 885.

[186]For instance, G. Finch, 'The Nuremberg Trial and International Law', *American Journal of International Law* 41 (1947): 21; M. Merle, *Le procés de Nuremberg et le chatiment des criminels de guerre* (Paris: Editions a. pedone, 1949), 98–9.

[187]A. Goodhart, 'Questions and Answers Concerning the Nuremberg Trials', *International Law Quarterly* 1 (1947): 527–8; W. Harris, *Tyranny on Trial, The Evidence at Nuremberg* (Dallas: Southern Methodist University Press, 1954), 557–8; R. Woetzel, *The Nuremberg Trials in International Law with a Postlude on the Eichmann Case* (London: Stevens & Sons Limited, 1962), 118–9.

[188]J. Insco, 'Defense of Superior Orders before Military Commissions', *Duke Journal of Comparative & International Law* 13 (2003): 398–9.

[189]I. D. Brownlee, 'Superior Orders - Time for a New Realism?', *Criminal Law Review* (1989): 410–11.

is significant 'just as in ordinary criminal law' with regard to the factors of the knowledge of illegality and manifest illegality.[190]

However, as mentioned before, manifest illegality itself is not generally recognized as a test of immunization. Further, especially in common law countries, a mistake of law cannot be deemed a defense. Therefore, it would be necessary to raise some other grounds besides the notion of subjective elements of crime. It might be possible, as Insco argued, to approve immunity on the ground of a lack of the knowledge of illegality and/or a lack of manifest illegality, especially for the case of superior orders, by emphasizing the importance of military discipline. Further, it might be thinkable to strengthen that military discipline more or less always brings about coercion. As already noted, it would be inappropriate to abstractedly understand a factor of coercion and recognize automatic immunity. Nonetheless, it might be possible to construe that whatever coercion which is caused by military discipline combines with a lack of the knowledge of illegality and/or a lack of manifest illegality, and leads to a multiplier effect of immunization.

Commentators who specifically refer to coercion as an immunizing ground have been comparatively restricted among those who approve immunity on the ground of a lack of the knowledge of illegality and/or a lack of manifest illegality. Stephan Glaser,[191] Dinstein,[192] Jescheck,[193] and Röling[194] are such discussants.[195]

---

[190]J. Starke, *Introduction to International Law*, 10th ed. (London: Butterworths, 1989), 557. Other arguments that recognize immunity on the ground of a lack of the knowledge of illegality and/or manifest illegality include H. Weber, 'Die Strafrechtliche Verantwortlichkeit für Handeln auf Befehl', *Monatsschrift für Deutsches Recht* 2 (1948): 37–8; T. Würtenberger, 'Der Irrtum über die Völkerrehtsmäßigkeit des höheren Befehls im Strafrecht', *ibid.*, 271–3. See also the literature cited in note 191–5 of this chapter. Ambos recognizes immunity on the test of manifest illegality except war crimes and crimes against humanity (K. Ambos, 'Zur Strafbefreienden Wirkung des "Handelns auf Befehl" aus Deutscher und völkerstrafrechtlicher Sicht', *Juristische Rundschau* 6 (1998): 224–6.

[191]S. Glaser, *Introduction a l'étude du droit international pénal* (Paris: Sirey, 1954), 111–31.

[192]Dinstein, supra n. 1, at 87–90.

[193]H. Jescheck, *Die Verantwortlichkeit der Staatsorgane nach Völkerstrafrecht – Eine Studie zu den Nürnberger Prozessen –* (Bonn: Ludwig Röhrscheid Verlag, 1952), 255–68.

[194]B. Röling, B. (ed. by A. Cassese), *The Tokyo Trial and Beyond, Reflections of a Peacemonger* (Cambridge: Polity Press, 1993), 109–110.

[195]See also G. Scelle, *Manuel de droit international public* (Paris: Editions domat-montcrrestien, 1948), 984–5; C. Eustathiades, 'Quelques aspects de la jurisprudence concernants les criminels de guerre: L'exception des ordres reçus et autres moyens de défense similaires', in D. Constantopoulos & H. Wehberg, *Gegenwartsprobleme des internationalen rechtes und der rechtsphilosophie: Festschrift für Rudolf Laun zu Seinem Siebzigsten Geburtstag* (Hamburg: Girardet & Co., 1953), 395–421; J. Rocca, 'Superior Orders as a Qualified Defense in International Law', in H. Miehsler et al., *Ius Humanitatis – Festschrift zum 90. Geburtstag von Alfred Verdross* (Berlin: Duncker & Humblot, 1980), 624; M. McDougal & F. Feliciano, *The International Law of War, Transnational Coercion and World Public Order* (Dordrecht: Martinus Nijhoff Pulishers, 1994), 691–4; J. Grayson, 'The Defence of Superior Orders in the International Criminal Court', *Nordic Journal of International Law* 64 (1995): 244–5, 252; Ambos, supra n. 190, at 225–6; K. Kittichaisaree, *International Criminal Law* (New York; London: Oxford University Press, 2001), 266–8.

For example, Glaser contended the validity of the two notions of the French *Penal Code*: moral constraint (*contrainte morale*), which recognizes the nonculpability (*non-culpabilité*) of the person who received orders on the ground that he/she was under pressure and the state of necessity (*l'état de nécessité*), which recognizes the person to sacrifice the interests of the third party for the sake of his/her own interest.[196] An example of the latter is the case in which a life of the person who received orders would be in peril as a consequence of disobedience.[197]

Jescheck also contended that immunity should be allowed if a state of necessity (*notstand*) had been brought about as a consequence of coercion under which the person who had received orders had been put.[198] This is an idea that the responsibility of subordinates should be denied as a legal conduct cannot be expected for them under the coercion by the government.[199] Consulting the national criminal laws of Germany, France, the United Kingdom, and the United States, Jescheck raised the following conditions under which *notstand* would be recognized: (1) a peril on the person who received orders was urgent and unavoidable, (2) legal interest that was in peril should be restricted to that of life and freedom of the person who received orders, (3) the proportionality of legal interest should severely be examined, (4) an intention of crime should have been brought about at the same time as the state of coercion emerged, and (5) an obligation of the person who received orders to endure certain perils in the line of duty (for example, perils as a consequence of being involved with the army) should be taken into consideration.[200]

Thus, the arguments that recognize immunity on the ground of coercion with specific reasons have been made mainly by those of continental law countries. They have based their discussions mainly on the theories of criminal laws of their own countries. Those who support the coercion defense have also included those of common law countries, but they have confined themselves to making a simple account and have not shown specific reasons for immunity. This would have something to do with the fact that common law has not recognized the coercion defense for serious crimes such as murder.

Meanwhile, there have also been some commentators who clearly deny immunity on the ground of coercion while supporting conditional immunity on the tests of the knowledge of illegality and/or manifest illegality. For instance, Morris Greenspan argues that moral choice is possible between a peril including capital punishment that would be caused by disobedience and another peril that would be brought about to the innocent third party.[201] Therefore, 'no man can excusably

---

[196] Glaser, supra n. 191, at 112–3, 124–6.

[197] *Ibid.*, 113.

[198] Jescheck, supra n. 193, at 261, 262–3, 268.

[199] *Ibid.*, 262–3.

[200] *Ibid.*, 262–8.

[201] M. Greenspan, *The Modern Law of Land Warfare* (Los Angeles: University of California Press, 1959), 494.

take the life of an innocent person in order to preserve his own'.[202] Christopher Blakesley also states that only the mitigation of punishment should be allowed on the ground of coercion for crimes such as murder.[203] Commentators such as Goodhart and Harris specifically denied the coercion defense but stayed ambiguous on the issues of the knowledge of illegality and/or manifest illegality.[204]

These arguments that do not approve immunity on the ground of coercion would be criticized from the viewpoint of the function and aim of criminal law. For instance, Shahabuddeen criticizes the *Erdemović* judgment of the ICTY Appeals Chamber from the viewpoint of the deterring function of criminal law.[205] He emphasizes that it is not in conformity with the notion of reasonableness to press a person to choose his/her own death rather than the death of innocent civilians.[206] Although the tribunal is responsible for warning on the legal consequences of violations, this warning should be reasonable. Otherwise, he argues, a general reaction to the tribunal would remain a certain level of distrust.[207] Actually, it would be difficult to expect the effect of deterrence by severely prosecuting those who conducted criminal act under coercion. Further, it would not be proper, from the viewpoint of retribution, to positively support responsibility for the person whose blameworthiness is questionable.

However, this position would sharply conflict with the other that, although recognizing the unreasonableness of such responsibility, still tries to keep 'absolute moral postulate'[208] not to kill innocent people. Brooks supports this latter position that the ICTY Appeals Chamber also held in the *Erdemović* case.[209] Brooks acknowledges that it cannot reasonably be expected for someone to sacrifice his/her own life in exchange for the lives of other people.[210] However, she points out that an essential problem is that international humanitarian law has been constructed on an optimistic 'belief in the ability of reason to prevail over violence and terror'.[211] Having said so, she concludes that a denial of the coercion defense could assume more reasonableness if one takes into consideration the process in which the person who was eventually coerced to conduct an illegal act ends up with such a result with various choices of his/her own.[212] Not all of those who appeal to

[202] *Ibid.*

[203] C. Blakesley, 'Atrocity and Its Prosecution: The Ad Hoc Tribunals for the Former Yugoslavia and Rwanda', in McCormack & Simpson, supra n. 130, at 220.

[204] Goodhart, supra n. 187, at 527–8; Harris, supra n. 187, at 557–8.

[205] Shahabuddeen, supra n. 169, at 571–3.

[206] *Ibid.*, 573.

[207] *Ibid.*

[208] Joint Separate Opinion of Judge McDonald and Judge Vohrah, *Prosecutor v. Dražen Erdemović*, IT-96-22-A (7 October 1997), 73.

[209] Brooks, supra n. 183, at 861–88.

[210] Brooks deems the common law rule which precludes the coercion defense to charges of homicide as even 'anomalous' (*ibid.*, 873).

[211] *Ibid.*, 861.

[212] *Ibid.*, 888.

the coercion defense would have driven themselves to the fatal situations by their own (mistake of) choices. However, in any event, any theory that approves immunity on the ground of coercion could not fully be persuasive in the face of such an argument that underlines the 'absolute moral postulate' of not killing innocent people. It seems difficult to support either a position to approve the coercion defense or another to deny the defense with some decisive arguments.

Thus, conditional immunity has widely been held in academic arguments after the Nuremberg Trial. This is in contrast with the fact that conditional immunity has neither been supported nor denied in a decisive manner in international rule-making. Most of those academic arguments that support conditional immunity have commonly approved immunity on the test of the knowledge of illegality and/or manifest illegality. On the other hand, those who approve immunity clearly on the ground of coercion have comparatively been limited. In addition, there are many who completely deny immunity by the coercion defense.

Throughout the process from the drafting of the Nuremberg Charter to the Subsequent Proceedings, it was the problem of coercion incidental to orders that showed the most serious fluctuation with regard to the debates on the superior orders defense. This factor of unstableness, which surfaced at the trials conducted under the Nuremberg Charter, could be said to have been reflected in the subsequent academic arguments exactly as it was.

Chapter 5
Change of the Structure of International Legal Order and 'Hesitation'

Abstract 'The denial of automatic immunity' specifically presented by the 'Nuremberg Principle' has generally been supported since the Nuremberg Trial. Meanwhile, with respect to the problem of conditional responsibility, the international society has not established any conclusive rule, especially regarding the issue of coercion, and restricted itself to showing its 'hesitation' in going so far as to deny immunity on the ground of actual coercion. It is noteworthy that the former 'Principle' constructively expanded the field of the regulation by international law, whereas the latter problem does not have such characteristics. Especially with respect to the issue of coercion, relevant national laws are considerably varied and future intervention by international law might bring about serious instability in the international legal order. It would thus be worth considering the possibility of self-restraint on the part of the international rule-making in relation to national law, by reevaluating the conventional pattern of the application of international criminal law.

5.1 The 'Nuremberg Principle' and the Present

What role did the Nuremberg Trial play in the development of international rules on the superior orders defense? An answer to this question is varied among discussants.

Some understand the notion of the possibility of moral choice presented by the IMT judgment as a test of mitigation of punishment and not of immunization. They connect the 'Nuremberg Principle' on the superior orders defense with the principle of absolute responsibility. On the other hand, those who understand the possibility of moral choice as a test of immunization consequently construe the 'Nuremberg Principle' as recognizing conditional immunity. They evaluate the IMT judgment as partially transforming the meaning of Article 8 of the Nuremberg Charter.

However, as was confirmed in Chapter 3, the position put forth through the drafting of the Nuremberg Charter and the judicial proceedings held under the Charter was neither the principle of absolute responsibility nor that of conditional immunity. What was specifically presented there remained the denial of automatic immunity under the superior orders defense.

H. Satō, *The Execution of Illegal Orders and International Criminal Responsibility*, DOI 10.1007/978-3-642-16753-9_5,

Meanwhile, it was not only the question of whether or not to recognize automatic immunity on the ground of superior orders that was examined at the Nuremberg Trial. The participants of the trials also paid attention to the issues of the knowledge of illegality and/or manifest illegality, and coercion that had conventionally been discussed with regard to the superior orders defense. The problem was how to consider these issues on deciding on responsibility in the cases where the superior orders defense mattered.

The debates on these problems bore unstable factors, that is, the swaying between absolute responsibility and conditional immunity. The issues of the knowledge of illegality and/or manifest illegality were not fully consulted throughout the whole judicial proceedings under the Nuremberg Charter. It is difficult to observe a transition of views of the participants. On the other hand, the situation was different with respect to the issue of coercion. What the drafters of the Nuremberg Charter meant was the rule to deny the superior orders defense even in considering the issue of coercion incidental to orders. Nonetheless, the IMT judgment presented the test of the possibility of moral choice, which left room for the interpretation that the tribunal approved immunity with regard to superior orders. Further, at the Subsequent Proceedings, the majority of the judgments suggested to approve immunity on the ground of coercion incidental to superior orders. Such a trend of the judgments also partially influenced the arguments of the prosecution.

Thus, the principle of absolute responsibility, which the drafters of the Nuremberg Charter intended to introduce, was amended or adjusted to some extent at the stage of the trials. The 'Nuremberg Principle' on the superior orders defense remained unstable; this allowed a wide range of interpretation from guilty to not guilty.

Such a swaying from absolute responsibility to conditional immunity that appeared under the Nuremberg Charter influenced the subsequent international rule-making. There were mainly two conflicts of views during the drafting of the Genocide Convention and Additional Protocol I. First, there was a conflict between automatic immunity and conditional immunity. With respect to the latter, various ideas were further presented on the details of immunizing conditions. The ILC from the outset had not supported automatic immunity which was clearly dismissed at the Nuremberg Trial and had consistently paid attention to the notion of moral choice of the IMT judgment. However, discussions on the details of this notion have not been developed up to the present. The Draft Code of Crimes against the Peace and Security of Mankind, which was adopted after the Second Reading, does not present a concrete solution for the problem.

The ICC Statute, which was concluded in 1998, recognizes immunity under the superior orders defense in the case of a lack of the knowledge of illegality and a lack of manifest illegality. It also recognizes duress (coercion) as a general defense under some conditions. However, this position of the ICC on the defense of duress conflicts with the judgment of the ICTY Appeals Chamber in the *Erdemović* case.

Thus, the problems of the knowledge of illegality and/or manifest illegality, and coercion incidental to superior orders have not been resolved to the present.

However, such situations do not necessarily indicate that there has not been any rule on the superior orders defense in international law. What should be noticed here is the principle of the 'denial of automatic immunity', which was clearly presented by the Nuremberg Charter and the trials held under the Charter. This principle has widely been held during the discussions at the ILC and by the international instruments as the ICC Statute. The exception has been limited to the arguments that were presented during the drafting of some multinational treaties up to the 1970s. The 'Nuremberg Principle' on the superior orders defense can be said, at least in this manner, to have been supported since the Nuremberg Trial, that is, the principle to deny automatic immunity on the mere fact of orders.

5.2 The 'Nuremberg Principle' – Denial of Automatic Immunity – and International Legal Order

Then, what was the theoretical consequence of the denial of automatic immunity under the superior orders defense? This question cannot be said to have been fully attended to during the drafting of the Nuremberg Charter and the subsequent trials. Article 8 of the Charter, which denied immunity under the superior orders defense, was introduced mainly from the viewpoint of removing obstacles for punishment.

Legal theories on the superior orders defense themselves had been varied especially until the end of World War II. First, there was the position to connect the superior orders defense with the theory of the immunity of state acts or the absolute character of military discipline. The latter included the view that emphasized military discipline from the viewpoint of state interest and another one that focused on the problem of coercion placed on soldiers who had received orders. Additionally, there were the influential positions that contended immunity by emphasizing the issues of a lack of the knowledge of illegality and/or a lack of manifest illegality, and actual coercion incidental to superior orders.

Thus, legal theories on the superior orders defense had been considerably varied depending on the commentators. Further, the Nuremberg Trial did not clarify what theory the IMT judgment rejected by denying the said defense. However, the fact that the IMT decisively rejected automatic immunity can be said to have at least objectively led to certain theoretical consequences. The tribunal completely denied the view to connect the superior orders defense with the theory of the immunity of state acts as well as another view to regard military discipline abstractedly as absolute. In other words, the tribunal dismissed such an idea to recognize immunity for whatever act of the state or the army without consulting the respective situations in which the subordinates had actually been set.

Article 8 of the Nuremberg Charter was surely, as Jackson stated in his report, a significant provision that enabled international criminal law to 'pierce' state sovereignty. The Nuremberg Trial brought about a constructive change in international criminal law by excluding the notion of the immunity of state acts and the understanding of military discipline as absolute. The degree and nature of the intervention of international legal order into the national legal order can be said to have largely been transformed.

The Allied Powers, which strengthened their interest in international criminal prosecution, questioned the idea of automatic immunity that would impede the application of international law. They then newly introduced the 'Nuremberg Principle' that denied automatic immunity. The 'Principle' indicated that even state acts, and especially military acts, were to be under the control of international criminal law. The introduction of this principle that reflected an expansion of international interest to the issues that had conventionally been deemed domestic was naturally accompanied by strong resistance. However, some dynamic power had been at work in the international society which experienced a turning point at the end of World War II.

In fact, it is very difficult to internationally prosecute individual state organs for their state acts. Such prosecution would be possible only in exceptional circumstances. For example, as in the Nuremberg Trial and the other war crimes trials after World War II, it would be possible when victorious countries intended to hold trials as postwar administration. It would otherwise be possible if the prosecution of the former regime is to be conducted by the newly established government. Nonetheless, the fact that the prosecution of state organs has theoretically been made possible under international law seems to have much significance regardless of how limited the possibility of the realization of such a theory would be.[1]

5.3 Remaining Problems

Then, what could be said with the remaining problems as the knowledge of illegality and/or manifest illegality, and actual coercion? How will the international rule-making proceed on these issues?

The possibility of immunity on the ground of a lack of the knowledge of illegality and/or a lack of manifest illegality, and of coercion, has not categorically been denied in the international rule-making process since the trials under the Nuremberg Charter.

In particular, the debates on the issue of coercion have been tracing a peculiar waver. Throughout the process from the drafting of the Nuremberg Charter, the Nuremberg Trial of the Major War Criminals, and the Subsequent Proceedings, a transition from absolute responsibility to conditional immunity in terms of coercion had been observed. Then, this significant swinging back kept influencing the succeeding international rule-making while narrowing its width of swaying.

Even an outline of rules on the issue of coercion has not been shown in the rule-making process at the international level. Although the ICC Statute approves the

[1]See Sect. 1.2 on this point.

defense of duress (coercion), its substantial meaning largely depends on the interpretation of the condition of proportionality. Further, it would be too early to predict what relationship the provisions of the Statue will construct with other international rules developing outside the ICC. Nonetheless, even in these circumstances, at least it can be said that the possibility of immunity on the ground of coercion has not ever been denied decisively. It would be said that the swinging back or 'hesitation' which was observed with the trials under the Nuremberg Charter has been lingering since then.

In light of these things, it could be said that immunity on the ground of coercion with regard to superior orders cannot easily be disapproved in international law. The argument of the ICTY Appeals Chamber that made use of the notion of 'policy consideration' and rejected the defense of duress (coercion) would be deemed too hasty.

Meanwhile, the case that was confirmed in this study would neither indicate that the coercion defense has been recognized in international law. What could be led from the whole relevant discussions is the conclusion that the coercion defense cannot easily be disapproved and not more than that. It seems extremely difficult to specify some conclusive international rules on this problem in the present circumstances.

Superior orders are accompanied by strong coercion in most cases. The treatment of the issue of coercion would bear determinative importance in examining the case of the superior orders defense. If a significant mitigation of punishment is to be allowed by the contention of the fact of coercion, it might be considered that it does not make much of a difference whether or not to recognize the coercion defense. However, if the coercion defense is recognized, the accused is to be immunized and deemed innocent. It does not seem that such a question as relevant to the decision on guilty or not guilty should be underestimated.

International law has not answered such an important question satisfactorily. The attitude of the international society remains halfhearted in avoiding a conclusion on the coercion defense. Since the Nuremberg Trial, the international society has 'hesitated' to unconditionally convict subordinates who acted under coercion. On the other hand, it has also kept hesitating to clearly recognize immunity on the ground of a certain level of coercion. As already noted, it is not without a reason for the international society to have kept hesitating for a long time, considering that the conflict of views on this problem is not easy to dissolve.

Now that things have come to such a pass, it seems necessary to reconsider a manner of international rule-making in order to get out of the blind alley.

What would be worth reminding here is the difference in the theoretical characters of the 'Nuremberg Principle' that have been confirmed in this study, that is, the denial of automatic immunity, and the remaining problems. While the problem of the superior orders defense has always been treated as unresolved, the substantial meaning of the expression 'the problem of the superior orders defense' and its theoretical implication in respective contexts of discussions have significantly been changed.

A legal consequence of actual coercion seems different in the theoretical aspect from that of the 'Nuremberg Principle' which was identified here. The former does not directly relate to the argument to prescribe *a priori* the degree of intervention by the international legal order into national legal order. Coercion incidental to superior orders would bear legal character in many cases. An evaluation of this 'legal compulsion' is not irrelevant to the question of how the tension between international and national legal orders influences individual criminal responsibility. However, such legal compulsion remains a factor to be analyzed in examining actual coercion in individual cases. There, the issue of coercion is no longer understood abstractedly and the idea of not prosecuting state acts or the army is completely rejected.

Thus, the 'Nuremberg Principle' recognized here and the remaining problems have a fundamentally different significance in the context of the international rule-making process. It is the former that directly brings about an effect to broaden the jurisdiction of international criminal law to act of state or the army.

Another point that seems worth noting here is the problem that generally accompanies rule-making in international criminal law. The United Nations has consistently, with a long intermission though, been involved in the codification of international criminal law. At present, the ICC Statute is functioning as the applicable law of the ICC. Further, the Draft Code of Crimes against the Peace and Security of Mankind was adopted by the ILC in its Second Reading and it provides for substantive rules of international criminal law. Since the trials under the Nuremberg Charter, the codification of international criminal law can be said to have been one of the most important agenda of the international society.

Meanwhile, international rule-making in international criminal law usually involves the intervention of international law into national legal order and sometimes brings about friction between international and national laws. In particular, in the case that national laws in question are considerably varied, such variation stands as a serious obstacle for international rule-making.

On the issue of coercion, which has been examined here, this obstacle has appeared conspicuously. As the ICTY Appeals Chamber pointed out in the *Erdemović* case, the treatment of the coercion defense differs particularly between common law countries and continental law countries. In the former, such as the United Kingdom, the United States, and Canada, the coercion defense cannot be recognized for serious crimes such as murder.[2] In contrast, continental law countries such as Germany, France, and Italy generally approve the possibility of immunity on the ground of coercion.[3] The countries that recognize the coercion

[2]Joint Separate Opinion of Judge McDonald and Judge Vohrah, *Prosecutor v. Dražen Erdemovic*, IT-96-22-A (7 October 1997), 48–51.

[3]Ibid., 41–8. In the theory of criminal law of Japan, the issue of coercion has been understood as relevant to necessity or 'the principle of impossibility of expectation (*Nichtzumutbarkeit*)' (T. Matsumiya, 'Kyōsei to Kinkyūhinan nitsuite (On Coercion and Necessity)', *Suzuki Shigetsugu Sensei Kokishukugaronbunshū (Jōkan) (Essays Celebrating Seventy Years of Age of Professor Suzuki Shigetsugu (First Part)* (Tokyo: Seibundō, 2007), 299–334; N. Inoue, 'Kyōsei to Kinkyū-hinan (Coercion and Necessity)', *Keihōzasshi* 46, no. 2 (2007): 1–13.

defense also include Morocco, Somalia (before the civil war), and Ethiopia,[4] that is, countries that have complex legal systems in succeeding the Islamic legal tradition. Such a variety contrasts with the fact that there has not been a significant difference between the positions of common law countries and continental law countries on the issues of the knowledge of illegality and/or manifest illegality *with regard to the superior orders defense*.[5]

Thus, in the case that the substantive rules of national criminal laws are varied among countries, a difficult task of coordination is to be required for international rule-making. That is, the international society should intervene to transform major rules of national laws that have been developed in the respective cultural and political circumstances. It would be natural that a serious tension is to be brought about between international and national laws.

Such a tension would further lead to another tension between the countries with specific legal culture and others. What if the positions of common law countries are to be consciously adopted to provide for general international rules? Would continental law countries, countries that have inherited Islamic legal systems, and the others approve of transforming their own national laws in conformity to common law? Of course, the question is the same in the opposite direction. It is symbolic at this point that Judge Cassese in the *Erdemović* case made the strong dissent in criticizing the common law thinking on policy consideration.[6]

---

[4]Ibid., 52–3. The *Erdemović* judgment mainly analyzes the continental criminal laws of various countries. Meanwhile, a country's rules on coercion provided in its military criminal laws are often similar to those provided in its continental criminal laws. For instance, Section 916(h) of the US Rule for Courts-Martial recognizes the coercion defense except the case where the killing of innocent persons matters (M. Davidson, *A Guide to Military Criminal Law* (Annapolis: Naval Institute Press, 1999), 114–5). The British Manual of Military Law also recognizes the coercion defense except the case of murders or treason (Manual of Military Law, 12th ed., Part I (London: Stationery Office, 1972), Chapter 6, Section 22). On the other hand, German military criminal law generally recognizes immunization on the ground of coercion (H. Jescheck & T. Weigend, *Lehrbuch des Starfrechts, Allgemeiner Teil* (Berlin: Duncker & Humblot, 1996), 483–4, 497–8), and the French military criminal law recognizes the application of the rule of the French criminal law with regard to this issue (Article 1 of the French *Code penal militaire*).

[5]With regard to the respective national laws and other legal instruments, see P. Gaeta, 'The Defence of Superior Orders: The Statute of the International Criminal Court versus Customary International Law', *European Journal of International Law* 10 (1999): 176–7; G. Nolte & H. Krieger, 'European Military Law Systems: General Comparative Report', in *European Military Law Systems*, ed. G. Nolte (Berlin: De Gruyter Recht, 2003), 171–2; J. Henckaerts & L. Doswald-Beck, *Customary International Humanitarian Law*, vol. II (Cambridge: Cambridge University Press, 2005), 3817–29. Regarding the Japanese law, Article 57 of the *Self-Defense Force Act* obliges subordinates to obey official orders by superiors. Meanwhile the *Handbook on Services* explains on this point that subordinates are not obliged to obey manifestly illegal orders and they shall be responsible for the execution of such orders (Jinji Kyōiku Kyoku, *Fukumu Handobukku* (Bureau of Personnel and Training, *Handbook on Services*) (2009), 31–2).

[6]With regard to the 'transcivilizational perspective' which emphasizes the importance of considering the diversity of civilizations in examining various issues of international law, see Y. Ōnuma, *Jinken, Kokka, Bunmei – Fuhenshugitekijinkenkan kara Bunsaitekijinkenkan e (Human Rights, State, and Civilization – From Universal Perspective of Human Rights to Transcivilizational*

Thus, there are some points or problems to be prudently consulted with regard to international rule-making, especially on the issue of the coercion defense. First, the coercion defense does not have anything to do with such a legal consequence as excluding state acts from the jurisdiction of international criminal law or allowing *a priori* judgment by abstractedly comprehending the ground of immunity. In addition, national laws are varied on this issue so that international rule-making should be attended to with considerable difficulties. In these circumstances, is it appropriate to approve or disapprove the said defense in international law for the purpose of making individual responsibility more lenient or severe? Is it indisputably desirable to provide for unified international rule on this issue?

Indeed, the significance of international rule-making in criminal matters cannot be denied solely by the examination of this study. It would not be proper to conclude on the manner of international rule-making in the future just by attaching much importance to the fact that the character of the debates on the superior orders defense has been changed. Nonetheless, what has been confirmed here on the remaining problems seems to somewhat decrease the significance of establishing internationally unified rules on them. With regard to the superior orders defense in international law, it might be thinkable to remain reconfirming the 'Nuremberg Principle' which was identified here, that is, the denial of automatic immunity. There might be an option to entrust the variety of national laws with the other problems remaining outside of the 'Principle'.

If one understands a realm of function of international criminal law as a limited one, the relevant rules of national criminal laws are to play crucial roles. Even at international tribunals, it would be thinkable to partially apply national criminal laws of relevant countries. Otherwise, it would also be possible to apply peculiar international rules at the international tribunals just in the realm of their jurisdiction. Although Article 10 of the ICC Statute has been introduced not to hinder the

Perspective of Human Rights) (Tokyo: Chikuma Shobō, 1998), 26–33, 319–37. With regard to discussions on a uniform penal code for the European Union (EU), it should be noted that the EU itself has not been competent enough to oblige its member states to formulate a concrete criminal legislation (G. Dannecker, 'Die Entwicklung des Strafrechts unter dem Einfluß des Gemeinschaftsrechts' *Juristische Ausbildung*, 1998, Heft 2 (1998): 79–80). The 'Corpus Juris' which is one possible model of EU's uniform penal code, is a draft criminal code with an aim limited to protecting the financial interests of the European Community (EC). The section on 'criminal liability' in the Corpus Juris contains a general discussion on 'mens rea', 'error', 'individual criminal responsibility' (the distinction between principal and accomplice), and 'attempts' (M. Delmas-Marty & J. Vervaele, *The Implementation of the Corpus Juris in the Member States, Penal Provisions for the Protection of European Finances* (Antwerpen: Intersentia, 2000), 192–4). Nonetheless, this restrictive attempt at drafting a uniform penal code continues to receive criticism; this resistance could either be because of the wide variations in the criminal legal systems of the European countries or the diversity of the criminal laws that reflect the differences in the ethical and political basis of the respective countries (Dannecker, supra n. 6 at 87; C. Harlow, 'Voices of Difference in a Plural Community', *American Journal of Comparative Law* 50 (2002): 339–67).

customary rules of international criminal law to develop outside the statute,[7] this provision seems important also in maintaining some vacuum of customary international law.

Attaching importance to the relevant national laws, the resolution of legal problems in the respective criminal cases would be varied as a matter of course. For example, a person who committed war crimes in foreign country A will possibly receive a largely different judgment in foreign country B that he/she fled to. The criminal law of country A might recognize the coercion defense whereas that of country B might not. The accused will thus be sentenced more severely in the latter. He/she might be convicted in country B for the crime on which country A has room for immunity. Yet, the prosecution in country B was brought about by running away from country A of the accused. It could be said that he/she should endure such a consequence if it were a result of the conduct with his/her own intention. To the contrary, if the criminal law of country B recognizes the coercion defense whereas that of country A does not, country A might possibly request his/her extradition from country B if there was an outcry of severe punishment back in country A.

Traditionally, on the application process of international criminal law, prudent adjustment has been made between international law and national law and room for discretion on the side of national law has consciously been left in order to ensure the universality of international criminal law.[8] Meanwhile, with regard to the problems such as war crimes, the 'limitation' of the intervention of international law into national law has simply been a result of the stagnation of the international rule-making process. How should such a consciously left or unwillingly brought about vacuum of international criminal law be evaluated in light of the present situations of international rule-making? Is an answer to this question indisputably negative?

These days, having been influenced by the establishment of several international criminal tribunals based on the resolutions of the United Nations Security Council or on the multinational treaty, rule-making on international criminal law has been rapidly proceeding. In particular, at the ICTY, it was pursued to maintain judgment at the international level by introducing the notion of policy consideration, which was expected to fill the gap in international rules. However, at least with regard to the problem of the superior orders defense, it would be necessary to take note of the fact that the focus of the legal arguments has largely been shifted from the Nuremberg Trial to the present. As was pointed out in this study, the debates on the superior orders defense have not been a single slab of rock. They have been developing as a complex which has been composed of several problems of largely different characters. The arguments have been transforming from what relates to

[7] L. Sadat, *The International Criminal Court and the Transformation of International Law: Justice for the New Millennium* (New York: Transnational Publishers, 2002), 261–74.

[8] With respect to this point, see S. Yamamoto, *Kokusaikeijihō (International Criminal Law)* (Tokyo: Sanseidō, 1991).

structural change in the international legal order to the individual issues that do not have a direct relation with such a structural problem but still involve the problem of tension with the general rules of national criminal laws. How should such a transformation influence international rule-making on the rules of the superior orders defense? It seems necessary to reexamine the problem in a flexible way in also paying attention to the option of conscious self-restraint on the part of international law.

Select Bibliography

Monographs (Including Microfilm)

Allen, M. (2005). *Textbook on Criminal Law,* 8th ed. Oxford: Oxford University Press, 85–94, 158–84.

Amnesty International. (1997). *The International Criminal Court, Making the Right Choices – Part 1, Defining the Crimes and Permissible Defences and Initiating a Prosecution.* London: Amnesty International.

Appleman, J. (1954). *Military Tribunals and International Crimes.* Indianapolis, IN: Bobbs-Merrill Company.

Asahishinbun Hōtei Kishadan. (1962). *Tōkyō Saiban (Tokyo Trial).* Tokyo: Tōkyō Saiban Kankōkai.

Asahishinbun Tōkyō Saiban Kishadan. (1983). *Tōkyō Saiban (Tokyo Trial).* Tokyo: Kōdansha.

Ball, H. (1999). *Prosecuting War Crimes and Genocide, The Twentieth-Century Experience.* Lawrence, KS: University Press of Kansas.

Bass, G. (2000). *Stay the Hand of Vengeance, The Politics of War Crimes Tribunals.* Princeton: Princeton University Press.

Bassiouni, M. (1999). *Crimes against Humanity in International Criminal Law,* Second revised ed. The Hague: Kluwer Law International, 448–91.

Bassiouni, M. (1998). *The Statute of the International Criminal Court: A Documentary History.* New York: Transnational Publishers.

Bassiouni, M. ed. (1998). *International Criminal Court: Compilation of United Nations Documents and Draft ICC Statute Before the Diplomatic Conference.* Rome: No Peace Without Justice.

Bell, J., ed. (1927). *Völkerreht im Weltkrieg 1914–1918,* vol. 3. Deutsche Vertlagsgesellschaft für Politik und Geschichte, M.B.H., 57–62.

Benton, W. & Grimm, G., eds. (1959). *Nuremberg, German Views of the War Trials.* Dallas, TX: Southern Methodist University Press.

Biddle, F. (1976). *In Brief Authority.* Westport, CT: Greenwood Press, 367–487.

Boissier, P. (1953). *Völkerrecht und Militärbefehl.* Stuttgart: K.F. Koehler Vertrlag Stuttgart, 30–52.

Boister, N. & Cryer, R., eds. (2008). *Documents on the Tokyo International Military Tribunal: Charter, Indictment and Judgments.* Oxford: Oxford University Press.

Bosch, W. (1970). *Judgment on Nuremberg, American Attitudes toward the Major German War-Crime Trials.* Chapel Hill, NC: The University of North Carolina Press.

Cassese, A. (2008). *International Criminal Law,* 2nd ed. Oxford: Oxford University Press.

H. Satō, *The Execution of Illegal Orders and International Criminal Responsibility,*
DOI 10.1007/978-3-642-16753-9, © Springer-Verlag Berlin Heidelberg 2011

Christopher, P. (1999). *The Ethics of War and Peace, An Introduction to Legal and Moral Issues*, 2nd ed. Upper Saddle River, NJ: Prentice Hall, 127–56.

Cross, R. & Jones, P. (1964). *An Introduction to Criminal Law*, 5th ed. London: Butterworths, 75–8.

Davidson, M. (1999). *A Guide to Military Criminal Law*. Annapolis, MD: Naval Institute Press, 111–21.

Dinstein, Y. (1965). *The Defence of 'Obedience to Superior Orders' in International Law*. Leyden: A.W. Sijthoff.

Donnedieu de Vabres, H. (1937). *Traité élémentaire de droit criminel et de législation pénale compare*. Paris: Librairie du recueil sirey, 246–7.

Draper, G. (1958). *The Red Cross Conventions*. London: Stevens & Sons Limited.

Dressler, J. (2001). *Understanding Criminal Law*, 3rd ed. New York: Lexis Publishing, 201–219.

Duguit, L. (1903). *Etudes de droit public, vol. 2, L'État, les gouvernants et les agents*. Paris: A. Fontemoing, 633–4.

Foreign Relations of the United States, Diplomatic Paper, The Conferences at Cairo and Teheran, 1943. (1961) Washington, DC: GPO.

Fuhrmann, P. (1963). *Der Höhere Befehl als Rechtfertigung im Völkerrecht*. Berlin: C. H. Beck'sche Verlagsbuchhandlung.

Fujita, H. (1983). *Kokusai Jindōhō (International Humanitarian Law)*, New edition. Tokyo: Yūshindō Kōbunsha.

Fujita, H. (1995). *Sensōhanzai towa Nanika (What is War Crime?)*. Tokyo: Iwanami Shoten.

Garçon, E. (1901–6). *Code pénal*, Tome premier. Paris: Librairie de la société du recueil général des lois et arrêts, 184–5.

Garner, J. (1920). *International Law and the World War*, vol. 2. London: Longmans, Green and company, 465–504.

Gerhart, E. (1958). *America's Advocate Robert H. Jackson*. Indianapolis, IN: The Bobbs-Merrill Company.

Ginsburg, G. (1996). *Moscow's Road to Nuremberg, The Soviet Background to the Trial*. The Hague: Martinus Nijhoff Publishers.

Glaser, S. (1954). *Introduction a l'étude du droit international penal*. Paris: Sirey, 111–31.

Glueck, S. (1994). *War Criminals, Their Prosecution & Punishment*. New York: Alfred A. Knopf, 140–245.

Green, L. (1976). *Superior Orders in National and International Law*. Leyden: A.W. Sijthoff.

Greenspan, M. (1959). *The Modern Law of Land Warfare*. Los Angeles: University of California Press, 477–511.

Harris, W. (1954). *Tyranny on Trial, The Evidence at Nuremberg*. Dallas, TX: Southern Methodist University Press.

Henckaerts, J. & Doswald-Beck, L. (2005). *Customary International Humanitarian Law*, vol. II. Cambridge: Cambridge University Press, 3814–53.

Higgins, R. (1994). *Problems and Process: International Law and How We Use It*. Oxford: Clarendon Press.

Hirano, R. (1981). *Hanzairon no Shomondai (Jō) Sōron (Problems of the Theory of Crime (Part One) General Part)*. Tokyo: Yūhikaku, 1–34.

Hoffmann, G. (1962). *Strafrechtliche Verantwortung im Völkerrecht, Zum Gegenwärtigen Stand des Völkerrechtlichen Strafrechts*. Frankfurt am Main: Alfred Metzner Verlag, 129–33.

Hosoya, C., Andō, N. & Ōnuma, Y. (1989). *Kokusai Shinpojiumu: Tōkyō Saiban wo Tou (International Symposium: The Problem of the Tokyo Trial)*. Tokyo: Kōdansha.

Jackson, R. (1971). *The Nürnberg Case*. New York: Cooper Square Publishers.

Jescheck, H. (1952). *Die Verantwortlichkeit der Staatsorgane nach Völkerstrafrecht – Eine Studie zu den Nürnberger Prozessen –*. Bonn: Ludwig Röhrscheid Verlag.

Jescheck, H., & Weigend, T. (1996). *Lehrbuch des Starfrechts, Allgemeiner Teil*. Berlin: Duncker & Humblot.

Jones, J. (2000). *The Practice of the International Criminal Tribunals for the Former Yugoslavia and Rwanda*, 2nd ed. New York: Transnational Publishers, 143.
Kahn, L. (1972). *Nuremberg Trials*. New York: Ballantine Books.
Keenan, J., & Brown, B. (1950). *Crimes against International Law*. Washington, DC: Public Affairs Press, 123–38.
Keijzer, N. (1978). *Military Obedience*. The Netherlands: Sijthoff & Noordhoff.
Kelsen, H. (1973). *Peace through Law*. New York: Garland, 71–124.
Kenny, C. (1936). *Outlines of Criminal Law*, 15th ed. Cambridge: Cambridge University Press, 75–90.
Kirchheimer, O. (1961). *Political Justice, The Use of Legal Procedure for Political Ends*. Princeton: Princeton University Press, 323–41.
Kittichaisaree, K. (2001). *International Criminal Law*. New York: Oxford University Press, 266–8.
Kiyose, I. (1967). *Hiroku Tōkyō Saiban (Secret Notes of the Tokyo Trial)*. Tokyo: Yomiuri Shinbunsha.
Klibanski, R. (1913). *Das Russische Militär-Strafrecht, Übersetzt und Bearbeitet*. Berlin: J. Guttentag, 29.
Knieriem, A. (1959). *The Nuremberg Trials*. Chicago, IL: Henry Regnery Company.
Korte, M. (2004). *Das Handeln auf Befehl als Strafausschließungsgrund: Die Wirkung des Befehls im Deutschen Recht und im Römischen Statut für den Internationalen Strafgerichtshof*. Baden-Baden: Nomos Verlagsgesellschaft.
Kojima, J. (1971). *Tōkyō Saiban* (Tokyo Trial). Tokyo: Chūōkōronsha.
Kyokutō Kokusaigunjisaiban Kankei Shiryōshūsei: Kokushikan Daigaku Fuzoku Toshokan Shozō: Eibun Sokkiroku (Compiled Documents on the International Military Trial for the Far East: Kokushikan University Library: Shorthand Notes in English) [microfilm]. (1994). Tokyo: Kashiwa Shobō.
Kyokutō Kokusaigunjisaiban Sokkiroku (Shorthand Notes of the International Military Trial for the Far East), 10 vols. (1968). Tokyo: Yūshōdō Shoten.
Lescure, K. (1994). *Le tribunal pénal international pour l'ex-Yugoslavie*. Paris: Editions Montchrestien – E. J. A.
Levie, H. (1978). *Prisoners of War in International Armed Conflict*. Newport, R.I.: Naval War College Press, 387–91.
Luckau, A. (1971). *The German Delegation at the Paris Peace Conference*. New York: H. Fertig.
McCormack, T. & Simpson, G., eds. (1997). *The Law of War Crimes, National and International Approaches*. Boston, MA: Kluwer Law International.
McDougal, M. & Feliciano, F. (1994). *The International Law of War, Transnational Coercion and World Public Order*. Dordrecht: Martinus Nijhoff Pulishers, 80–82, 690–99.
Maeda, M. (2006). *Keihō sōron Kōgi (Lectures on the General Part of Criminal Law)*, 4th ed. Tokyo: University of Tokyo Press.
Maogoto, J. (2003). *State Sovereignty and International Criminal Law: Versailes to Rome*. New York: Transnational Publishers.
Maser, M. (1977). *Nürnberg Tribunal der Sieger*. Düsseldorf: Econ Vertlag.
Maugham, V. (1951). *U.N.O. and War Crimes*. London: John Murray.
Maunoir, J. (1956). *La répression des crimes de guerre devant les tribunaux français et allies*. Genève: Editions Médecine et Hygiène, 144–5.
Maurach, R. (1950). *Die Kriegsverbrecherprozesse gegen deutsche Gefangene in der Sowjetunion*. Hamburg, 32–5, 37–41.
Merle, M. (1949). *Le procés de Nuremberg et le chatiment des criminels de guerre*. Paris: Editions a. pedone.
Morris, V. & Scharf, M. (1995). *An Insider's Guide to the International Criminal Tribunal for the Former Yugoslavia, A Documentary History and Analysis*, vol. 1. New York: Trasnational Publishers, 101–111.

Mullins, C. (1921). *The Leipzig Trials, An Account of the War Criminals' Trials and a Study of German Mentality*. London: H. F. & G. Witherby.
Myerson, M. (1944). *Germany's War Crimes and Punishment, The Problem of Individual and Collective Criminality*. Toronto: The Macmillan Company, 147–65.
Nakayama, K., Nishihara, H. & Miyazawa K., eds. (1977). *Keihō no Kisoriron (Basic Theory of Criminal Law)*. Tokyo: Seibundō, 231–53.
Neave, A. (1978). *On Trial at Nuremberg*. Boston, MA: Little, Brown and Company.
Nill-Theobald, C. (1998). *"Defences" bei Kriegsverbrechen am Beispiel Deutschlands und der USA, Zugleich ein Beitrag zu einem Allgemeinen Teil des Völkerstrafrechts*. Freiburg im Breisgau: Edition Iuscrim, 65–107, 159–67, 245–51, 276–80.
Nishida, N. (2006). *Keihō Sōron (General Part of Criminal Law)*. Tokyo: Kōbundō.
Nomura J. (1993). *Nachisu Saiban (Trials of Nazis)*. Tokyo: Kōdansha.
Nyurunberugu Saiban Kiroku (Records of the Nuremberg Trial). (1947). Tokyo: Jijitsūshinsha.
Ōnuma, Y. (1998). *Jinken, Kokka, Bunmei – Fuhenshugitekijinkenkan kara Bunsaitekijinkenkan e (Human Rights, State, and Civilization – From Universal Perspective of Human Rights to Transcivilizational Perspective of Human Rights)*. Tokyo: Chikuma Shobō, 77–139.
Ōnuma, Y. (1975). *Sensōsekininron Josetsu (Introductory Study on the Responsibility for War)*. Tokyo: University of Tokyo Press.
Ōnuma, Y. (1997). *Tōkyōsaiban kara Sengosekinin no Sisō e (From the Tokyo Trial to the Idea of Postwar Responsibility)*, 4th ed. Tokyo: Tōshindō.
Oppenheim, L. (1906). *International Law, vol. 2, War and Neutrality*. London: Longmans, Green and Company, 263–70.
Oppenheim, L. (1921). *International Law, 3rd ed. by R. Roxburgh, vol. 2, War and Neutrality*. London: Longmans, 341–4.
Oppenheim, L. (1926). *International Law, 4th ed. by A. McNair, vol. 2, Disputes War and Neutrality*. London: Longmans, Green, 409–13.
Oppenheim, L. (1935). *International Law, 5th ed. by H. Lauterpacht, vol. 2, Disputes, War and Neutrality*. London: Longmans, Green, 452–6.
Oppenheim, L. (1940). *International Law, 6th ed. by H. Lauterpacht, vol. 2, Disputes, War and Neutrality*. London: Longmans, Green & Co., 450–55.
Oppenheim, L. (1944). *International Law, Revised, 6th ed. by H. Lauterpacht, vol. 2, Disputes, War and Neutrality*. London: Longmans, Green & Company, 450–53.
Oppenheim, L. (1952). *International Law, 7th ed. by H. Lauterpacht, vol. 2, Disputes, War and Neutrality*. London: Longmans, Green & Company, 566–86.
Osiel, M. (1999). *Obeying Orders, Atrocity, Military Discipline & the Law of War*. New Brunswick, NJ: Transaction Publishers.
Paust, J. et al., eds. (2000). *International Criminal Law, Cases and Materials*, 2nd ed. Durham, NC: Carolina Academic Press.
Pella, V. (1926). *La criminalité collective des états et le droit penal de l'avenir*, deuxiéme ed. Bucarest: Imprimerie de l'État, 179–94.
Phillipson, C. (1916). *Termination of War and Treaties of Peace*. London: Fisher Unwin, 243–50.
Poljokan, I. (1923). *La responsabilité pour les crimes et délits de guerre*. Paris: Jouve et cie, Éditeurs, 35–97, 147–65.
Ratner, S. & Abrams, J. (2001). *Accountability for Human Rights Atrocities in International Law, Beyond the Nuremberg Legacy*, 2nd ed. Oxford: Oxford University Press, 228–52.
Report of Robert H. Jackson, United States Representative to the International Conference on Military Trials, London, 1945. (1949). Washington: GPO.
Röling, B. (ed. by A. Cassese). (1993). *The Tokyo Trial and Beyond, Reflections of a Peacemonger*. Cambridge: Polity Press, 107–110.
Sadat, L. (2002). *The International Criminal Court and the Transformation of International Law: Justice for the New Millennium*. New York: Transnational Publishers, 53–75, 216–20.
Scelle, G. (1948). *Manuel de droit international public*. Paris: Editions domat-montcrrestien, 983–5.

Schwarzenberger, G. (1943). *International Law and Totalitarian Lawlessness*. London: J. Cape, 57–81.
Shahabuddeen, M. (1996). *Precedent in the World Court*. Cambridge: Cambridge University Press, 152–6.
Shinobu, J. (1941). *Senjikokusaihō Kōgi (Lectures on International Laws of War)*, vol. 3. Tokyo: Maruzen, 382–495.
Sumimoto, T. (1952). *Senryō Hiroku (Ge) (Secret Notes on the Occupation (The Second Part)*. Tokyo: Mainichi Shinbunsha.
Smith, B. (1981). *The Road to Nuremberg*. New York: Basic Books.
Starke, J. (1989). *Introduction to International Law, 10th ed*. London: Butterworths, 552–8.
Stimson, H. & Bundy, M. (1947). *On Active Service in Peace and War*. New York: Happer & Brothers, 1948.
Sunga, L. (1992). *Individual Responsibility in International Law for Serious Human Rights Violations*. Dordrecht: Martinus Nijhoff Publishers.
The Henry Lewis Stimson Diaries in the Yale University Library. (1973). Yale University Library, roll 9, vol. 48 [microfilm]. Modern Japanese Political History Materials Room, National Diet Library, Japan, DHS-1.
The Memoirs of Cordell Hull, vol. 2. (1948). New York: The MacMillan Company.
The United Nations War Crimes Commission. (1948). *History of the United Nations War Crimes Commission and the Development of the Laws of War*. London: HMSO.
Thielke, O. (1911). *Gehorsam und Schuld des Staatsbeamten und des Soldaten bei gesetzwidrigen Befehlen des Vorgesetzten*. Königsberg: Druck von Karg und Manneck, 62–72.
Thorneycroft, E. (1961). *Personal Responsibility and the Law of Nations*. The Hague: Martinus Nijhoff, 41–7.
Trainin, A. (translated by A.Rothstein). (1945). *Hitlerite Responsibility under Criminal Law*. London: Hutchinson & Company.
Trial of the Major War Criminals before the International Military Tribunal, Nuremberg, 14 November 1945 – 1 October 1946, 42 vols. (1947–9). Nuremberg.
Trials of War Criminals before the Nuernberg Military Tribunals under Control Council Law No. 10, 15 vols. (1949–52). Washington: GPO.
Triffterer, O., ed (1999). *Commentary on the Rome Statute of the International Criminal Court, Observer's Notes, Article by Article*. Baden-Baden: Nomos Verlagsgesellschaft.
Turner, J. (1964). *Russell on Crime*, 12th ed., vol. 1. London: Stevens & Sons, 87–90.
United Nations – General Assembly, International Law Commission. (1949). *The Charter and Judgment of the Nürnberg Tribunal, History and Analysis (Memorandum Submitted by the Secretary-General)*. New York.
van Sliedregt, E. (2003). *The Criminal Responsibility of Individuals for Violations of International Humanitarian Law*. The Hague: T.M.C. Asser Press, 225–341.
War Department: Office of the Chief of Staff. (1914). Rules of Land Warfare. Washington: GPO.
War Office. (1899). *Manual of Military Law*. London: HMSO.
War Office. (1907). *Manual of Military Law*. London: HMSO.
War Office. (1914). *Manual of Military Law*. London: HMSO.
Wegner, A. (1925). *Kriminelles Unrecht, Staatsunrecht und Völkerrecht*. Hamburg: W. Gente, 28.
Williams, G. (1961). *Criminal Law, The General Part*, 2nd ed. London: Stevens & Sons, 296–301.
Winthrop, W. (1920). *Military Law and Precendents*, 2nd ed. Washington, DC: GPO, 296–7.
Woetzel, R. (1962). *The Nuremberg Trials in International Law with a Postlude on the Eichmann Case*. London: Stevens & Sons Limited.
Yamamoto, S. (1991). *Kokusaikeijihō (International Criminal Law)*. Tokyo: Sanseidō.

Articles

Adachi, S. (1972). Kokusaihōjō no Meirei to Fukujū no Kankei (Relationship between Orders and Obedience in International Law). *Bōeidaigakkō Kiyō* 24: 319–46.
Address by Lord Cave, Minutes of the Proceedings of the Seventh Annual General Meeting. (1923). *Transactions of Grotius Society* 8: xix–xliii.
Aichi, M. (1999). Kokusaikeijisaibansho Kitei no Keihōsōsokuteki Kitei – Keijihō no Shiten kara – (Provisions of the Statute of the International Criminal Court on General Principles of Criminal Law – From the Perspective of Criminal Law –). *Kokusaihō Gaikō Zasshi* 98, no. 5: 132–65.
Alvarez, J. (1999). Crimes of States/Crimes of Hate: Lessons from Rwanda. *Yale Journal of International Law* 24: 365–483.
Ambos, K. (1996). Establishing an International Criminal Court and an International Criminal Code, Observations from an International Criminal Law Viewpoint. *European Journal of International Law* 7: 519–44.
Ambos, K. (1998). Zur Strafbefreienden Wirkung des 'Handelns auf Befehl' aus Deutscher und völkerstrafrechtlicher Sicht. *Juristische Rundschau* 6: 223–6.
Amerasinghe, C. (1999). The Canadian Experience. In M. Bassiouni (Ed.), *International Law, 2nd ed., vol. 3, Enforcement* (pp. 243–72). New York: Transnational Publishers.
April, N. (1946). An Inquiry into the Judicial Basis for the Nuremberg War Crimes Trial. *Minnesota Law Review* 30: 313–31.
Arbour, L. (1998). History and Future of the International Criminal Tribunals for the Former Yugoslavia and Rwanda. *American University International Law Review* 13: 1498–1508.
Arriaza, N. (2001). The Pinochet Precedent and Universal Jurisdiction. *New England Law Review* 35: 311–19.
Aubert, M. (1988). The Question of Superior Orders and the Responsibility of Commanding Officers in the Protocol Additional to the Geneva Conventions of 12 August 1949 and Relating to the Protection of Victims of International Armed Conflicts (Protocol I) of 8 June 1977. *Revue International de la Croix Rouge* 70: 105–20.
Bantekas, I. (2004). Defences in International Criminal Law. In McGoldrick, D & Rowe, P. & Donnelly, E. *The Permanent International Criminal Court, Legal and Policy Issues* (pp. 263–84). Oxford and Portland Oregon.
Barthélémy, J. (1914). L'influence de l'ordre hiérarchique sur la responsabilité des agents. *Revue du droit public et de la science politique en France et a l'étranger* 31: 32–508.
Bartlett, H. (1919). Liability for Official War Crimes. *Law Quarterly Review* 35: 177–92.
Bassiouni, M. (1974). An Appraisal of the Growth and Developing Trends of International Criminal Law. *Revue internationale de droit pénal* 3.4: 405–33.
Bassiouni, M. (1997). From Versailles to Rwanda in Seventy-Five Years: The Need to Establish a Permanent International Criminal Court. *Harvard Human Rights Journal* 10: 11–62.
Bassiouni, M. (1999). The Sources and Content of International Criminal Law: A Theoretical Framework. In M. Bassiouni (Ed.), *International Criminal Law, 2nd ed., vol. 1, Crimes* (pp. 3–125). New York: Transnational Publishers.
Bassiouni, M. (2001). Universal Jurisdiction for International Crimes: Historical Perspectives and Contemporary Practice. *Virginia Journal of International Law* 42: 81–162.
Bassiouni, M. & Blakesley, C. (1992). The Need for an International Criminal Court in the New International World Order. *Vanderbilt Journal of Transnational Law* 25: 151–82.
Battle, G. (1921). The Trials before the Leipsic Supreme Court of Germans Accused of War Crimes. *Virginia Law Review* 8: 1–26.
Bellot, H. (1925). Draft Statute for the Permanent International Criminal Court. *Report of the International Law Association, 1924*: 75–111.
Bellot, H. (1917). War Crimes: Their Prevention and Punishment. *Transactions of Grotius Society* 2: 31–55.

Bennouna, M. (1990). La création d'une juridiction pénale internationale et la souveraineté des états. *Annuaire français de droit international* 36: 300–306.
Beres, L. (1991). The United States Should Take the Lead in Preparing International Legal Machinery for Prosecution of Iraqi Crimes. *Virginia Journal of International Law* 31: 381–9.
Berger, J. (1944). The Legal Nature of War Crimes and the Problem of Superior Command. *American Political Science Review* 38: 1203–8.
Blewitt, G. (1999). The Australian Experience. In M. Bassiouni, (Ed.), *International Law, 2nd ed., vol. 3, Enforcement* (pp. 301–24). New York: Transnational Publishers.
Boissier, P. (1948). La repression des ⟨⟨petits⟩⟩ crimes de guerre. *Revue internationale de droit penal* 293–309.
Bos, A. (1996). The Establishment of an International Criminal Court. *Foreign Relations Journal* 11: 42–8.
Bower, G. (1916). The Laws of War: Prisoners of War and Reprisals. *Transactions of Grotius Society* 1: 15–31.
Bowers, A. (2003). A Concession to Humanity in the Killing of Innocents – Validating the Defences of Duress and Superior Orders in International Law. *Windsor Review of Legal and Social Issues* 15: 31–72.
Brand, G. (1949). The War Crimes Trials and the Laws of War. *British Yearbook of International Law* 26: 414–27.
Brierly, J. (1927). Do We Need an International Criminal Court? *British Yearbook of International Law* 8: 81–8.
Brierly, J. (1958). The Nature of War Crimes Jurisdiction. In J. Brierly. *The Basis of Obligation in International Law* (pp. 297–305). Clarendon Press.
Broms, B. (1996). The Establishment of an International Criminal Court. In Y. Dinstein & M. Tabory (Eds.), *War Crimes in International Law* (pp. 183–96). The Hague: Martinus Nijhoff Publishers.
Brooks, R. (2003). Law in the Heart of Darkness: Atrocity & Duress. *Virginia Journal of International Law* 43: 861–88.
Brownlee, I. D. (1989). Superior Orders – Time for a New Realism? *Criminal Law Review* 396–411.
Burns, P. (1994). An International Criminal Tribunal: The Difficult Union of Principle and Politics. *Criminal Law Forum* 5: 341–80.
Carnahan, B. (1998). Lincoln, Lieber and the Laws of War: The Origins and Limits of the Principle of Military Necessity. *American Journal of International Law* 92: 213–31.
Carnegie, A. (1963). Jurisdiction over Violations of the Laws and Customs of War. *British Yearbook of International Law* 39: 402–24.
Cassese, A. (1999). The Statute of the International Criminal Court: Some Preliminary Reflections. *European Journal of International Law* 10: 144–71.
Clunet, E. (1921). Les criminels de guerre devant le Reichsgericht, à Leipzig. *Journal du droit international* 440–47.
Cohn, E. (1941). The Problem of War Crimes Today. *Transactions of the Grotius Society* 26: 125–51.
Colby, E. (1923). Courts-Martial and the Laws of War. *American Journal of International Law* 17: 109–15.
Colby, E. (1924–5). War Crimes. *Michigan Law Review* 23: 606–34.
Colby, E. (1923). War Crimes and Their Punishment. *Minnesota Law Review* 8: 40–6.
Commission of Jurists to Consider and Report upon the Revision of the Rules of Warfare. (1938). General Report. *American Journal of International Law, Supplement* 32: 1–56.
Commission on the Responsibility of the Authors of the War and on Enforcement of Penalties. (1920). Report Presented to the Preliminary Peace Conference. *American Journal of International Law* 14: 95–154.
Coste-Floret, P. (1945). La répression de crimes de guerre et le fait justificatif tiré de l'ordre supérieur. *Recueil dalloz de doctrine de jurisprudence et de législation – Chronique* 21–2.

Cotler, I. (1996). International Decision – Regina v. Finta. *American Journal of International Law* 90: 460–76.
Cotler, I. (1995). War Crimes Law and the Finta Case. *Supreme Court Law Review* 6, no. 2: 577–646.
Cowles, W. (1945). Universality of Jurisdiction over War Crimes. *California Law Review* 33: 177–218.
Crawford, J. (1995). Prospects for an International Criminal Court. *Current Legal Problems* 48: 303–26.
Crawford, J. (1995). The ILC Adopts a Statute for an International Criminal Court. *American Journal of International Law* 89: 404–16.
Crawford, J. (1994). The ILC's Draft Statute for an International Criminal Tribunal. *American Journal of International Law* 88: 140–52.
D'Amato, A. (1986). Superior Orders vs. Command Responsibility. *American Journal of International Law* 80: 604–11.
David, E. (1978–9). L'Excuse de l'ordre superieur et l'etat de necessite. *Revue Belge de Droit International* 14: 65–84.
Delhaye, C. (1984). L'Etat de nécessité comme cause de justification dans le chef de l'individu en cas d'infractions graves aux conventions de genève. *Revue de droit penal militaire et de droit de la guerre* 23: 277–82.
Denson, W. (2001). The Obligation to Disobey Superior Orders under International Law. *Touro International Law Review* 9: 175–82.
Descheemaeker, J. (1946). Le Tribunal Militaire International des grands criminels de guerre. *Revue générale de droit international public* 50: 210–311.
Des sanctions contre les violations du droit des gens. (1915). *Réforme sociale* 69: 181–213.
Deutsche Juristen! (1922). *Deutsche Juristen – Zeitung* 106–7.
Dinstag, A. (1982). Fedorenko v. United States: War Crimes, the Defense of Duress, and American Nationality Law. *Columbia Law Review* 82: 120–83.
Dinstein, Y. (2000). Defences. In G. McDonald & O. Swaak-Goldman (Eds.), *Substantive and Procedural Aspects of International Criminal Law, The Experience of International and National Courts*, vol. 1 (pp. 371–88). The Hague: Kluwer Law International.
Dinstein, Y. (1985). International Criminal Law. *Israel Law Review* 20: 206–42.
Dinstein, Y. (1996). The Distinctions between War Crimes and Crimes against Peace. In Y. Dinstein & M. Tabory (Eds.), *War Crimes in International Law* (pp. 1–18). The Hague: Martinus Nijhoff Publishers.
Donnedieu de Vabres, H. (1947). Le proces de Nuremberg devant les principes modernes du droit pénal international. *Recueil des cours* 70: 559–73.
Dufour, G. (2000). La défense d'ordres supérieurs existe-t-elle vraiment? *Revue internationale de la Croix-Rouge* 82: 969–92.
Dugard, J. (1997). Obstacles in the Way of an International Criminal Court. *Cambridge Law Journal* 56: 329–42.
Dunbar, N. (1951). Some Aspects of the Problem of Superior Orders in the Law of War. *Juridical Review* 63: 234–61.
Eagleton, C. (1943). Punishment of War Criminals by the United Nations. *American Journal of International Law* 37: 495–9.
Eser, A. (1995). 'Defences' in War Crime Trials. *Israel Yearbook on Human Rights* 24: 201–22.
Eustathiades, C. (1953). Quelques aspects de la jurisprudence concernants les criminels de guerre: L'exception des ordres reçus et autres moyens de défense similaires. In Constantopoulos, D. & Wehberg, H., *Gegenwartsprobleme des internationalen rechtes und der rechtsphilosophie: Festschrift für Rudolf Laun zu Seinem Siebzigsten Geburtstag* (pp. 395–421). Hamburg: Girardet & Company.
Ferencz, B. (1992). An International Criminal Code and Court: Where They Stand and Where They're Going. *Columbia Journal of Transnational Law* 30: 375–99.

Ferencz, B. (1981). The Draft Code of Offences against the Peace and Security of Mankind. *American Journal of International Law* 75: 674–9.
Finch, G. (1920). Jurisdiction of Local Courts to Try Enemy Persons for War Crimes. *American Journal of International Law* 14: 218–23.
Finch, G. (1943). Retribution for War Crimes. *American Journal of International Law* 37: 81–8.
Finch, G. (1921). Superior Orders and War Crimes. *American Journal of International Law* 15: 440–45.
Finch, G. (1947). The Nuremberg Trial and International Law. *American Journal of International Law* 41: 20–37.
Fletcher, G. (2001). Criminal Law: Criminal Theory in the Twentieth Century. *Theoretical Inquiries in Law* 2: 265–86.
Fletcher, G. (1974). The Individualization of Excusing Conditions. *Southern California Law Review* 47: 1269–1309.
François, J. (1923). L'Avenir du sous-marin. *Revue general de droit international public* 30: 34–50.
Fujita, H. (1998). Kokusaikeijisaibansho Kitei Saitaku no Igi to Genkai (The Significance and Problems of the Adoption of the Statute of the International Criminal Court). *Sekai* 652: 207–16.
Fujita, H. (1999). Kokusaikeijisaibansho Kōsō no Tenkai – ICC Kitei no Ichizuke (The Development of the Idea of the International Criminal Court – The Position of the ICC Statute). *Kokusaihō Gaikō Zasshi* 98, no. 5: 31–62.
Fukatsu, E. & Kita, Y. (1993). 'Jōkanmeirei no Kōben' ni Kansuru Kokusaihōtenka wo Meguru Shomondai – Dainijisekaitaisen Izen no Sagyō – (Problems on International Codification on "Superior Orders Defense" – The Work before World War II). *Hōgaku Kiyō (Nihondaigaku Hōgakubu Hōgakukenkyūjo)* 34: 173–227.
Gaeta, P. (1999). The Defence of Superior Orders: The Statute of the International Criminal Court versus Customary International Law. *European Journal of International Law* 10: 172–91.
Garner, J. (1920). Punishment of Offenders against the Laws and Customs of War. *American Journal of International Law* 14: 70–94.
Garraway, C. (1999). Superior Orders and the International Criminal Court: Justice Delivered or Justice Denied. *International Review of the Red Cross* 836: 785–94.
Genet, R. (1938). The Charge of Piracy in the Spanish Civil War. *American Journal of International Law* 32: 253–63.
Gianaris, W. (1992–3). The New World Order and the Need for an International Criminal Court. *Fordham International Law Journal* 16: 88–119.
Ginsburg, G. (1959–60). Laws of War and War Crimes on the Russian Front during World War II: The Soviet View. *Soviet Studies* 253–85.
Glaser, S. (1948). La Charte du Tribunal de Nuremberg et les nouveaux principes du droit international. *Schweizerische Zeitschrift für Strafrecht* 63: 13–38.
Glaser, S. (1952–3). L'ordre hiérarchique en droit pénal international. *Revue de droit pénal et de criminologie* 33: 283–330.
Goodhart, A. (1930). Determining the ratio decidendi of a Case. *Yale Law Journal* 60: 161–83.
Goodhart, A. (1947). Questions and Answers Concerning the Nuremberg Trials. *International Law Quarterly* 1: 525–31.
Graefrath, B. (1990). Universal Criminal Jurisdiction and an International Criminal Court. *European Journal of International Law* 1: 67–88.
Grant, S. (1995). Dispensing International Justice: The Yugoslav and Rwandan Criminal Tribunals. *Interights Bulletin* 9: 39–42.
Graven, J. (1950). Principes fondamentaux d'un code repressif des crimes contre la paix et la securite de l'humanite. *Revue de droit international de sciences diplomatiques et politiques* 28: 173–204, 361–92.
Grayson, J. (1995). The Defence of Superior Orders in the International Criminal Court. *Nordic Journal of International Law* 64: 243–60.

Green, L. (1988). Canadian Law, War Crimes and Crimes against Humanity. *British Yearbook of International Law* 59: 217–35.
Green, L. (1997). Drazen Erdemovic: The International Criminal Tribunal for the Former Yugoslavia in Action. *Leiden Journal of International Law* 10: 363–81.
Green, L. (1989). Superior Orders and Command Responsibility. *Canadian Yearbook of International Law* 167–202.
Green, L. (1970). Superior Orders and the Reasonable Man. *Canadian Yearbook of International Law* 61–103.
Greenberg, M. (1992). Creating an International Criminal Court. *Boston University International Law Journal* 10: 119–42.
Gregory, S. (1919). Criminal Responsibility of Sovereigns for Willful Violations of the Law of War. *Virginia Law Review* 6: 400–421.
Hafner, G. et al. (1999). A Response to the American View as Presented by Ruth Wedgwood. *European Journal of International Law* 10: 108–123.
Halleck, H. (1911). Military Tribunals and Their Jurisdiction. *American Journal of International Law* 5: 958–67.
Herzog, J. B. (1960). Le principes juridiques de la répression des crimes de guerre." *Schweizerische Zeitschrift für Strafrecht* 277–304.
Hirobe, K. (1979). Hanzai no Kokusaika to Sono Taiō (The Internationalization of Crimes and Countermeasures). *Jurist* 681: 58–65.
Hirose, Y. (1984). 'Heiwa ni Taisuru Tsumi' to Kokusaihō ('Crimes against Peace' and International Law). *Meijigakuin Ronsō* 350: 1–30.
Horwitz, S. (1950). The Tokyo Trial. *International Conciliation* 465: 473–584.
Husak, D. (1998). Partial Defenses. *Canadian Journal of Law & Jurisprudence* 11: 167–92.
Hyde, C. (1917). Attacks on Unarmed Enemy Merchant Vessels. *Proceedings of American Society of International Law* 26–37.
Inoue, N. (2007). Kyōsei to Kinkyūhinan (Coercion and Necessity). *Keihōzasshi* 46, no. 2: 1–13.
Insco, J. (2003). Defense of Superior Orders before Military Commissions. *Duke Journal of Comparative & International Law* 13: 389–418.
Johnson, D. (1985). The Defence of Superior Orders. *Australian Yearbook of International Law* 9: 291–314.
Jones, J. (1996). The Implications of the Peace Agreement for the International Criminal Tribunal for the former Yugoslavia. *European Journal of International Law* 7: 226–44.
Judgment in the Case of Commander Karl Neumann. Judicial Decisions Involving Questions of International Law. (1922). *American Journal of International Law* 16: 704–8.
Judgment in the Case of Lieutenants Dithmar and Boldt, Hospital Ship 'Llandovery Castle'. Judicial Decisions Involving Questions of Internaitonal Law. (1922). *American Journal of International Law* 16: 708–724.
Kawai, H. (2003). Erdemović Jiken – Jōkanmeirei Oyobi Kyōhaku no Kōben wo Chūshin ni – (The Case of *Erdemović* – Mainly on the Defenses of Superior Orders and Duress –). *Hōgaku Jānaru (Kansai Daigaku)* 73: 184–208.
Kelsen, H. (1948). Collective and Individual Responsibility for Acts of State in International Law. *Jewish Yearbook of International Law* 226–39.
Kelsen, H. (1943). Collective and Individual Responsibility in International Law with Particular Regard to the Punishment of War Criminals. *California Law Review* 31: 530–71.
King, H. (2001). Universal Jurisdiction: Myths, Realities, Prospects, War Crimes and Crimes against Humanity: The Nuremberg Precedent. *New England Law Review* 35: 281–6.
King, H. & Theofrastous, T. (1999). From Nuremberg to Rome: A Step Backward for U.S. Foreign Policy. *Case Western Reserve Journal of International Law* 31: 47–106.
Kirby, M. (1993). War Crimes Prosecution: An Australian Update. *New Zealand Law Journal* 12–5.

Kita, Y. (1993). Kokusaihōjō no Mensekijiyū toshiteno Jōkanmeirei no Mondai – Gakusetsu no Kentō – Sonoichi (The Problem of Superior Orders as an Exempting Factor in International Law – Examination of Academic Arguments – Part 1). *Nihon Hōgaku* 58, no. 3: 247–80.

Kita, Y. (1993). Kokusaihōjō no Mensekijiyū toshiteno Jōkanmeirei no Mondai – Gakusetsu no Kentō – Sononi (The Problem of Superior Orders as an Exempting Factor in International Law – Examination of Academic Arguments – Part 2). *Nihon Hōgaku* 61, no. 1: 75–116.

Kita, Y. (1994). Sensōhanzainin Saiban to Jōkanmeirei no Kōben – Nyūrunberugu Saiban no Baai – (Trials of War Criminals and Superior Orders Defense – the Case of the Nuremberg Trial –). *Nihon Hōgaku* 60, no. 2: 103–51.

Kita, Y. (1993). Sensōhanzainin Saiban to Jōkanmeirei no Kōben – Nyūrunberugu Saiban no Baai – (Trials of War Criminals and Superior Orders Defense – the Case of the Nuremberg Trial –). *Nihon Hōgaku* 59, no. 2: 205–44.

Lador-Lederer, J. (1984). The Eichmann Case Revisited. *Israel Yearbook on Human Rights* 14: 54–79.

Lahav, P. (1992). The Eichmann Trial, the Jewish Question, and the American-Jewish Intelligentsia. *Boston Unviersity Law Review* 72: 555–75.

Lasok, D. (1962). The Eichmann Trial. *International and Comparative Law Quarterly* 11: 355–74.

Lauterpacht, H. (1944). The Law of Nations and the Punishment of War Crimes. *British Yearbook of International Law* 21: 58–95.

Levie, H. (1991). The Rise and Fall of an Internationally Codified Denial of the Defense of Superior Orders. *Revue de droit militaire et de droit de la guerre* 30: 183–209.

Levy, A. (1945). Criminal Responsibility of Individuals and International Law. *University of Chicago Law Review* 12: 313–32.

Lewy, G. (1961). Superior Orders, Nuclear Warfare, and the Dictates of Conscience: The Dilemma of Military Obedience in the Atomic Age. *American Political Science Review* 55: 3–23.

Linton, S. (1999). Reviewing the Case of Drazen Erdemović: Uncharted Waters at the International Criminal Tribunal for the Former Yugoslavia. *Leiden Journal of International Law* 12: 251–70.

Lippman, M. (2002). Genocide: The Trial of Adolf Eichmann and the Quest for Global Justice. *Buffalo Human Rights Law Review* 8: 45–121.

Lippman, M. (2001). The Development and Scope of the Superior Orders Defense. *Penn State International Law Review* 20: 153–251.

Lippman, M. (1997). International Law and Human Rights Edition: Crimes against Humanity. *Boston College Third World Law Journal* 17: 171–273.

Lippman, M. (1998). The Pursuit of Nazi War Criminals in the United States and in Other Anglo-American Legal Systems. *California Western International Law Journal* 29: 1–100.

Liwerant, O. (2000). Les executants. In H, Ascensio, E. Decaux et A. Pellet (Eds.), *Droit international penal* (pp. 211–24). Éditions a.pedone.

Malkin, H. (1922–3). The Washington Conference (November 12, 1921 – February 6, 1922). *British Year Book of International Law* 3: 179–82.

Mangoldt, H. (1948). Das Kriegsverbrechen und Seine Verfolgung in Vergangenheit und Gegenwart. *Jahrbuch für internationales und Auslandisches offentliches Recht* 2–3: 307–9.

Manner, G. (1943). The Legal Nature and Punishment of Criminal Acts of Violence Contrary to the Laws of War. *American Journal of International Law* 37: 407–35.

Marquardt, P. (1995). Law Without Borders: The Constitutionality of an International Criminal Court. *Columbia Journal of Transnational Law* 33: 73–148.

Matsumiya, T. (2007). Kyōsei to Kinkyūhinan nitsuite (On Coercion and Necessity). In *Suzuki Shigetsugu Sensei Kokishukugaronbunshū (Jōkan) (Essays Celebrating Seventy Years of Age of Professor Suzuki Shigetsugu (First Part))* (pp. 299–334). Tokyo: Seibundō.

Mayama, A. (1999). Kokusaikeijisaibansho Kitei to Sensō Hanzai (The Statute of the International Criminal Court and War Crimes). *Kokusaihō Gaikō Zasshi* 98, no. 5: 99–131.

Mayer, M. (1908). Der rechtswidrige Befehl des Vorgesetzten. In *Festschrift Paul Laband* (pp.148-62). Verlag von J. C. B. Mohr.

Maynard, J. (1946). Crimes et criminels de guerre probleme, Etudie par un groupe de juristes aux Etats-Unis. *Revue internationale de droit penal* 333–42.

McCoubrey, H. (2001). From Nuremberg to Rome: Restoring the Defence of Superior Orders. *International and Comparative Law Quarterly* 50: 386–94.

Mérignhac, A. (1920). De la responsabilité pénale des actes criminels commis au cours de la guerre de 1914–1918. *Revue de droit international et de législation comparée, Troisième sirie* 1: 34–70.

Mérignhac, A. (1917). De la sanction des infractions au droit des gens commises, au cours de la guerre européenne, par les empires du centre. *Revue générale de droit international public* 24: 5–56.

Mérignhac, A. (1922). Le désarmement, les traités de paix de 1919–1920, la conférence de Washington de 1921–1922. *Revue général de droit international public* 29: 105–51.

Merkel, R. (2002). Gründe für den Ausschluss der Strafbarkeit im Völkerstrafrecht. *Zeitschrift für die Gesamte Strafrechtswissenschaft* 114: 437–54.

Meron, T. (1996). The Normative Impact on International Law of the International Tribunal for Former Yugoslavia. In Y. Dinstein & M. Tabory (Eds.), *War Crimes in International Law* (pp. 211–31). The Hague: Martinus Nijhoff Publishers.

Meron, T. (1998). War Crimes Law Comes of Age. *American Journal of International Law* 92: 462–8.

Morgan, J. (1947). Nuremberg and After. *Quarterly Review* 285: 318–36.

M. Salem's comment. (1916). *Revue penitentiaire et de droit pénal* 40: 39–42.

Nast, M. (1919). Le sanctions penales de l'enlèvement par les allemands du matériel industriel en territoires français et belges occupés par leurs troupes. *Revue générale de droit international public* 26: 111–28.

Newman, S. (2000). Duress as a Defense to War Crimes and Crimes against Humanity – Prosecutor v. Drazen Erdemovic. *Military Law Review* 166: 158–71.

Nichols, D. (1976). Untying the Soldier by Refurbishing the Common Law. *Criminal Law Review* 181–90.

Nolte, G. & Krieger, H. (2003). Comparison of European Military Law Systems. In G. Nolte, *European Military Law Systems* (pp. 19–182). Berlin: De Gruyter Recht.

Oellers-Frahm, K. & Specht, B. (1998). Die *Erdemovic*-Rechtsprechung de Jugoslawien-tribunals: Probleme bei der Entwicklung eines Internationalen Strafrechts, Dargestellt am Beispiel des Notstands. *Berichte und Urkunden* 58: 389–414.

Okada, I. (1996). 'Jindō ni Taisuru Tsumi' Shobatsu no Konnichiteki Tenkai – Kokunai Rippō oyobi Kokunaisaiban ni Chūmoku shite – (The Recent Development of the Punishment of 'Crimes against Humanity' – With the Focus on National Legislation and National Trials –). *Sekaihō Nenpō* 49–70.

Okuhara, T. (1973). Kokusairengō to Sensōhanzai (The United Nations and War Crimes). In T. Kamiya (Ed.), *Kokusairengō no Kihonmondai (Basic Problems of the United Nations)* (pp. 251–320). Tokyo: Sakai Shoten.

Onuma Y. (2003). International Law in and with International Politics: The Functions of International Law in International Society. *European Journal of International Law* 14: 105–139.

Orentlicher, D. (2003). Striking a Balance: Mixed Law Tribunals and Conflicts of Jurisdiction. In M. Lattimer & P. Sands, *Justice for Crimes against Humanity* (pp. 213–35). Oregon: Hart Publishing.

Owada, H. (1999). Kokusaikeijisaibansho Setsuritsu no Igi to Mondaiten (The Significance and Problems of the Establishment of the International Criminal Court). *Kokusaihō Gaikō Zasshi* 98, no. 5: 1–30.

Patel, F. (1990). Crime without Frontiers: A Proposal for an International Narcotics Court. *International Law and Politics* 22: 709–47.

Paust, J. (1999). Superior Orders and Command Responsibility. In M. Bassiouni (Ed.), *International Criminal Law, 2nd ed., vol. 1, Crimes* (pp. 223–37). New York: Transnational Publishers.

Pic, P. (1916). Violation systmatique des lois de la guerre par les austro-allemands. Les sanctions necessaries. *Revue général de droit international public* 23: 243–68.

Pollock, F. (1919). The Work of the League of Nations. *Law Quarterly Review* 138: 193–8.

Puttkamer, E. (1948/1949). Die Haftung der Politischen und Militärischen Führung des Ersten Weltkriegs für Kriegsurheberschaft und Kriegsverbrechen. *Archiv des Volkerrechts* 1: 439–40.

Renault, L. (1918). De l'application du droit pénal aux faits de guerre. *Revue générale de droit international public* 25: 5–29.

R. Garraud's Report on 'L'application du droit pénal aux faits de guerre; compétence et procédure'. (1916). *Revue penitentiaire et de droit pénal* 40: 20–42.

Roberts, A. (1995). The Laws of War: Problems of Implementation in Contemporary Conflicts. *Duke Journal of Comparative & International Law* 6: 11–78.

Robinson, D. (1997). Trials, Tribulations, and Triumphs: Major Developments in 1997 at the International Criminal Tribunal for the Former Yugoslavia. *Canadian Yearbook of International Law* 179–213.

Rocca, J. (1980). Superior Orders as a Qualified Defense in International Law. In H. Miehsler et al, *Ius Humanitatis – Festschrift zum 90. Geburtstag von Alfred Verdross* (pp. 607–30). Berlin: Duncker & Humbolt.

Röling, B. (1976). Criminal Responsibility for Violations of the Laws of War. *Revue belge de droit international* 12: 8–26.

Röling, B. (1961). The Law of War and the National Jurisdiction since 1945. *Recueil des cours de l'Académie de droit international de la Haye* 100: 329–456.

Rogers, A. (1990). War Crimes Trials under the Royal Warrant: British Practice 1945–1949. *International and Comparative Law Quarterly* 39: 780–800.

Rowe, P. (1998). Duress as a Defence to War Crimes after Erdemovic: A Laboratory for a Permanent Court? *Yearbook of International Humanitarian Law* 1: 210–28.

Roxburgh, R. (1922–3). Submarines at the Washington Conference. *British Yearbook of International Law* 3: 150–58.

R. R. B. (1951). The Municipal and International Law Basis of Jurisdiction over War Crimes. *British Yearbook of International Law* 28: 382–93.

Sack, A. (1944). Punishment of War Criminals and the Defence of Superior Order. *Law Quarterly Review* 60: 63–8.

Sadat, L. (2003). International Criminal Law and Alternative Modes of Redress. In A. Zimmermann (Ed.), *International Criminal Law and the Current Development of Public International Law, Proceedings of an International Symposium of the Kiel Walther Schücking Institute of International Law, May 30 – June 2, 2002* (pp. 161–94). Berlin: Duncker & Humbolt.

Saland, P. (1999). International Criminal Law Principles. In R. Lee (Ed.), *The International Criminal Court, The Making of the Rome Statute* (pp. 189–216). The Hague: Kluwer Law International.

Sarooshi, D. (1999). The Statute of the International Criminal Court. *International and Comparative Law Quarterly* 48: 387–404.

Schabas, W. (1998). General Principles of Criminal Law in the International Criminal Court Statute (Part III). *European Journal of Crime, Criminal Law and Criminal Justice* 6: 400–28.

Scharf, M. (2000). Justice versus Peace. In S. Sewall & C. Kaysen, *The United States and the International Criminal Court, National Security and International Law* (pp. 179–93). New York: Rowman & Littlefield Publishers.

Schick, F. (1947–8).War Criminals and the Law of the United Nations. *University of Toronto Law Journal* 7: 27–67.

Schneeberger, E. (1947). The Responsibility of the Individual under International Law. *Georgetown Law Journal* 35: 481–9.

Schwarzenberger, G. (1947). The Judgment of Nuremberg. *Tulane Law Review* 21: 329–61.

Schwarzenberger, G. (1950). The Problem of an International Criminal Law. *Current Legal Problems* 3: 263–96.

Scott, J. (1921). The Trial of the Kaiser. In E. House & C. Seymour (Eds.), *What Really Happened at Paris: the Story of the Peace Conference, 1918–1919, by American Delegates* (pp. 231–58). London: Hodder & Stoughton.

Shahabuddeen, M. (2000). Duress in International Humanitarian Law. In C. Barea et al., *Liber Amicorum 'In Memoriam' of Judge José María Ruda* (pp. 563–74). The Hague: Kluwer Law International.

Shestack, J. (1996). A Review and Critique of the Statute of the International Tribunal. In Y. Dinstein & M. Tabory (Eds.), *War Crimes in International Law* (pp.197–210). The Hague: Martinus Nijhoff Publishers.

Shibata, M. (1980). Kokusaihanzai no Gainen ni Kansuru Ichikōsatsu (A Study on the Notion of International Crimes). *Chibashōdai Ronsō* 18, no. 2: 399–418.

Shick, F. (1947-8). War Criminals and the Law of the United Nations. *University of Toronto Law Journal* 7: 27–67.

Simon, P. (1919). La clause d'amnistie dans les traités de paix. *Revue général de droit international public* 26: 245–61.

Simpson, G. (1997). War Crimes: A Critical Introduction. In T. McCormack & G. Simpson (Eds.), *The Law of War Crimes, National and International Approaches* (pp. 1–30). The Hague: Kluwer Law International.

Solis, G. (2000). Obedience of Orders and the Law of War: Judicial Application in American Forums. *American University International Law Review* 15: 481–526.

Stephen, H. (1901). Superior Orders as Excuse for Homicide. *Law Quarterly Review* 17: 87–9.

Suikkari, S. (1995). Debate in the United Nations on the International Law Commission's Draft Statute for an International Criminal Court. *Nordic Journal of International Law* 64: 205–21.

Taijudō, K. (1980). Kokusaihanzai no Gainen to Kokusaihō no Tachiba (The Notion of International Crimes and the Position of International Law). *Jurist* 720: 67–72.

Takayama, K. (2003). Kokusai Keijisaibanken (International Criminal Jurisdiction)(1). *Hōgaku Ronsō* 154, no. 1: 1–26.

Takayama, K. (2003). Kokusai Keijisaibanken (International Criminal Jurisdiction)(2). *Hōgaku Ronsō* 154, no. 2: 22–60.

Takigawa, Y. (1950). Keihō ni okeru Kōseiyōken no Kinō (The Function of the Definition of the Crime in Criminal Law). *Keihō Zasshi* 1, no. 2: 145–71.

Taylor, T. (1949). Nuremberg Trials, War Crimes and International Law. *International Conciliation* 450: 243–371.

Tomuschat, C. (1996). Crimes against the Peace and Security of Mankind and the Recalcitrant Third State. In Y. Dinstein & M. Tabory (Eds.), *War Crimes in International Law* (pp. 41–63). The Hague: Martinus Nijhoff Publishers.

Turns, D. (1998). The International Criminal Tribunal for the Former Yugoslavia: The Erdemovic Case. *International and Comparative Law Quarterly* 47: 461–74.

Verhaegen, J. (2002). Le refus d'obéissance aux ordres manifestement criminal. *Revue internationale de la Croix-rouge* 84: 35–50.

Vogler, T. (1973). The Defense of 'Superior Orders' in International Criminal Law. In C. Bassiouni & V. Nanda (Eds.), *A Treatise on International Criminal Law*, vol. 1 (pp. 619–35). Springfield, IL: Charles C Thomas.

Weber, H. (1948). Die Strafrechtliche Verantwortlichkeit für Handeln auf Befehl. *Monatsschrift für Deutsches Recht* 2: 34–42.

Wedgwood, R. (2000). National Courts and the Prosecution of War Crimes. In G. McDonald & O. Swaak-Goldman (Eds.), *Substantive and Procedural Aspects of International Criminal Law, The Experience of International and National Courts*, vol. 1 (pp. 391–413). The Hague: Kluwer Law International.

Wedgwood, R. (1999). The International Criminal Court: An American View. *European Journal of International Law* 10: 93–107.

Wedgwood, R. (2000). International Criminal Law and Augusto Pinochet. *Virginia Journal of International Law* 40: 829–47.
Weinschenk, F. (1976). Nazis before German Courts: The West German War Crimes Trials. *International Lawyer* 10: 515–29.
Weinschenk, F. (1999). 'The Murderers among Them' – German Justice and the Nazis. *Hofstra Law & Policy Symposium* 3: 137–54.
Wright, Q. (1920-21). The Effect of the War on International Law. *Minnesota Law Review* 5: 515–39.
Wright, Q. (1919). The Legal Liability of Kaiser. *American Political Science Review* 13: 120–28.
Wright, Q. (1925). The Outlawry of War. *American Journal of International Law* 19: 76–103.
Wright, Q. (1945). War Criminals. *American Journal of International Law* 39: 257–85.
Würtenberger, T. (1948). Der Irrtum über die Völkerrehtsmäßigkeit des höheren Befehls im Strafrecht. *Monatsschrift für Deutsches Recht* 2: 271–3.
Wyman, R. (1984, March–April). The First Rules of Air Warfare. *Air University Review* 94–102.
Yamamoto, S. (1987). Kokusaihanzai no Kisei wo meguru Kokusaihō to Kokunaihō no Kankei (The Relationship between International Law and National Law on the Regulation of International Crimes). *Jurist* 875: 232–6.
Yee, S. (1997). The Erdemovic Sentencing Judgement: A Questionable Milestone for the International Criminal Tribunal for the Former Yugoslavia. *Georgia Journal of International and Comparative Law* 26: 263–309.
Yokota, K. (1930). Rondonkaigi to Sensuikanshiyōhōki (The London Conference and the Rules on the Use of Submarines). *Kokusaihō Gaikō Zasshi* 29, no. 6: 1–23.
Zakr, N. (2001). L'imputabilité des faits et actes criminels des subalterns au supérieur hiérarchique devant le tribunal pénal international pour le Rwanda. *Revue de droit international et de droit compare* 78: 51–73.
Zimmermann, A. (2002). Superior Orders. In A. Cassese, P. Gaeta & J. Jones (Eds.), *The Rome Statute of the International Criminal Court: A Commentary* (pp. 957–74). Oxford: Oxford University Press.

Index

FSC
www.fsc.org
MIX
Papier | Fördert
gute Waldnutzung
FSC® C083411

Kolibri 360 GmbH
Ferdinand-Jühlke-Straße 7
99095 Erfurt, Deutschland
produktsicherheit@kolibri360.de